Public Policy and the Aesthetic Interest

Published with the assistance of
the John M. Olin Foundation, Inc.

Public Policy and the Aesthetic Interest

Critical Essays on Defining Cultural and Educational Relations

Edited by

Ralph A. Smith and Ronald Berman

University of Illinois Press
Urbana and Chicago

Manufactured in the United States of America
1 2 3 4 5 C P 5 4 3 2 1

This book is printed on acid-free paper.

Library of Congress Cataloging-in-Publication Data

Public policy and the aesthetic interest : critical essays on defining cultural and educational relations / edited by Ralph A. Smith and Ronald Berman.
p. cm.
Includes bibliographical references and index.
ISBN 0-252-01899-0 (cl).—ISBN 0-252-06244-2 (pb)
1. Art and state—United States. 2. United States—Cultural policy. 3. Arts—Scholarships, fellowships, etc.—United States. 4. Art patronage—United States. I. Smith, Ralph Alexander. II. Berman, Ronald.
NX730.P79 1992
700'.1'03—dc20 91-27335
CIP

Contents

Acknowledgments

The editors are grateful to the writers and their publishers for permission to reprint the following:

"Washington: The Artificial City" by Charles Frankel is from his book *High on Foggy Bottom: An Outsider's Inside View of the Government* (New York: Harper and Row, 1969), pp. 94–95, 101–6. © 1968, 1969, 1971 by Charles Frankel. Reprinted by permission of Harper-Collins Publishers. "Washington" was added to the title.

"Government and the Arts in the United States" by Kevin V. Mulcahy is adapted from *The Patron State: Government and the Arts in Europe, North America, and Japan,* ed. Milton C. Cummings, Jr., and Richard S. Katz (New York: Oxford University Press, 1987), pp. 311–24. © 1987 by Oxford University Press.

"Art and the General Welfare" by Albert William Levi is from the *Journal of Aesthetic Education* 7, no. 4 (October 1973): 39–48. © 1973 by the Board of Trustees of the University of Illinois.

"Art and the Public Interest" by Edward C. Banfield is from *Controversies in Art and Culture* 1, no. 1 (1987): 19–29.

"Aesthetic Welfare, Aesthetic Justice, and Educational Policy" by Monroe C. Beardsley is from the *Journal of Aesthetic Education* 7, no. 4 (October 1973): 39–48. © 1973 by the Board of Trustees of the University of Illinois.

"Should the Government Subsidize the Arts?" by Ernest van den Haag is reprinted with permission from the fall 1979 issue of *Policy Review,* the flagship publication of the Heritage Foundation, 214 Massachusetts Avenue, NW, Washington, D.C. 20002.

"A Surfeit of Fine Art" by Jacques Barzun is from his book *The Culture We Deserve,* ed. Arthur Krystal (Middletown, Conn.: Wesleyan University Press, 1989), pp. 120–28.

"Can Government Funding of the Arts Be Justified Theoretically?" by Noel Carroll is from the *Journal of Aesthetic Education* 21, no. 1 (Spring 1987): 21–35. © 1987 by the Board of Trustees of the University of Illinois.

"Democracy and Excellence" by Sir Roy Shaw is from his book *The Arts and the People* (London: Jonathan Cape, 1987), pp. 77–88. © 1987 by Jonathan Cape.

"American Popular Culture and High Culture in a Changing Class Society" by Herbert J. Gans is from *Art, Ideology, and Politics,* ed. Judith H. Balfe and Margaret J. Wyszomirski (New York: Praeger, 1985), pp. 40–57. © 1985 by Praeger.

"Arts versus the Arts" by Ronald Berman is from his book *Culture and Politics* (Lanham, Md.: University Press of America, 1984), pp. 127–44. © 1984 by the University Press of America.

"Arts Education as a Political Issue: The Federal Legacy" by Laura Chapman is reprinted by permission of the publisher from Chapman, *Instant Art, Instant Culture: The Unspoken Policy for American Schools* (New York: Teachers College Press, 1982), pp. 113–30. © 1982 by Teachers College, Columbia University. All rights reserved.

"Policy for Arts Education: Whither the Schools, Whither the Public and Private Sectors?" by Ralph A. Smith is from *Design for Arts in Education* 89, no. 4 (March/April 1988): 2–11, published by Heldref Publications, 4000 Albemarle Street, NW, Washington, D.C. 20016. © 1988. Reprinted by permission of the Helen Dwight Reid Educational Foundation.

"The Role of the National Endowment for the Arts [Today]" is excerpted from *Toward Civilization: A Report on Arts Education by the National Endowment for the Arts* (Washington, D.C.: National Endowment for the Arts, 1988), pp. 161–76.

"The NEA: Looking Back and Looking Ahead" by Samuel Lipman is from *The New Criterion* 7, no. 1 (September 1988): 6–13. © 1988 by the Foundation for Cultural Review, Inc.

"The Museum in the City" by Mark Lilla is from the *Journal of Aesthetic Education* 19, no. 2 (Summer 1985): 79–91. © by the Board of Trustees of the University of Illinois.

"Art, Culture, and Identity" by John Wilson is from the *Journal of Aesthetic Education* 18, no. 2 (Summer 1984): 89–97. © 1984 by the Board of Trustees of the University of Illinois.

"The Artists-in-Schools Program of the National Endowment for the Arts: Analysis and Criticism" by Ralph A. Smith is from *Art Education* 30, no. 5 (September 1977): 12–19. © 1977 by the National Art Education Association. The title has been slightly modified.

"The Arts in Alternative Schools: Some Observations" by Barbara Leondar is from the *Journal of Aesthetic Education* 5, no. 1 (January 1971): 75–91. © 1971 by the Board of Trustees of the University of Illinois.

"Is Art above the Laws of Decency?" by Hilton Kramer is from the *New York Times,* 2 July 1989, sec. 2, pp. 1, 7. © 1989 by the New York Times Company.

"Artistic Freedom: An Art World Paradox" by E. Louis Lankford is from the *Journal of Aesthetic Education* 24, no. 3 (Fall 1990): 15–28. © 1990 by the Board of Trustees of the University of Illinois. This essay has been slightly edited and updated.

"An Overview of the Strategic Issues in American Arts Education" by Samuel Hope is from the *Journal of Aesthetic Education* 21, no. 4 (Winter 1987): 25–40. © 1987 by the Board of Trustees of the University of Illinois.

Preface

Since the establishment of the National Foundation for the Arts and Humanities and their respective endowments in 1965, we have witnessed the development of a new genre of writing, a policy literature devoted to the positive and negative aspects of government support for the arts and arts education. With the advent in 1990 of the twenty-fifth anniversary of the legislation that established the endowments, there were numerous assessments of the legislation's overall contribution to the health of the arts and culture in the society. The essays in this collection provide material for a continuing assessment, with particular emphasis on the National Endowment for the Arts and the role this agency plays in defining cultural and educational relations.

Toward the end of encouraging better policymaking, this volume contains essays both supportive and critical of government subsidy of the arts and arts education. The collection is partisan only in the intellectual bias it reflects toward the need to scrutinize policy based on the experiences of the past. Liberal and conservative alike can thus find ideas worth their serious consideration. And students, whether preparing to enter teaching or the cultural services field, can benefit from examining the arguments presented.

A few words may be helpful about the order of the essays. The collection opens with some observations made by Charles Frankel during his tenure as assistant secretary of state for cultural and educational affairs during the Johnson administration, a position since abolished. It was Frankel's hope that by giving greater attention to cultural concerns the nation's capital would become less one-dimensional, a city not totally preoccupied with political decision making. It was also one of the benefits of Frankel's position to have discovered firsthand what the term *culture* means to Washington's official inhabitants, namely, the dead hand of the past, opening nights at performing arts centers, people-to-people activities, and cultural lag—all, Frankel observed, benign meanings of the term.

The National Endowment for the Arts has now contributed its view of culture, a sense of which Kevin V. Mulcahy provides in his description of the kinds of decisions the new agency has made, decisions that are, of course, subject to change and updating. In a democratic society a continuing critique of such decisions is always in order. Accordingly, the question of government support for the arts is addressed, in dialectical manner, by Albert William Levi, Monroe C. Beardsley, Sir Roy Shaw, and the agency itself, all in favor of it, while Edward C. Banfield, Ernest van den Haag, Noel Carroll, Ronald Berman, and Jacques Barzun raise questions.

The remaining essays discuss critically the ways cultural and educational relations have been defined since the Endowment's inception, the direction future policymaking should take, and some of the issues that have been and should be addressed. Laura Chapman, Ralph A. Smith, and Samuel Lipman express reservations about the Endowment's past educational policies, while Herbert J. Gans, Mark Lilla, John Wilson, and Barbara Leondar address the issues of high versus popular culture, the civic role of the museum, cultural and personal identity, and alternative arts education. As this volume was being prepared for submission to the publisher, the question of government support for artists whose work segments of the public and the art world found objectionable was being hotly discussed in the press and government. It seemed fitting that the volume address this issue, hence the inclusion of the essays by Hilton Kramer and E. Louis Lankford. The collection concludes with a review by Samuel Hope of some of the basic problems facing policymaking for arts education in the future. Here, then, are some thoughtful reflections, criticisms, and recommendations for further thinking about support for the arts and arts education, assembled by editors with cultural and educational interests.

This collection should prove valuable to all those at government, state, and local levels who are involved in policymaking, to members of the cultural services field, and to prospective teachers of art in the schools and those who prepare them. Interested citizens trying to decide whether their tax dollars should be spent in support of the arts and arts education, or how they should be spent, will also find something to help them.

Ralph A. Smith
Ronald Berman

1

Washington: The Artificial City

Charles Frankel

If the government often seems strangely deaf to messages from the outside, its information system isn't the only reason. Life in the government of the United States is a special kind of life because it is life in Washington.

The Founding Fathers invented Washington. They were thoughtful men, and one must suppose that they knew what they were doing, but it is difficult to think so. They wanted a capital that would have no ties to any state, and the result was an artificial city, constructed on a site that had been shunned as a place of urban habitation during the hundred and fifty years in which settlers had roamed up and down the Atlantic seaboard looking for places to live. The Founding Fathers wanted a city that would belong neither to the North nor to the South. They got what they wanted, and we still have it—a capital too far north to escape the snows, and too far south ever to be prepared for them, a neutral, in-between place, of mixed styles and uncertain tastes, where the magnolias bloom in the slush. Washington, as John Kennedy said, is a city of Southern efficiency and Northern charm.

Yet Washington has, of course, a distinctive flavor. It is, to begin with, two cities, not one. The larger city is composed of people who have fled to a federal enclave in the hope of escaping poverty, degradation, and the aftermath of slavery. The other and smaller city—Washington Northwest and its suburban appendages—is inhabited by a ruling minority, most of whom think of someplace else as home. Like the rulers of Taiwan, their eyes are on a continent over which they claim authority, and they have only a tangential interest in the place where they reside. And in this Washington a culture, a way of life, prevails unlike that of any other major city I know. Alone among the great capitals of the world, Washington—Washington Northwest—is a one-business town. Every view in it is a political view, and practically every avenue to success is an avenue through government.

Looking back, however, I think that perhaps the most broadening result of my exposure to Washington was my education in the meaning of culture. As assistant secretary for cultural affairs, I had an opportunity to do research in "culture" which has been vouchsafed to only a few. It may be helpful to the anthropologist, philosophers, and many others who have argued about culture to record the fact that in Washington, the center of power in the world, there are four principal definitions of the word.

Definition Number One is probably the most popular. It is illustrated in sentences like "He spends his evenings in cultural pursuits" or "He went to the Cultural Center." "Culture," in this definition, stands for the performing arts. The novel doesn't quite fit—not if *Lolita* is a novel. And neither does poetry, which is usually produced and enjoyed in private and requires an active effort from the reader as well as the writer before it can be enjoyed. "Culture," in the public, political sense of the word, requires celebrities, crowded places, opening nights, and ample intermissions.

I was the only secretary of any kind in Washington with the word *Culture* in his title. It had its pleasant side. I could go backstage whenever I wished and meet ballet dancers. But congressmen who have spent ruined evenings at concerts their wives had made them attend were a little suspicious of me, and I often had the impression, in my meetings with hardheaded bureaucrats and administrators, that they felt a certain initial hesitation about talking to me about money or politics for fear that such talk might wound my sensibilities.

However, it was the lovers of Culture who gave me my greatest trouble—or perhaps it was I who troubled them. Somehow, I was not the man they hoped to find: my tastes were a bit too catholic. I like Ray Bolger as well as Paul Taylor, Zero Mostel as much as Oliver, and there was music written after Wagner which, apparently, I could tolerate. In fact, I had difficulty tolerating Wagner. In a survey I once conducted surreptitiously during an intermission at Constitution Hall—I recorded its results on the back of an envelope—I was able to determine that 2.56 of every 4 people in Washington who love Culture (Definition One) expect it to be refined and uplifting. This gives them, these days, a restricted field in which to roam. Deplorable language is used on the stage; ballet is too explicit; music upsets the digestion. Culture in its basic sense has been reduced, for most of them, to *Swan Lake*—and not all of that. Besides, *Swan Lake* belongs to the Russians, which limits its usefulness in American foreign policy. In Washington, caught between the Culture haters and the Culture lovers, an assistant secretary of state for cultural affairs walks a thin line.

The second definition of "culture" that prevails in Washington produced problems too. I usually encountered it among economists and technicians. They used the word *culture* as in *cultural lag.* Culture (not to equivocate) is what is wrong with the world. Why hasn't foreign assistance worked out in Country X? Answer: Country X's culture is an obstacle. Why doesn't a multinational organization like the United Nations Educational Scientific and Cultural Organization achieve all the purposes that had been hoped? Answer: cultural differences. Why, despite the brilliant performance of the American economy, are there still people who complain about it and say that it turns out too many useless and ugly things? Answer: cultural prejudices.

The practical consequences of this view of culture were somewhat unsettling. If an assistant secretary for cultural affairs says that it is important to promote "cultural exchanges," he is likely to be interpreted as proposing an exchange of vices between nations. He is perceived as a brake on the wheels of progress, a man concerned with the traditional and the outmoded. One of the difficulties of my job, during working hours and afterward, was that the word *culture* set up all sorts of reverberations—the humanities against the sciences, books and other useless things against technical progress, the soft side of life against the realities of power, money, and politics. There was always a latent question whether I belonged in a serious meeting.

Washington's third definition of "culture" is achieved by dividing Definition One by Definition Two, as follows:

$$\frac{\text{Culture: Performing Arts}}{\text{Culture: The Dead Hand of the Past}}$$

Knowledge of the new mathematics is not required to work out the quotient: "Culture" equals the dead arts, the monuments of times gone by. It is the nonperforming, noncontroversial side of a country—Williamsburg, the Temple of Abu Simbel, Canterbury, Chartres, Venice, the paintings of Picasso in the United States (but not his opinions), the opinions of Picasso in the Soviet Union (but not his paintings). "Culture," in a word, is a subject that offers a common ground to people who would otherwise disagree.

This definition of "culture" was by all odds the easiest for me to live with. So conceived, "culture" gave me a unique function to perform in Washington's foreign policy community: as assistant secretary of state for cultural affairs, I was the man who was kept around to change the subject whenever things got hot. This definition of "culture" permitted me to live with the handicaps of my position and to carve out a niche for myself just the same. Still, I confess that I was a little restive under this definition of my role. I couldn't quite manage to stand for nothing but neutrality. "Are you still sending that dancer, Josie Lemon, abroad?" a congressman once asked me, and I had to confess that if it wasn't José Limon it was probably another dancer named Alvin Ailey. "My God, who?" he asked.

I ran into difficulties with the Russians too. They have reasons, philosophical and political, for preferring the idea of culture as something inert. The Russians once turned down an American candidate for the exchange program who proposed to study contemporary Moscow dialect. When they were asked why, they said that they could not provide him with facilities to do his research. Translated, this meant that his research would require him to walk around the streets and talk to living people, which, under the Russian definition, would not be cultural exchange but cultural penetration. This example may suggest why, although I wanted to do my bit to dispel the clouds of the cold war, I sometimes had disagreements with my Russian colleagues. I found it hard to subscribe to a definition of culture which reduced it to the customs house definition of an antique: something that can be imported duty-free because it is purely decorative and is more than a hundred years old.

My view of culture as active was the subject of a conversation between a Russian diplomat and myself. The United States and Soviet governments were in the midst of negotiating the renewal of the cultural exchange agreement, and the negotiation wasn't going well. The Russians blamed it on the war in Vietnam, which they said had created a bad atmosphere for negotiation. At a reception in a neutral embassy, I ran into the Russian cultural attaché, a cheerful, vigorous man with whom I had agreeable relations. I said to him that I hoped he realized, and would tell his ambassador, that there were no political obstacles on the American side to the conclusion of a new agreement.

He replied: "Mr. Secretary, I am happy to have this reaffirmation of intentions from your side and will tell my ambassador. But you are a philosopher and you should know that culture is a frail flower; its health depends on the soil in which it is planted, and that soil is the soil of politics. The soil now, I am sorry to say, is not good. It has turned—how do you say?—sour."

Thus did the representative of one great superpower speak. And I, the representative of the other, replied: "No, culture is not a frail flower. Culture is a busy bee. It flies from flower to flower, and in the process fertilizes the plants and enriches the soil. Culture can change politics."

"One can see, Mr. Secretary," said the attaché, "that you are not a Marxist, nor a materialist. You believe that culture can change the base, that the superstructure can affect the foundation."

"Yes," I said, "I do. And on this point I am in full agreement with Engels, who said that Marx and he weren't so foolish as to imagine that ideas had no influence."

"It is unfair of the Americans," said the attaché, smiling, "to appoint a professor of philosophy to their government."

The agreement was in time signed. Unhappily—or perhaps happily—nowhere in it, as I recall, is there a formal agreement on the definition of culture.

It was the fourth definition of "culture" which I ran across in Washington that had the greatest possibilities. In this definition, "culture" stands for anything that takes people away from government, politics, business, or anything organized. These are formal and impersonal. Culture in contrast is informal and personal. "Cultural relations" means "people-to-people" relations—and diplomats, businessmen or officials, it goes without saying, are not people.

There is something to be said for this point of view, I suppose. At any rate, a good deal was said in favor of it in my hearing in Washington. I met some enthusiasts for this definition of culture, however, who rather startled me. One evening, after a dinner at the house of one of Washington's patrons of the arts, I was buttonholed by an advocate of the people-to-people technique in international affairs. He urged me to propose a massive exchange of persons with the Russians: we would send ten of our best colleges and universities—students, faculties, families, and all—and install them in permanent enclaves in the Soviet Union, where they would pursue their normal American activities. The Russians would do the same thing to or for us, sending their best people and institutions of learning. Through such people-to-people exchanges, the gentleman argued, each side would be deterred from dropping bombs on the other. After absorbing this thought for a moment, I intimated to my companion that he was proposing an exchange of hostages and not what was normally meant by an exchange of persons. He looked at me with disappointment and mumbled something about the conservatism of the State Department. But by that time I was already beginning to play with the idea. If we could send some people I knew, and if the Russians sent us some of theirs, and if we could just arrange to let the trade stand . . . But I didn't let him in on my thinking. In Washington you have to play your cards close to your vest.

2

Government and the Arts in the United States

Kevin V. Mulcahy

Historically, government support for the arts in the United States has been very limited. However, some public patronage never has been completely absent. The Smithsonian Institution, chartered by Congress in 1846 as a nonprofit corporation, has grown from the "nation's attic" to a vast holding company of museums and special collections. States and localities administer and support a variety of art, historical, and natural science museums as well as commemorative sites and cultural parks. Since the nineteenth century, national copyright laws have protected individual artistic creators while subsidized postal rates have dramatically enhanced the publication and fund-raising activities of cultural organizations. More recently, the federal government has sponsored international cultural exchange programs. The federal government also allows tax deductions for individuals and corporations making donations to cultural organizations, and localities typically exempt these organizations from paying property taxes.[1]

Significant as this support for the arts has been, until recently its impact was indirect, episodic, and largely marginal. No public arts agency existed on the national level comparable to the British Arts Council, let alone to the state-run cultural institutions found in either France or Germany. The principle of public subsidy was also the subject of harsh partisan and ideological debate. It is difficult to disagree with Milton Cummings that for the arts in the United States before 1965, "there was no large-scale and continuous tradition of direct subsidy by the government, such as was common in Europe."[2]

Government support for the arts in the United States has developed since the 1960s with the political legacy of the New Deal arts program of the 1930s still uppermost in the minds of policymakers and the interested members of the public.[3] The political controversies that resulted from the cultural projects of the Works Progress Administration served to dramatize the dangers as well as the benefits for the arts that might come with an official embrace. Public arts agencies have been very sensitive to any charges of ideological or aesthetic biases and, in both their organizational structures and programmatic policies, have sought to prevent their occurrence. As America's preeminent public patron, the National Endowment for the Arts (NEA) has been particularly aware of these precedents and problems and has sought to develop a model of public patronage that would avoid previous political pitfalls. In the discussion of public support for the arts that follows, certain major themes will recur that reflect the ongoing concern with political acceptability and popular approval.

First, public patronage and public arts agencies have played a highly circumscribed role in the nation's culture. The NEA has not functioned as a national "ministry of culture"—that is, a Cabinet-level department responsible for comprehensive cultural policymaking and for administering the nation's artistic activities—but has promoted the arts in strictly limited ways.

Second, the NEA, while a highly circumspect public patron, has developed close relationships with state arts agencies. These "little NEAs" have complemented the federal agency in supporting a broad range of national cultural policies including increased public funding.

Third, the delimited nature of federal commitment to the arts has been underscored by the limited public funding that has been made available. Not only have appropriations for the Arts Endowment and related agencies remained small, but the federal government has chosen not to provide operating subsidies, assume responsibility for artistic production, or become the guarantor of a national cultural heritage.

Fourth, the history of past cultural controversies has led the NEA to adopt a political strategy that avoids extremes both in funding and in programming. The guiding decision-making principle has been a commitment to "cultural pluralism"—that is, a definition of the arts capacious enough to allow broadly distributed support for a diversity of cultural expressions.

Overall, the Arts Endowment has sought to build a broad base of public support, from within the arts world and without, while also broadening the nation's cultural base in both its variety and availability. Public support has come to be associated with greater access to, and awareness of, the arts, even as the NEA has sought not to become identified with particular aesthetic values. On the other hand, the NEA's record has also been cause for much criticism; government support for the arts has proven no more immune from political controversy than other public policies.

Public Law 89-209 created the National Foundation for the Arts and Humanities in 1965; this enabling legislation defined the arts broadly as including but not limited to "music (instrumental and vocal), dance, drama, folk arts, creative writing, architecture and allied fields, painting, sculpture, photography, graphic and craft arts, industrial design, costume and fashion design, motion pictures, television, radio, tape and sound recording, the arts related to the presentation, performance, execution, and exhibition of such major art forms, and the study and application of the arts to human environments." While this discussion is almost exclusively about the NEA, some observations should also be offered about the National Endowment for the Humanities (NEH). The National Endowment's administrative twin, the NEH, provides public support for studies in the following academic disciplines: "history, philosophy, languages, linguistics, literature, archeology, jurisprudence, history and criticism of the arts, ethics, comparative religion, and those aspects of the social sciences employing historical or philosophical approaches."

The creation of the Arts and Humanities Endowments represented the first permanent commitment by the federal government to support cultural programs. (The WPA projects were only "emergency relief.") Yet, the role of the federal government was to be limited and indirect, lest it become a state-imposed culture at odds with the American pluralist tradition.[4] As grant-making agencies (similar to the National Science Foundation or the National Institutes of Health), the Endowments normally provide only discretionary funding on a competitive basis to underwrite partially the costs of specific projects undertaken by private or locally supported cultural institutions.

The NEA is involved primarily with execution, exhibition, and performance while the NEH places greater emphasis on aesthetic criticism and philosophy. More important, the NEH may be seen as an agency of the major research universities in the United States, while the NEA is closely related to the major arts organizations. Although the political and budgetary fates of the NEA and NEH have been closely linked, the Humanities Endowment has had a more difficult time in creating a public identity and solidifying political support. The enabling legislation provided for a Federal Council on the Arts and Humanities as a coordinating agency, but this council largely has been inactive, and the two endowments have functioned as separate administrative entities.

In addition to the endowments, there are other public cultural agencies of somewhat lesser importance. Prominent are the museums located in Washington, D.C., whose operations are directly underwritten by the federal government, even if they are technically autonomous institutions. These are the National Gallery of Art and the Smithsonian complex, the latter receiving a larger appropriation than the NEA. The Institute of Museum Services, an independent executive branch agency, is endowed with a small budget to provide museums nationwide with technical and management assistance. The Interior Department supports historic preservation efforts in cooperation with the (private) National Trust for Historic Preservation and maintains the National Register of Historic Places. Interior's Park Service also maintains a number of commemorative sites and historic monuments.

The Corporation for Public Broadcasting (CPB) serves as a conduit for federal funds to the various not-for-profit radio and television stations around the country that provide noncommercial cultural and public affairs programming. These stations may be either privately run or operated by local governmental authorities such as state departments of education or public universities. The stations form a loose network with locally supported member stations providing the bulk of the programs. CPB itself is a government-owned corporation, yet is not a government agency; however, since funds are appropriated by Congress, that may be a fine distinction.

This summary of the federal government's involvement with culture does not include government programs that are involved with cultural matters, but as ancillary activities. The Library of Congress and National Archives are important cultural institutions; however, the former is at root a legislative reference service and the latter is a document-preservation arm of the General Services Administration. In one of the few examples of direct patronage by the national government, the General Services Administration commissions artwork to decorate federal buildings. The United States Information Agency (USIA) supports international, cultural, and educational exchange programs which, along with informational activities such as Voice of America and Radio Marti, export American arts and artists to audiences abroad.

For all this, there is no ministry of culture in the United States. The cultural programs of the federal government are highly fragmented, located in a variety of administrative agencies, overseen by different congressional committees, supported by and responsive to a variety of interests, and articulating the policy perspectives of discrete segments of the cultural constituency. This institutional fragmentation reflects both the diffuse nature of artistic activity in the United States and a fear of the effects that a unified cultural bureaucracy might have on artistic expression. The United States has eschewed the idea of establishing an official culture in which the state would act as the sole, or even the most influential, patron of the arts. The government has seen itself as a minority stockholder in the nation's culture. Consequently, public spending on the arts in the United States remains small. Despite a major spurt in the 1970s, funding remains at approximately 0.2 percent of the entire federal budget.

The National Endowment for the Arts, while but one of the arts agencies of the federal government, is the paramount actor in cultural policymaking.

No other public arts agency enjoys its prestige in the arts world or exercises comparable influence on cultural institutions. Though not a cabinet department, the NEA as an independent agency reports directly to the president and enjoys considerable political prestige. Its chief administrative officer is its chairman, appointed by the president for a four-year term upon Senate confirmation. The chairman is responsible to a twenty-six-member National Council on the Arts appointed by the president and confirmed by the Senate to staggered six-year terms. The chairman may appoint any such subordinate officials—for example, deputy chairmen—as is deemed necessary, and administrative arrangements have varied with different incumbents. At the same time, the basic building blocks of the NEA's administrative structure have remained the various program areas that embody the legislative intent of PL 89-209. Each of these programs—for example, music, museums, opera theater, visual arts, arts education—represents a major interest in the cultural community. It is the program personnel—staff and advisory panelists—who largely determine the NEA's grant-making decisions and create its cultural guidelines.

By statutory provision, all grant-making decisions are made by the chairman; while this means that the NEA chairman may approve or disapprove grant applications at will, this has occurred only rarely.[5] Each of the NEA's program areas advises the National Council and the chairman about grants to be awarded on the basis of recommendations provided by specialized panels. The panels are, in many ways, the bedrock of the Arts Endowment's administrative organization. Panel members are appointed by the NEA chairman for terms of up to four years on the recommendation of the NEA staff, arts lobbyists, cultural administrators, council members, elected officials, and other concerned parties from the cultural community. On one level, these advisory groups serve to provide expert, and presumably disinterested, evaluations of the grant proposals submitted to the program areas into which the Endowment is organized. On another level, the panels represent an effort to minimize "cultural porkbarrelling" and to keep "politics" out of the grant-making process. More basically, these panels serve as the principal means for insulating the NEA from adverse criticism about the wisdom of having made a particular grant.

As is typical of groups of outside consultants, the panels cannot be convened more than five or six times a year and for periods of only a few days. Although proposals are distributed to panelists in advance, the average panel has about eleven days a year in which it must evaluate perhaps one thousand grant applications. The bases for making a grant are, of course, the artistic value or the proposed project and its contribution to the community's cultural development.[6] Panel members also serve as individuals and not as representatives of their institutions. However, it is not always easy to ascertain when an institutional interest may influence decision making or when, as with any group of successful professionals, NEA panelists make decisions on the basis of predetermined assumptions about what constitutes a good project. These professional norms may serve to create a bias in favor of proposals from applicants whose work is familiar. However, the cause of any such biases seems less rooted in organizational favoritism than in the unanalyzed assumption that, if an applicant's work is unknown, it is not worth knowing.[7]

Because of lack of time, divided attention, and incomplete information, panels cannot provide fully independent evaluations and instead depend on the Endowment staff (as does the National Council) for structure, direction, and guidance. Inevitably, the values of NEA staff members, especially those of the program directors who are recruited largely from major cultural institutions, will strongly influence granting decisions.[8] Since policy consensus is as strong in the cultural sphere as it is in other policy areas (although policy views are certainly never monolithic anywhere), it should not be surprising that panelists and staff members share common values. To suggest, however, that these administrative arrangements skew the decision-making process is unwarranted. The primary influence that staff members exercise on panelists is to push them along a demarcated bureaucratic path.

In sum, panels serve four important functions that reflect the current goals and past history of public support for the arts in the United States. First, the selection of panelists allows for the representation of relevant interests from the arts world in the process of cultural policymaking. Second, the panels are important assurances that government support for the arts is not politics as usual, but represents an effort to allow merit and need to determine grant decisions. Third, by actively involving artists and arts administrators in the grant-making process, the NEA secures a large measure of legitimation for its decisions and also emphasizes the partnership goal of its funding arrangements. Fourth, the panel system helps to protect the Arts Endowment from political interference and censorship. It allows the chairman to justify his opposition to such intrusions as deferring to the considered judgment of a group of experts rather than asserting the superiority of his own opinion or that of the NEA staff.

Given the criticism of the New Deal arts projects as unrepresentative of community preferences, ideologically motivated, politically unaccountable, and in need of censorship, the administrative procedures of the Arts Endowment reflect a good sense of bureaucratic politics. Whether the NEA's political tactics are to be judged a success depends ultimately on one's assessment of the cultural outcomes. Nonetheless, it cannot be overemphasized that the policies and programs of the National Endowment for the Arts are not simply an administrative convenience. These arrangements reflect the realities of American politics. In particular, the history of cultural politics in the United States strongly suggests the advisability of a grant-making agency with limited authority and indirect responsibility rather than a comprehensive cultural department with direct responsibility for artistic production.

Eighteen state arts councils existed before the creation of the NEA, but with the distinct exception of the New York State Arts Council, these public arts agencies were not particularly active. Following the NEA's creation, the number of these councils quickly grew to include each of the states and territories. Now all states serve as official patrons of the arts and have departments responsible for the administration of a cultural budget. The impetus for this spectacular growth came from provisions of the Endowment's enabling legislation that required the existence of a state arts agency as a condition for receipt of federal funds and provided for a once-only basic grant of $50,000 to establish an arts agency if none existed. While this sort of an organizational requirement may seem like an administrative formality, it did lay the foundation for a locally based NEA constituency and stimulated state arts appropriations.

State arts agencies range considerably from the New York State Arts Council, which until the mid-1970s outspent the NEA, to the councils of Nevada and most of the territories whose budgets remain below $100,000 per year. Most states administer their cultural programs according to the following model: an independent agency with a small staff; a council or commission with an average of fifteen members appointed by the governor to staggered terms to formulate policy; and advisory panels to review grant applications and recommend awards.[9] Seven states have some form of cabinet-level department of cultural resources with responsibility for the arts council and a variety of other cultural activities such as historic preservation, public broadcasting, and a state library.[10] The Arts Task Force of the National Conference of State Legislatures has recommended that all states have a unified cultural department both to enhance coordination of activities among cultural agencies and to increase the political visibility of the arts. Decisions about awarding grants typically are made by the appointed members of the state arts councils acting on the recommendations of advisory panels whose members are experts in particular art forms. Most states also provide for direct representation of professionals from the visual, literary, or performing arts on their councils.[11]

Nineteen state arts agencies delegate responsibility for grant distribution to local entities. This administrative decentralization is advocated because of the ability of local agencies better to assess audience demand and to identify deserving projects. Moreover, local arts agencies, by accepting responsibility for making certain grants, may serve to deflect criticism from the state agency in controversial allocations. Locally oriented arts agencies sometimes are criticized for funding programs that are decidedly amateur, if not actually "hobbies." On the other hand, these programs may provide the only cultural activities that further community participation and identification. This debate has raged at all levels of public cultural funding and has led to the criticism that the public arts agencies are subsidizing artists and audiences where few actually exist. Yet, the dearth of opportunities outside of major metropolitan areas is precisely the situation which state and local arts agencies are seeking to correct. Dick Netzer, who is not uncritical of the funding decisions of public arts agencies, makes the following observation:

> In the last decade hundreds of thousands if not millions of Americans have discovered through publicly supported programs some form of the arts and found it so fascinating that continuing experience with that art form—at some level—will be part of the rest of their lives. The emphasis of the public funding agencies on wider availability has made ordinary Americans more familiar and comfortable with the arts than their counterparts in other large countries seem to be. And this development may in time result in significant audience expansion.[12]

From its inception, the NEA envisioned active participation by the states in the grant-making process. Indeed, not less than 20 percent of the Arts Endowment's budget must be distributed to the states, with no state (or territory) receiving less than $200,000. These funds then are distributed by the state arts agency as the "federally-mandated conduit."[13] Total spending by the states and territories in 1988 was greater than the NEA's budget. While a few states (especially New York) stand out as particularly generous, forty-three of the fifty-six states and territories appropriate more funds for the arts than they receive from the NEA.

In distributing funds, most states follow the NEA's decision-making model—that is, they are grant-making agencies in which councils act after reviews of advisory panels. Twenty states, however, have "line-item" appropriations for one or more of their arts institutions. This direct legislative support varies from authorizing bonds for a specific capital project (such as a performing arts center) to underwriting the operating expenses of a cultural institution (such as a symphony or museum). Clearly, line items in the state budget are welcomed by institutions as more stable and predictable sources of financial support than those provided by the grants programs of the various state arts agencies. For many arts administrators, however, these direct appropriations violate the council and panel review system that was designed to ensure the allocation of arts funds based on cultural need or value rather than due to political pressure. Allegations of playing politics with public culture are particularly intense if an arts organization's line-item appropriation constitutes a disproportionate share of the arts budget, or if a line item has been sought to override a decision by the state arts agency.[14] These budgetary decisions raise the specter of a line itemization of the arts budget and an end to decision-making autonomy. Opponents of the line item prefer that the legislature appropriate an overall amount for all cultural spending and allow the state arts agency to decide which institutions to fund and at what level.

State arts agencies support a variety of programs and in general these follow the guidelines established by the NEA for its programmatic divisions. The majority of states have programs such as the "Arts in School" or "Arts in the Community." Dance, theater, and music touring groups are supported widely as are major, private arts organizations. Public cultural institutions such as state museums or state libraries usually have a line item in state budgets and separate administrative organizations. States also provide significant support for local arts agencies—some of which, like the San Francisco Arts Council and the New York City Cultural Affairs Commission, have national significance. Many state and localities have also instituted special devices to support the arts such as hotel/motel taxes, income tax checkoffs, dedicated portions of sales taxes, special assessment districts, and in Massachusetts a state lottery to benefit the arts.[15]

State arts agencies came into existence reflecting a wide variety of legislative intentions usually expressing vague, broad-based goals such as the "cultivation of arts appreciation" and the "nourishment of artistic quality and creativity." Typically, state legislation provides little specific programmatic guidance; moreover, many state arts agencies originally were established simply to quality for NEA funds. Given the absence of a tradition of arts administration in the states in the early years, the Arts Endowment became the source of guidance about policies, programs, and administrative organization. These agencies functioned in effect as "little NEAs" in their close association with the national arts agency and its cultural goals.

As state arts agencies have developed their own cultural identity and administrative autonomy, friction between them and their national parent over policy questions has increased. Regardless, the NEA realizes important political goals through its close partnership with the state arts agencies. Endowment officials are able to recite the specific local uses of cultural funds when testifying before congressional committees with specific mention of NEA-supported institutions in the districts of the committees' members.

The cultural institutions funded, with their administrators, boards of trustees, and clienteles, constitute the constituency base of the Endowment. These arts advocates, disproportionately well off and well educated, are able to articulate concerns about the nation's cultural condition while focusing on specific issues and local concerns. In sum, state arts agencies, with an understandable instinct for bureaucratic self-preservation, have become institutionalized advocates for the NEA's general policies and the principle of continued and increased public funding.

The administration of New Deal arts projects involved the government in a variety of allocational, supervisory, employment quota, and subject-matter conflicts which left a negative association with government support for the arts. Given the government's role as direct patron of the artist, this may have been inevitable, but it nevertheless served to involve these projects in debilitating political controversies. The Arts Endowment, by contrast, has operated on the principle of indirect sponsorship through matching grants (up to 50 percent of the cost) for special projects to be undertaken by private cultural institutions and state and local arts councils. The NEA, typically, does not subsidize the operating costs of cultural institutions, make grants to individual artists, or commission works of art. Avoiding direct patronage has not completely spared the NEA from being tarred by the brush strokes of controversial projects. While sharing responsibility with cultural institutions in the private sector and relying on the panel system for grant-making was designed to help the NEA avoid the political criticism that undermined the effectiveness of the New Deal arts program, the recent controversy associated with the Helms amendment has shown the fallibility of the NEA's strategy.

By the end of Richard Nixon's tenure in office, the basic contours of the cultural budget had been established as the Arts Endowment successfully passed through its "initial survival threshold." A sign of having navigated this passage is the allocation of enough resources so that an agency "can rapidly expand to meet the needs its members have long been advocating."[16] During the 1970s, the endowments (with the NEH just behind the NEA) had a regular, steady upward increase in appropriations that was only slowed in the face of efforts by the Reagan administration to impose sharp budgetary cutbacks. While the Arts Endowment has not enjoyed the high yearly gains in budgetary growth in the 1980s that was the case during the Carter and Nixon administrations, it has maintained its budgetary position—in part because of the legislative protection afforded by Congressman Sidney Yates (D–Ill.) and Senator Claiborne Pell (D–R.I.). The NEA's appropriation in 1988 was approximately $168 million compared to about $150 million a decade earlier. This appropriation level was reached despite repeated rhetoric about cutting the "nonessential" elements in the federal budget.

The Reagan budget cuts, which were announced in 1981 by then Director of Management and Budget (OMB) David Stockman, were perhaps a healthy shock to an overly complacent cultural community that had come to expect steady increases in the cultural budget and strong presidential support—regardless of party. OMB proposed cutting the 1982 appropriations for the Arts Endowment almost in half—from $158 million to $88 million and the Humanities Endowment from $155 million to $85 million. Stockman's proposed budgetary reductions were "premised on the notion that the (Reagan) administration should completely revamp federal policy for arts and humanities support." The Arts Endowment was sharply criticized for "promoting the notion that the federal government should be the financial patron of first resort for . . . artistic and literary pursuits."[17]

In assessing the probable reaction to the drastic cuts that it would propose, OMB officials forecast (correctly) that there would be strong opposition: "The Arts and Humanities Endowments have broad and articulate public constituencies, ranging from university presidents to museum directors to individual artists and scholars. In addition, most artistic and cultural institutions maintain strong ties to business and corporations through honorary appointments on boards of directors."[18] The cultural constituency indeed had become a very well connected group, and members of the NEA's National Council, like Beverly Sills, were very vocal in their opposition to the proposed cuts.

In all the controversy about the Endowment's programs and the Reagan budget cuts, it is very easy to lose sight of the magnitude of the issue in monetary terms. The NEA's budget amounts to less than 0.1 percent of total federal spending; moreover, public funds from all sources account for only about 15 percent of the operating expenses of arts organizations in the United States. Nonetheless, this makes the Endowment the biggest single source of support for the arts in the nation and means that it exerts an influence vastly greater than the dollar amounts would suggest. Since the importance of NEA support is in inverse proportion to the size of the cultural institutions, only the largest would be likely to survive if there were a sharp decline in federal funding. Moreover, even for the large arts organization, public support often may determine the hours that a museum can be open or what a symphony orchestra's scheduling arrangements will be.

Besides the financial margin of survival that the NEA sometimes provides, it is possible to identify three qualitative contributions provided by government support for the arts. First, an NEA grant constitutes an imprimatur for the smaller and newer arts organizations; that is, it provides a respected and recognized official seal of approval. In the amorphous arts world, this can be particularly helpful in generating funds from foundation and corporate sources. Second, an Endowment grant often allows cultural institutions to do what they would otherwise be unable to consider. Among these activities are concerts for groups outside the usual subscription clientele; exhibitions and performances in smaller communities, at the workplace, custodial facilities, and shopping malls; and support for nontraditional artists through commissions and fellowships. Third, as a public arts agency, the Endowment properly has addressed itself to concerns of cultural equity that cannot be addressed by a private arts institution. The Endowment's policies have sought to further the accessibility of culture to people of different socioeconomic and ethnic backgrounds than have usually constituted the culture-consuming public even as it continues its support for elite, standard-setting arts institutions.

In sum, a primary goal of Endowment policy had been to get the arts to the people. Government support for the arts cannot be characterized simply as a "transfer payment for the upper-middle class," nor as a form of "cultural imperialism" that threatens the artistic autonomy and cultural vitality of "non–high cultural taste publics."[19] Critics of the NEA's outreach efforts might note the following survey findings describing the condition of culturally less developed respondents.

> The responses of those without high-school diplomas to cross-sectional survey questions indicate that a sizeable group of Americans are, in fact, cultural dropouts, individuals with no apparent artistic or cultural interests. . . . Cultural deprivation then is not a matter of choosing performances of hobbies that diverge from upper-middle class norms; rather, it consists of having no creative or expressive pastimes, enjoying no performances of any kind, and being equally immune to the claims of galleries, zoos, or public parks.[20]

It is this unrepresented cultural constituency to whom the Endowment has addressed much of its efforts through nontraditional programming and support for community-based cultural activities. The NEA thus seeks to reconcile high culture with the mass public and to gain the broad support that is necessary for such a specialized public policy. It also bears repeating that small nonestablishmentarian arts groups will be badly, if not mortally, wounded by substantial reductions in public support. The major orchestras, opera companies, dance troupes, and museums will continue to operate regardless of public subsidy. Rich patrons and large corporations could still guarantee their basic operation expense even if public funding were abolished or dramatically reduced. Less likely to survive are community-based and minority-oriented institutions that depend almost solely on NEA, or NEA-generated, funds. Many of the needs of these special cultural constituencies are being addressed by local arts agencies; however, these agencies are themselves heavily dependent on NEA funds. The result of any drastic cuts in the arts budget would be a step from past public commitments to aesthetic pluralism and cultural democratization.

Notes

1. See Alan L. Feld and others, *Patrons Despite Themselves: Taxpayers and Arts Policy* (New York: New York University Press, 1983). In this Twentieth Century Fund Report, the authors argue that two-thirds of public support for the arts comes in an indirect form, principally through federal income tax deductions and local property tax exemptions.

2. Milton C. Cummings, Jr., "To Change a Nation's Cultural Policy," in *Public Policy and the Arts,* ed. Kevin V. Mulcahy and C. Richard Swaim (Boulder, Colo.: Westview Press, 1982), p. 142.

3. See William F. McDonald, *Federal Relief Administration* (Columbus: Ohio State University Press, 1968); Jerre Mangione, *The Dream and the Deal* (Boston: Little Brown, 1972); Richard McKinzie, *The New Deal for Artists* (Princeton: Princeton University Press, 1973); Jane DeHart Matthews, *The Federal Theatre, 1935–1939* (Princeton: Princeton University Press, 1967); Lawrence Mankin, "The National Government and the Arts: From the Great Depression to 1973" (Ph.D. dissertation, University of Illinois, 1976); Karal Ann Marling, *Wall to Wall America: A Cultural History of Post Office Murals in the Great Depression* (Minneapolis: University of Minnesota Press, 1982).

4. Kevin V. Mulcahy, "The Rationale for Public Cultures," in *Public Policy and the Arts,* pp. 52–55. See also Mulcahy, "The Public Interest in Public Culture," *Journal of Arts Management and Law* 21 (Spring 1991): 5–27.

5. Margaret J. Wyszomirski reports that in Frank Hodsoll's first year as NEA chairman, he exercised a "chairman's veto" on twenty out of a total of nearly six thousand panel-endorsed applications. Yet such an action was considered highly unusual. "Hodsoll's predecessor, Livingston Biddle, could not remember one instance of his overruling either a panel of Council recommendation during his entire four-year tenure." See "The Reagan Administration and the Arts, 1981–1983," paper prepared for presentation at the annual meeting of the American Political Science Association, Chicago, 1–4 September 1983, p. 14.

6. For a discussion of the panel system, see Committee on Appropriations, House of Representatives, *Report on the National Endowments for the Arts and Humanities,* U.S. Congress, House, 96th Congress, 1st Session, vol. 1, pp. 865–1041; see also Michael Straight, *Twigs for an Eagle's Nest: Government and the Arts, 1965–1978* (Berkeley: Devon Press, 1980), pp. 77–80.

7. For a contrary view, see Michael Macdonald Mooney, *The Ministry of Culture* (New York: Wyndham Books, 1981), pp. 330–74, but one should be advised that his discussion is often widely off the mark. See Kevin V. Mulcahy, "Public Culture and the Public," *Western Political Quarterly* 34 (September 1981): 461–70.

8. These characteristics of the panel system reflect the observations of the various NEA staffers interviewed by C. Richard Swaim for the "National Endowment for the Arts" in *Public Policy and the Arts,* pp. 169–204. This writer has reached similar conclusions during the time in which he has served as a panelist for the Louisiana Council on the Arts and for the Arts and Humanities Council of Greater Baton Rouge.

9. Arthur Svenson in Kevin V. Mulcahy, "Government and the Arts: A Symposium," *Journal of Aesthetic Education* 14 (October 1980): 36–37. See also Arthur Svenson, "State and Local Arts Agencies," in *Public Policy and the Arts,* p. 200.

10. Not all states with a "cultural department" include all of these cultural agencies under the departmental umbrella. See *Arts and the States* (Denver: National Conference of State Legislatures, 1981), pp. 41–42.

11. Ibid., p. 42.

12. Dick Netzer, *The Subsidized Muse: Public Support for the Arts in the United States* (New York: Cambridge University Press, 1978), p. 162.

13. "The Interrelationship of Funding for the Arts at the Federal, State, and Local Levels," *Report by the Committee on Government Operations,* U.S. Congress, House, 98th Congress, 1st Session, pp. 14–15.

14. *Arts and the States,* p. 47.

15. "The Interrelationship of Funding," pp. 32–33.

16. Anthony Downs, *Inside Bureaucracy* (Boston: Little Brown, 1966), p. 9.

17. Quoted in the U.S. House of Representatives, Democratic Study Group, "Special Report: The Stockman Hit List," mimeograph, 7 February 1981, p. 35.

18. Ibid.

19. For a discussion of different taste cultures and the aesthetic preferences involved, see Herbert Gans, *Popular Culture and High Culture* (New York: Basic Books, 1979); also see Gans, "American Popular Culture and High Culture in a Changing Class Structure," in *Art, Ideology and Politics,* ed. Judith Balfe and Margaret J. Wyszomirski (New York: Praeger, 1985), pp. 40–57 (reprinted in this volume).

20. Paul DiMaggio and Michael Useem, "The Arts and Cultural Participation," *Journal of Aesthetic Education* 14 (October 1980): 65.

3

Art and the General Welfare

Albert William Levi

Our judgment of the level of civilization of any specific epoch in Western culture may well hinge upon the propositions which it takes for granted. Today, for example, one is forced to ask, Does art promote the general welfare? What, after all, does culture contribute to the common good or general enlightenment? Such questions indicate an aesthetic skepticism endemic to a narrowly pragmatic or commercial age, where the cash nexus reigns supreme and even the arts themselves have become corrupted by the values of mechanical efficiency and private profit. Le Corbusier thinks that a city street is a machine for traffic to pass through as efficiently as possible. Other urban architects are under the quaint delusion that a home is a housing project. And serious books are now written with the title "Art as Investment" to aid collectors whose collections perform the same role as portfolios of blue chip stocks and bonds.

In other ages it was profoundly different. Cosimo de Medici, Sigismondo Malatesta, and Federigo da Montefeltro were also great collectors, and in some cases great businessmen, but they would have been scornful and contemptuous of a collector's passion guided by the principles of investment and tax deduction. The streets of the agora in Athens permitted rapid passage when necessary, but Alcibiades used them to meet and greet his friends, and Socrates lingered in them talking ethics and politics with sophists and young aristocrats as if they were a private club. And when Bess, Countess of Shrewsbury, commissioned Hardwick Hall in Derbyshire at about the time that Shakespeare was writing his first plays, it took three years to build and, however much the plan was symmetrical and the detail Italian, it was meant to service the exigencies of her life and no other.

I do not mean that the contrast has always been so black and white. Sometimes, as under the Protestant bourgeoisie of the Netherlands, it has been a mixed picture. But even there the plastic arts began as a necessity of civilized life. In Antwerp in 1560, with only 169 bakers and 78 butchers, there were said to be over 300 masters busy with painting and the graphic arts, proving that a fine landscape or portrait seemed no less a necessary food for the soul than bread and meat for the body. No philosopher, aesthetician, or educator of the Dutch seventeenth century would have bothered to ask the question, Does art promote the general welfare? The answer would have been only too obvious.

It is obvious to me, too, . . . and in a society which has within the last eight years established a National Foundation of the Arts and a National Foundation of the Humanities, funded through congressional appropriation and budgeted for the coming year at well over $150,000,000, I think it is slowly becoming obvious in the United States generally also. I shall not therefore present arguments to *prove* that art promotes the general welfare; rather, I shall attempt to indicate the way in which I think this promotion can best be accomplished and in so doing indirectly show why the issue is of the clearest relevance to a program of career education for the cultural services field.

In this task I shall use the terms *art* and *the general welfare* in restricted senses. A broad meaning of aesthetic welfare would include all acts of private enjoyment, appreciation, and enlightenment. For example, in seventeenth-century Holland there was an enormous private market for paintings. Terborch and Metsu worked for the very wealthy, de Hoogh and Vermeer for a somewhat less distinguished clientele, Jan Steen and Nicolaes Maes for the poorer class. But a passion to own and continually view works of art was universal; they were sold like gloves and fans at the Rotterdam fair and in the end managed to appear on the walls of even the most modest houses. Here art could indeed be said to work for the general welfare but, distributively rather than collectively, in the service of private rather than public acts of appreciation. This is not the sense of the general welfare that I will have in mind.

But the spirit of art can also be twofold. It has always been possible to judge the intentions of artists and the consequences of their work sociologically—that is, according to the Marxist criterion as to whether it serves to underwrite or to undermine the society within which it originates. The sculptures of Verrocchio and Donatello, commissioned for Florence, expressed acceptance of her needs and values. Giovanni Bellini, as "Pittore di Stato" in Venice, and his contemporary Carpaccio painted solemn processions and happy festivals to express the awe and respect they felt for their beloved Republic. But in a much later age Daumier's prints knew the rottenness of establishment "justice," George Grosz hated the smug sensualism of capitalist decadence, and Ben Shahn busied himself with urban poverty with all the irony of a man profoundly mistrustful of a commercial society and its cruel standard of distributive justice. In our own time Herbert Marcuse, always subtle and imaginative (if profoundly wrongheaded) in his treatment of the arts, interprets literature, painting, and all expressions of "high culture" as if they were by nature "oppositional"—that is to say, an imaginative bastion against the status quo, containing important transcending elements which stand over against and "refute" the given social reality.

But this also is not the kind of art with which I wish to deal in showing how art promotes the general welfare. For, with respect to the cultural services field today, the private sector of the general welfare and the critical function of art is less relevant than an art socially accepted and directed toward the public sector.

The mutual dependence of politics and culture is an old story. When Leonardo Bruni wrote his famous *Laudatio* ("Eulogy of the City of Florence") in 1404, he was elegiac not only of her liberal constitution, but also of her aesthetic order and proportions: "For just as harpstrings are attuned to each other so that, when they are twanged, a single harmony arises from all the different tones . . . just so this farsighted city has so adapted all her parts to each other that from them results a harmony of the total structure of the Republic. . . . Nothing in this state is ill-proportioned, nothing improper, nothing incongruous, nothing left vague; everything occupies its proper place which is not only clearly defined but also in the right relation to all others." With such classic principles of harmony and proportion applied at once to the physical structure of the city and to its legal constitution, it is not difficult to see here the inspiration for Jacob Burckhardt's contention that every major city-state of the Italian Renaissance was essentially a "work of art."

It was a point of view also congenial to the Founding Fathers of the American Republic—to Adams and Madison and above all to Jefferson, whose ideas of the separation and cooperation of the orders of classical Greek architecture were probably not unlike his ideas of the separation and cooperation of powers in the new Constitution. But the former must seem less credible to the contemporary inhabitants of Birmingham, Newark, or Detroit, where ruined countryside and sprawling commercial ugliness constrict the spirit and suggest rather the relationship between economic lawlessness and physical decay.

There is a contrast here which invites our consideration of the Renaissance alternative, for the acknowledged and crucial intimacy between art and the general welfare gives to the cities of the Italian Renaissance an exemplary character still striking even to the modern tourist. Consider the case of Florence. Today the busy modern city of Florence surges with endless traffic. To the visitor, the cathedral with its baptistry and bell tower, the old city hall, the Bargello, the Or San Michele, the churches—Santa

Maria Novella, Santa Croce, and the others—with their vast interior treasures, seem like some surviving museum of fabulous wonders out of a dead past. But the past in its own day was anything but dead: it was the product of order and plan, of artistic competitions and outright commissions, in the service of a single noble idea to which a varied and heterogeneous collection of groups and individuals contributed.

Already in the first great period of civic development (1280–1350) the pattern was set. In the late thirteenth century the wealthy merchant guild of cloth processors assumed the expenses for the maintenance and improvement of the baptistry of the cathedral, faced its outer walls with marble, and a few decades later commissioned the design and construction of its three magnificent bronze doors. At the same time the cathedral itself was enlarged and decorated through funds raised by an automatic levy on every city expenditure and by a small head tax on every male citizen, although in the early fourteenth century the funding and construction were given into the hands of the wool manufacturers—the richest guild in the city.

Meanwhile, other edifices were coming into being at prodigious cost. The Dominicans laid the foundations of Santa Maria Novella; not to be outdone, the Franciscans began Santa Croce. Arnolfo di Cambio, architect of the cathedral, also designed the new town hall. Giotto was put in charge of design and construction of the new bell tower. And on the site of the old grain market Orcagna was instructed to design and construct the most beautiful shrine possible for the great altarpiece which Bernardo Daddi had just been commissioned to paint. All of this took place early—a full century before Brunelleschi created the dome of the cathedral, the Foundling Hospital, and the church and sacristy of San Lorenzo; Michelozzo the cloister of San Marco and the Medici palace; and Donatello the great marble sculpture for the exterior niches of Or San Michele.

What is important is the continuity of the effort and the spirit in which it is undertaken. For the new burgher mentality—whatever the sordid conditions of its wealth—also represented aspirations growing out of civic pride and ambition: a sense of community founded upon the recognition that art is essential to the general welfare and that a polity growing daily in wealth and power should express this fact visibly through outer garments devised by the noblest imaginative products of its great architects, sculptors, and painters. And, if one finds here much of the mentality of the *nouveau arrivé*—of citizens who wish their city not only to *be* the first in the world but to *appear* as such—today's observer of Giotto's tower and the sculptures in the Bargello finds the sentiment easy to forgive.

True, there is little expression here of the ideals of equality and true democracy. Florence experienced the consistent economic crises of uncontrolled capitalism; during most of the Renaissance she was run by a clique of very rich merchants and bankers led by the Medici family. Morally, these men had little to recommend them. Politically, their motive was self-interest, and they continually used their power to siphon the city's riches into their own pockets. Yet these early rulers had one saving grace: they had been born into a tradition of civic patronage. Their ancestors had endowed churches, monasteries, and charitable foundations. The sense of sin which still hung over the practice of usury seemed to demand restitution, but even those rich merchants and bankers clearly deficient in the sense of sin still felt the need to express gratitude for their good fortune through civic donations and endowments.

A century later these generous habits were securely buttressed by the theories and the attitudes of classical humanism. Those in the governing circles of Florence became convinced that their great city was the true heir of republican Rome. The great oligarchs, in their leisure from conducting diplomacy and collecting taxes, read Plato and above all Cicero, and they began to feel as never before that the good life was only possible if a man devoted himself to civic virtue. Civic humanism thus became the true presupposition of the doctrine that art is essential to the promotion of the general welfare. It was true then, and if art is ever in our own time to be reestablished as an ingredient in the general welfare, civic humanism will once more have to come into its own.

During the half-century of Medician power, Florence dominated the intellectual and artistic life of the Italian Renaissance. Cosimo de Medici poured out a fortune on buildings, sculptures, and paintings for the public good—so much so that his grandson Lorenzo the Magnificent, astounded by the staggering sums spent by his grandfather, found it cheaper simply to patronize philosophers. However, he did not completely turn his back upon the traditions of his family, and Florentine civic life continued to prosper and express itself in the public accumulation of magnificent works of fine art.

Nevertheless, when one considers the full two centuries of Florentine greatness, it is impossible to attribute it to the munificence of a single family. In fact, what is enormously impressive is to consider the extent to which its benefactors are heterogeneous in name and composition: the great noble families like the Medici, Strozzi, and Rucellai, the great monastic orders of the church, and the enormously wealthy and powerful craft guilds like the cloth processors, goldsmiths, wool manufacturers, and leatherworkers. This is heartening to remember in a mixed economy and power structure like our own, where government agencies and private philanthropists, giant corporations and mammoth unions could turn their attention to the rehabilitation of America—if only the ideology were available and the civic attitudes revivified.

But in considering the case of Florence, there is one thing more to remember. The slow formation of a true humanistic culture which renewed the foundations of knowledge by re-creating the classic past and which, in so doing, at once interpreted anew man's place in nature and his importance as a creature of history and tradition, made her the first to view and to publicize the activities of city life as the heart of an organized society. No longer a mere association of trading and commercial interests, the city itself, in its meaning and historical accretions, became a product of reason and fine art. In the new elite which assumed control over the political and cultural life of the city, there was a special place for those whose imagination of the city combined the requirements of reason and beauty. The most cultivated and influential artists—and those closest to the centers of political power—were the architects. But they were architects whose elaborate designs were for the revision of the older city layout by the creation of new urban vistas and wide regular squares, for the addition of new sections to the city and the construction of structures whose masses were meant to monitor the development of the future homes and public edifices of the developing urban center. It is no accident that treatises on architecture in the fifteenth and sixteenth centuries were full of ideal cities and that many of the proposed vistas are suggestive of stage designs. The architectural designs of Leon Battista Alberti in the mid-1400s and of Andrea Palladio a hundred years later show that the specific problems of individual buildings have become subordinate to the global aspects of the city plan.

The organic interconnection between the fine arts which this entails is obvious. Paintings and sculptures become part of the idea of the building and integral to its meaning and valuational expression, just as these same buildings become the jewels in the total setting which constitutes the urban plan. The very metaphor of "jewel" is not inappropriate, since the orientation from tradition of civic humanism for the first time brings to the fore the importance of "the historical monument" and causes the architect–city planner to design in full awareness of the importance of his city's "cultural resources." From this perspective the shape and meaning of the city should depend, not upon its modes of production or commercial advantages, but upon its great historical monuments. Thus, however much the great architectural planners played with the geometrical forms of "the ideal city," their actual work was based less on logic than on history.

The essence of the monument is that it is a building or edifice which symbolizes and expresses historical and ideological values of moral and spiritual importance to the community. When the architect or city planner is "a man of culture," he senses instinctively that what makes a city valuably historical or traditional is its fortunate accumulation of cultural assets—

universities, libraries, collections of antiquities, great churches with their works of art, monuments to wars and heroes, noble theaters, academies of music and fine art—which are at once a valuable heritage and a source of civic pride. In this perspective the arts contribute to the general welfare even in the humble and inglorious corners of civic life, as, for example, its charitable and remedial aspects. When Brunelleschi is asked to give artistic form to an orphanage (Ospedale degli Innocenti) and Rembrandt to paint one of his noblest canvases for the public poorhouse in Amsterdam, this expresses an attitude which our Department of Health, Education, and Welfare and our state boards of education and housing would do well to follow.

It may seem that I have dwelt too long and self-indulgently on the aesthetic history of Renaissance Florence. But my purpose has been by indirection to focus attention upon that civic humanism which was her glory—and, as I see it, the only possibility of our own American restoration. I have long been convinced that the future of the arts and the humanities, both as lived and as taught, is bound up with the rehabilitation of our cities and the elimination of the worst of their degradation and ugliness.

It is surely not necessary to dwell upon the obvious—the forms of pathology which afflict our civic life: fragmentation, loss of immediacy and close communication, isolation, mechanization, impersonality, retreat into unconcern. The abstractions are terrifying, but they stand for all that we recognize in our current diminution and impoverishment, and they are often simply the effects of the unrestrained bent for profit at any cost, poverty, brutality, and racial injustice with which the last American decades have been afflicted.

Size, industrialization, and the automobile have been against us. The Athenians believed that the range of democracy was the range of the orator's voice. Analogously, I firmly believe that the range of real community is the range of the pedestrian possibility. The isolationism of the suburban mentality is a disaster, but it springs in part from an impulse which is good—an effort to limit the size of the urban unit in the attempt (however fruitless) to reestablish the lost cohesiveness of neighborhood.

History seems to show that cultural achievement and social living flourish best in the organic community of manageable size: Periclean Athens, Medician Florence, the Venetian Republic of the fourteenth and fifteenth centuries, Baroque Vienna under Maria Theresa, where painting, sculpture, architecture, music, and drama, as well as reading and good talk, flowered within an environment of social cohesion and civic concern. Urban life has always been the fountainhead of culture, and the contemporary metropolitan crisis, with its erosion of public safety, flight to the suburbs, and the physical decay of the central city, bodes ill for the humanist as well as for the human future. Not until the urban environment is once again manageable in size, walkable, proud of its monuments and open spaces, and the locus of a revived civic and cultural concern will an American future be secure.

How to bring this about? The mind boggles at the immensity and complexity of the task. It means new principles of economic adjustment between productive responsibility and consumer need, new patterns of distributive justice, new concepts respecting the civic duties of the public and private sectors of the economy. But it will also require new attitudes about civic virtue, the concept of the city, and the necessary role of the arts in relation to the general welfare.

Consider first the simple but almost insoluble difficulty which the automobile and the economic separation of functions have produced in our attitude toward the city. If the central city is viewed as a business locale *only,* then all is lost. Historically, the city is a social congregation of people, for business certainly, but also for pleasure, education, and ceremony. One has only to attend to Lorenzetti's frescoes in the town hall in Siena, Carpaccio's civic processions in Venice, and Canaletto's great baroque cityscapes of Venice, Vienna, and Dresden to know that a great, flourishing, active city means citizens in the streets, and to recognize the hollowness of Le Corbusier's conception of a city street as a machine for traffic to pass through rather than a square—market, cathedral, town hall, theater, or university, as the case may be—in which citizens may stroll, linger, and discourse. If in the modern world we turn out to be merely family men or organization men, our isolation and boredom are irreparable. One of our utopian city planners long ago voiced the dreadful possibility: "It is possible that this (Greek, Mediaeval, or Renaissance) urban beauty is a thing of the past. Perhaps there are no longer real occasions for social congregations in the square. The larger transactions of business occur at a distance by 'communication,' not face to face. Politics is by press, radio, and ballot. Social pleasure is housed in theaters and dance halls. If this is so, it is a grievous and irreparable loss. There is no substitute for the spontaneous social conflux whose atoms unite, precisely, as citizens of the city. If it is so, our city crowds are doomed to be lonely crowds, bored crowds, humanly uncultured crowds."

These words were written over twenty-five years ago, before racial discord, rampant industrial pollution, and increasing poverty and drug-connected crime had turned our cities into a living hell. Ironically, in this radical worsening may lie the very possibility of salvation. I think it is now clear that American civilization faces a single option: either reform and redesign and resurrect, or perish.

In this redesigning and reconstruction we shall need city planning architects like those of the Renaissance, with economic resources provided as then by the multiple economic establishments of a pluralistic society. But the lead must be taken by federal, state, and local governments, and behind it all must lie the concept of the city: not the city as a vast industrial complex supported by housing projects sustaining an urban proletariat with its middle-class managers and professionals, but the city as an exemplification of history and of culture, with theaters, museums, universities, concert halls, libraries, churches, and schools becoming monuments of function *and* aesthetic expressiveness. Only in terms of such a program of massive urban reconstruction does it make sense to raise questions about "career education" for the future, with the arts and the humanities as related ingredients of an "occupational cluster," and to view this education as preparatory for entrance into "the cultural services field." Otherwise our efforts will be temporary and ad hoc, and we shall not see the forest for the trees.

With such a global reorientation, it goes without saying that the contribution of the arts and humanities to the general welfare will be considered not as secondary—as the fortuitous bloom upon the peach of economic prosperity—but as an essential ingredient in that humane way of life for which the peach itself is but necessary nourishment. The quaint reversal of the economic and the aesthetic factors in civilization (so prevalent in a dangerously acquisitive society) will be set right once more, and a truer relationship between intrinsic and instrumental value will service the life which is desirable (and possible) under the aegis of civic humanism.

4

Art and the Public Interest

Edward C. Banfield

Toward the end of Balzac's great novel, *Cousin Bette,* a kindly and thoughtful courtesan raises the question that I wish to discuss. Josepha, the former mistress of Baron Hulot, has taken pity on his distraught and impoverished wife. If you only had the skills of a courtesan, she tells the baroness, you would be able to keep your husband from running after the likes of me. A practical woman, she sees the problem here: How is a virtuous woman to learn the tricks of a courtesan? But she also sees the solution to the problem: "The government," she says, "ought to start a school for respectable women."

Well, why not?

If one supposes that a government ought to do whatever will give its people—a majority of them, or perhaps any minority that can get legislation passed—pleasure, or whatever it is that they want. If one supposes this, what objection can be made to Josepha's proposal? Is there any limit to the sphere of a democratic government? Are there principles which enable one to say government may properly do this but not that? If so, what are they? This, in its most general form, is the question I mainly wish to discuss.

Let us narrow the question, first, by limiting ourselves to the American government. If there are principles of the sort that I am looking for, they may be different from place to place and time to time. Josepha was a child of the French Revolution. We are the great-great-grandchildren of the American Revolution. So the question is, In the light of American tradition and American present-day reality, are there limits to the scope of government? If there are, what are they?

Although we are looking for general answers to these questions, it will be convenient to discuss them in the context of a particular subject matter: art, especially visual art. What is the justification, if any, for public, i.e., taxpayer, support of art and artists?

As you doubtless know, since 1965 the National Endowment for the Arts has given grants, some large and some small, to individuals and to organizations who, or which, in the judgment of panels of artists and other "qualified" persons, will thereby be enabled to make a larger contribution to cultural life. By comparison with most Federal subsidy programs—say, those for farm products—those for the arts are picayune: a very tiny drop in the federal budget deficit. By far the largest part of what the public gives for the support of art is in the form of indirect, rather than direct, subsidies; various tax exemptions are far more important to the budgets of art institutions than are direct grants from the National Endowment or other governmental sources. But even taking indirect subsidies into account, the sums of public money involved are small by comparison with almost anything else that the federal government does.

My reason for singling out for discussion the public subsidy of art (rather than, say, the growing of tobacco) is that art presents—or rather *seems* to present—a hard case. To anyone but a thorough-going Philistine it may seem obvious that the support of art is a proper, even a highly desirable, activity of government. It is easy to make a case against public subsidy of tobacco-growing. But what can be said against the subsidy of art?

Let us look at the American political tradition as it bears upon these matters, especially the principles of the Founders—principles laid down in the Declaration of Independence and the Constitution.

I use the phrase "natural law liberalism" to characterize the *political* theory of the Founders. The element of *liberalism* in the American tradition is epitomized by the ringing words of the Declaration of Independence: All men are endowed by their Creator with certain unalienable rights; among these are life, liberty, and the pursuit of happiness. To secure these rights governments are instituted. For the philosopher John Locke, whose writings these words echo, the only justification for the infringement of liberty is its preservation. As you know, Jefferson, the author of the Declaration, was an extremist in defense of liberty.

But the Founders were the heirs of Aristotle as well as of Locke, and the idea of individual liberty was wholly alien to the thought of the ancients. "What the statesman is . . . anxious to produce," Aristotle wrote, "is a certain moral character in his fellow citizens, namely, a disposition to virtue and to the performance of virtuous actions." Most of the state constitutions written before the federal one contained provisions to encourage "civic virtue," without which, the constitution-makers thought, individual liberty would be no blessing at all. In the deliberations of the Constitutional Convention at Philadelphia, however, there was no discussion of civic virtue. Even those like James Madison who wished to supplant the states with a national government did not contemplate a morally improving function for the new government. The Preamble of the Constitution declares its purpose: to form a more perfect Union, establish justice, ensure domestic tranquility, protect for the common defense, secure the blessings of liberty.

There had been, you will remember, a stiff contest between those who wanted to preserve the sovereignty of the states and those who wanted to subordinate the states to the national government. In the end, there was a compromise. Article I, Section VIII of the Constitution enumerates the powers given to the national government, all others being (by the Tenth Amendment) reserved to the states and to the people thereof.

If you look down that list of the eighteen enumerated powers—to lay and collect taxes, to borrow money, to establish a uniform rule of naturalization, and so on—you will not find one that could conceivably authorize a program for the support of art, culture, or even moral improvement. (There is a power "to promote progress of science and useful arts." This is the patent clause, an altogether different matter.) As the authors of the *Federalist* declared, the powers of the national government were "few and defined." How few and how sharply defined Washington discovered when he recommended to Congress the establishment of a national university. Madison, as president, made that same recommendation, accompanying it with an acknowledgment that a constitutional amendment would be necessary to make it possible.

The powers of the federal government are no longer "few and defined"; they are many and undefined. The change has come about in recent decades through interpretation by the Supreme Court of the "general welfare" and the "necessary and proper" clauses of the Constitution. In my opinion the Court's rulings violate the intention of the Framers and of the voters who ratified the Constitution. (Need I say that mine is a minority opinion?)

One may argue that, whatever the intentions of the Framers and Ratifiers, the course of events in the past two hundred years has made it necessary to enlarge the federal sphere. Perhaps this is so. But the enlargement of that sphere has not been the consequence of any general public discussion and has not been guided by any general principles. So I think it is fair to say that the American *tradition,* although not the American *practice,* still gives the federal government only such powers as were delegated to it.

If Americans have never entirely agreed, or been entirely clear, about the scope of the two great and more or less conflicting purposes of government—the protection of the individual in the exercise of his rights and his improvement as a citizen—they *have* agreed that government ought always to serve *public,* as opposed to private, interests. The Vermont constitution of 1793 contained a provision typical of those in many other state constitutions: "That government is or ought to be instituted for the common benefit, and not for the particular emolument or advantage of any single man, family, or set of men, who are only part of that community."

What Americans have agreed to is the *principle* that government, state or national, should do only such things as will serve *public* interests. Obviously the application of this principle presents difficulties in a large and heterogeneous society—difficulties that would not exist in a small and homogeneous one. What exactly can it mean to speak to an interest common to the community when the community is not a village, or even a society like that of the Founders (consisting of about 3 million persons, slaves not counted), but rather a society as large and complex as our own? Is there any interest that *all* Americans share? Clearly it is not always possible to say what is in the common interest and what is not. Nevertheless I cannot agree with those who say that the idea is entirely without content.

In thinking about what is meant by "the common benefit" it seems to me essential to distinguish between two quite different conceptions. One I'll call the "welfare" conception. This derives from utilitarianism, the slogan of which was (and is) "the greatest good of the greatest number"—*good* here meaning whatever the individual chooses provided it does not harm others. According to this conception one is "better off" when he gets what he wants, whatever that may be. The term *general welfare* refers to the welfare of individuals viewed in the aggregate: it is the level of satisfaction of the members of the society considered as private persons, each with his or her set of wants, desires, tastes, whims, or whatever.

The other, contrasting conception is of "the public interest." This refers to those wants that people have when in the role of citizen, that is, as members of a public. The very idea of a "society" implies that those who constitute it share some guiding conceptions of right and of justice, of how matters that affect them collectively are to be decided, of the necessity of coping collectively with problems, some actual and pressing and others yet unknown but sure to arise eventually, and therefore of the necessity of preserving and if possible improving their capacity to respond effectively to unspecifiable needs over what seems to be an endless future—endless because the collectivity is mortal in the sense that the individuals who compose it are.

I believe that the principal concern of government ought to be with the public interest, not the general welfare. I do not say that assisting individuals—"consumers"—to get more of what they want is *never* a proper function of government. But I *do* say that the *principal,* the *overriding,* task of government, is with matters that concern "citizens." In other words, "welfare," what individuals in their private capacities think good for themselves, ought to be subordinate to the "public interest," what individuals in their capacity as members of a public think good for the public.

By way of illustration, I suggest that a courthouse is justified in a way that a statue in front of it is not. The courthouse exists for the performance of a function—the administration of justice—that is indispensable to the well-being and good order of a public, a function that can *only* be served by government. The statue is there to give pleasure to the eye of the passerby.

So much for political theory. I turn now to its bearing on governmental support of art. The National Endowment and other public agencies give to all of the arts—music, the dance, theatre, literature, as well as visual art. I limit myself now to visual art. What I have to say about public support of it has some application to the other arts. But the question of how much application I will have to set aside.

The key question for me is this: Is the promotion of visual art in the public interest? Is it like the courthouse or like the statue in front of the courthouse? If one examines the arguments that were made for the establishment of the National Endowment one finds that its proponents (there were hardly any opponents) couched their arguments in public interest terms. The "culture industry" of New York City was the most powerful single proponent. Supporters of the bill mentioned, but did not rest their case on, the benefits that would accrue to hotels, restaurants, and shops from the tourist trade that subsidies to New York's cultural institutions would attract. What they emphasized was that government support would give "official recognition" to art and culture and, by so doing, "improve the image" of the United States and "raise its prestige." No politician was fooled by this rhetoric, of course. There was a general sense that it was unseemly to point to naked commercial interests. They had to be clothed in the rhetoric of the public interest.

Curiously this rhetoric did not claim benefits to the public from art as aesthetic experience; the claims were mostly on grounds that had only an incidental relation to art. Subsidy of art would not only "improve the image" of the United States; it would also improve international understanding, benefit the poor, and relieve tensions in the urban ghettoes. These alleged benefits were of course all ones that could be achieved—if they could be achieved at all—as well or better by means entirely different than the support of art.

A century or more ago, more plausible connections between art—I speak now of visual art only—and the public interest were asserted, although in support of demands on government. After the Civil War, when the great museums were founded, art was seen by the Protestant elite that ran things as a means of moralizing the growing populations of the large cities—of inculcating the domestic and civic virtues which (so the elite supposed) the largely immigrant underlying population lacked. Frederick Law Olmstead, for example, who was one of the creators of Central Park in New York and also a trustee of the Metropolitan Museum of Art, wrote that "public parks, gardens, galleries of art and instruction in art, music, athletic sports, and healthful recreations" were all "means of cultivating taste." To the reformers of the time it appeared that the underlying population lacked "habits of discipline." Cultural institutions, the historian David D. Hall has written, were seen as a way of imposing an "ethic of deference to 'the best.' "

This view of the social function of art rested upon a particular conception of the nature of art. In the middle of the nineteenth century the great opinion-maker in the art world was John Ruskin, for whom beauty, truth, and goodness were all one. Art being something that would elevate and refine the popular mind, it was certainly plausible for the reformers to build museums. This was done on a large scale, but mainly through private philanthropy; local governments gave land, but in the last century—indeed until after the Second World War—hardly anyone thought it constitutional for the federal government to support the arts directly.

The great museums had hardly been built when Ruskin's doctrines were declared obsolete and the art world defined art in altogether different terms. Walter Pater and others declared that art existed for its *own* sake—that it had nothing to do with truth and morality. There have since been successive reformulations by artists, critics, and philosophers on the nature of art, each one bringing it into a more abstract and esoteric realm, a realm farther from popular interest and understanding. Today it is hard to find an artist of any standing who thinks that his or her work has, or ought to have, a morally or otherwise improving effect upon the viewer. There is much disagreement as to what is properly to be called "art," but I think it is safe to say—with respect to *visual* art—that art is now widely understood to pertain to a world that is radically separated from that of ordinary experience. Much contemporary art is intended to jolt the viewer out of his normal perception of the world—to shock or surprise him into seeing the world as absurd, irrational, or as something that does not matter. Consider, for example, the message of Ad Reinhardt's work, *Abstract Painting*. He has described it as follows:

> A square (neutral, shapeless) canvas, five feet wide, five feet high, as high as a man, as wide as a man's outstretched arms (not large, not small, sizeless), trisected (no composition), one horizontal form negating one vertical form (formless, no top, no bottom, directionless), three more or less dark (lightless), non-contrasting (colorless) colors, brushwork brushed out to remove brushwork, a mat, flat, free-hand painted surface (glossless, texture-less, non-linear, no hard edge, no soft edge) which does not reflect its surroundings—a pure, abstract,

non-objective, timeless, spaceless, changeless, relationless, disinterested painting, an object that is self-conscious (no unconsciousness), ideal, transcendent aware of nothing but art (absolutely no anti-art).

If one thinks, as I do, that the proper function of government is to attend to *public* matters—that is, to what concerns the *citizen* as opposed to the consumer—one cannot justify governmental support of visual art, not at least as art is understood by the art world today. If one thinks that art is a public matter one ought, to be consistent, to favor government censorship, or suppression, of such art as is deemed injurious to the public.

If, in the tradition of Aristotle, one identifies "the good" with what is most distinctively human—with reason above all, but also the love of the beautiful—one must conclude that what exalts the distinctively human is admirable and what debases it is the reverse. Art which debases man, which tells him that human life is absurd, or disgusting, must, if words are used properly, be called obscene. The protection of the public against obscenity is, and always has been, a proper function of government. It is part of what we call environmental protection.

I do not want to be understood as saying that contemporary art is obscene and should be suppressed. Most of it claims to be—and I suppose is—quite irrelevant to any public concern. As for that which *is* obscene, I doubt that as a practical matter it has enough effect on the quality of the society to justify incurring the dangers inherent in censorship. But we should recognize that the claim for governmental intervention must cut both ways: if government should support some art on public interest grounds, then—in principle—it should suppress some on the same grounds.

Whether or not art is improving from a *public* standpoint, there is no doubt at all that it is a source of private satisfaction to a great many people. (I say "satisfaction" rather than "pleasure" because the aesthetic experience is not necessarily pleasurable: sometimes it is unsettling, even painful). If you go to an exhibition of, say, French Impressionists you are likely to find crowds so thick that it is difficult to see the paintings. That surely is evidence that large numbers of people "enjoy," or get satisfaction from, viewing that kind of art. Thus art can contribute to the "welfare" of individuals even when it does not serve the public interest.

Subsidies can, and doubtless do, increase the amount of art consumed. They make it possible, for example, for museums to exhibit more works and to exhibit them more often. They make artworks more accessible to people who live at a distance from great museums. They help to introduce school children to aesthetic experience, a dimension of life many might otherwise miss.

Tibor Scitovsky, an eminent economist, has written persuasively in *The Joyless Economy* of the high rate of return that is to be had from improving one's tastes. A predictable happy ending or a too-simple piece of music, he says, yields less satisfaction than one would get if one learned to enjoy something more complex. An investment of time and money to improve one's tastes, Scitovsky says, will pay off handsomely. The justification for public support of the arts—he believes that it is the *only* justification—arises from this opportunity to increase welfare by improving tastes. I have two objections to this argument for public support. The first you have already heard: Giving people pleasure is not the proper business of government.

My other objection to the claim that government ought to invest in the improvement of tastes is that individuals have ample incentive to make such investments on their own. I grant that it is often very difficult to know how to invest wisely in the improvement of one's tastes—how much time and effort (not to mention money) will be required to acquire a new taste? And how much satisfaction will the newly acquired taste yield? These considerations discourage investment, I have no doubt. But it is a fact of everyday experience that most people are constantly endeavoring to acquire new tastes, tastes they expect will yield them more and better satisfactions than the old ones. Think of all the people who are employed to teach others to ski, to play the violin, to do gourmet cooking, to distinguish vintage wine from *vin ordinaire,* and so on.

Some may ask, Why shouldn't government do what it can to help consumers get whatever satisfactions they want (subject only to the provision that these satisfactions be not injurious to others)? That the founders limited the scope of government to *public* purposes is a fact of history, but the world today is very different from the world of two hundred years ago. The democratic principle—some may say—requires that government, the servant of the people, do whatever the people want.

I doubt if anyone will want to carry this argument all the way. No one thinks that 51 percent of the people are entitled to do as they please with the other 49 percent. Indeed, no one thinks that a majority *however large* is entitled to infringe the rights of a minority *however small.* There is no escaping the need to limit the sphere of government. And there is no escaping the conclusion that, whatever government does, it ought to serve a *public* purpose. This is so because everything that government does involves the exercise of coercion, or the threat of it, and no *private* purpose can justify coercion.

These are the decisive considerations. There are others—of a prudential nature—that support the conclusion that public support of art is undesirable. Let me list some. (No importance is to be attached to the order of the listing.)

1. Government support of art involves a transfer of income in the wrong direction: that is, from the less well-off to the more well-off. Museumgoers and concertgoers are mostly relatively prosperous as compared to the average taxpayer. Why should the "poor" subsidize the "not poor"?

2. Economists can demonstrate rigorously that a competitive market will allocate goods and services efficiently—that is, in a way that cannot be improved upon if consumers' tastes are the standard. Admittedly, many markets are not truly competitive, and some goods are by their nature such that they cannot be allocated by a market. These limitations have little application to the art world, however. A museum is no less able than a movie house to charge an entrance fee. Nowadays most museums *do* charge, but they charge less than the full cost of what they provide—and less, incidentally, than any movie house. If, like the movie, the museum charged what would yield it the greatest "profit" (that is, difference between income and costs), one could be sure that it was not wasting resources. Insofar as subsidies take the place of a price set by the market, one cannot know whether resources are being wasted or not. Imagine a heavily endowed museum, the displays of which no one wants to see. Such a museum might exist indefinitely, occupying a choice site and filling its storerooms with costly objects; even though it served no one, there would be no way of bringing it to an end. Imagine, by contrast, a museum that, like the movie house, depends entirely on its earnings. It would have a strong incentive to find ways to please its customers, and one could be reasonably sure that a customer who paid its entrance fee expected to get at least as much satisfaction from its displays as he would from any other use of his money.

3. One may oppose governmental intervention—even in some matters that serve the public interest—on the grounds that there is a limit to what government can do effectively and that this limit has been reached or perhaps overreached. The argument is that we ought to forgo doing some things that are of lesser importance in order that we may do better those that are absolutely essential—national defense, for example. Several years ago the Advisory Commission on Intergovernmental Relations, a body established by Congress to monitor the working of the federal system, urged the president to initiate a national debate on the topic "What is a 'national purpose'?" The idea was to see if national programs could be grouped according to priority—some as "paramount" (national defense and the economy), others "primary" (e.g., the postal system), "secondary" (the lesser regulatory programs), "tertiary" (state and local activities involving the federal government), and, finally, those "of no real concern." The proposal was never taken seriously, perhaps because everything that the national government does is of "paramount" importance in the eyes of its beneficiaries.

A sacrifice of effectiveness from trying to do too much is perhaps most easily recognized as an administrative phenomenon: there is a natural limit to the number of talented executives as well as to the number and range of problems to which any one executive can give attention. But the problem has a political dimension as well. It is impossible for even the most conscientious voter to be reasonably well informed about even the most important issues of our day. The more numerous the matters that he must pass upon the less competent he must be and—what is surely no less important—the less confidence he can have in his own and in his fellow citizens' judgments.

4. Finally, I want to argue that governmental support of art tends to confuse people about the nature of art and, indeed, to substitute for aesthetic values other values that are unrelated to it. This criticism applies to *direct* subsidies such as those of the National Endowment, not to indirect ones via tax exemptions. The objection to the direct subsidies is that they give rise to an art "establishment" intent upon the expansion of any publicly supported activities to which the word *art* can with the slightest plausibility be attached. Since 1965, when direct aid began, there has been brought about into existence a coalition of interests—private associations, state art agencies (every state has one), the congressional art caucus, and of course the National Endowment itself—that is devoted to the enlargement of the sphere of public support. From the standpoint of those who think that government ought *not* to support the arts the emergence of this coalition is obviously something to be deplored. But it ought to also be deplored by those who want government to support "real" art—art which affords a genuine aesthetic experience. Like all public agencies, the tendency of the National Endowment and of the other art agencies is to magnify their callings—to respond to the demands of their various constituencies by establishing new programs and extending old ones, and also to create new constituencies to which they can point when they come to OMB and congressional appropriations hearings. The NEA, according to Ronald Berman, a former chairman of its sister agency, the National Endowment for the Humanities, has sanctioned the idea that the primary purpose of support of art is the distribution of funds. The arts constituency, he writes, "determines what the definition of art of 'the arts' will be. And that constituency has in the most determined way exempted artistic activity from critical standards. Art is whatever is done, whether crafts, hobbies, or simply the display of intentions. It is an ennobled form of middle-class entertainment."

What Berman calls the "redefinition of art" must be expected to continue and even to gain momentum as the agencies and their constituencies succeed in enlarging each other. The impulse to expand without much regard to direction arises from the very nature of organization, and since the potential supporters of "real" art are relatively few, art will be "redefined" to suit the most popular taste. Ironically, then, agencies created to raise popular taste end by succumbing to popular taste.

5

Aesthetic Welfare, Aesthetic Justice, and Educational Policy

Monroe C. Beardsley

The concept of *aesthetic welfare*—if it can be framed clearly and concretely—ought to be useful in our thinking about some broad and fundamental problems. It could identify a distinguishable area of concern as a subject of public policy, in terms of which a basic educational goal might be defined. It could contribute to our understanding of what is involved in some difficult political choices and help to make these choices more rational.[1]

One way of framing this concept is to begin by noting that our experience during different stretches of time may differ considerably in the degree to which it is marked by aesthetic quality—that is, in its aesthetic level. By "aesthetic quality" I mean the kind of pleasure or sense of satisfaction and fulfillment that comes from awareness of the way elements of experience interrelate in order to bring about the formation of complex unities that are marked by emergent regional qualities. I do not extend the aesthetic dimension of experience to include sheer sensuous agreeableness or local pleasure, but neither do I claim that the lines of demarcation are sharp. Still, I would say that, in designing a public transportation system, a concern for harmonious color combinations and good proportions is aesthetic, but a concern for quiet operation and comfortable seats is not.

The aesthetic level of experience ranges from the neighborhood of zero to utter absorption, such as is likely to occur only in the presence of great works of art or rare natural settings. The level is dependent on what is available in one's surroundings, for the surroundings are the occasion for aesthetically qualified experience and provide the ingredients for it. It is also dependent on the will of the experiencer, who may choose to ignore what is around him, or to attend only fitfully and selectively.[2] We can nevertheless speak of the *capacity* of objects, situations, events, etc. (including, of course, literary works of art and the intentional worlds they project), to raise the aesthetic level of experience significantly, when they are encouraged to. This capacity is what I take to be aesthetic value—with the important qualification that to say that an object has aesthetic value is, I hold, to say not only that it has the capacity to raise the aesthetic level of experience significantly but also that to do this is itself desirable. Judgments of aesthetic value are, in one aspect, estimates of a particular capacity, but they are not reducible to empirical estimates, for they have an ineradicable normative character.

That it can be not only enjoyable but also desirable for experience to have a high aesthetic level is a proposition I shall have to assume without argument here. I do not say that this is the only feature of experience that makes it worth having, and I do not deny that it is incompatible with other desirable features and so must often be sacrificed for their attainment. But when a rise in the aesthetic level of experience occurs without loss of other desirable qualities, experience always becomes more desirable. And that a person's experience in general has recurrent aesthetic quality and sometimes reaches high aesthetic levels is (I claim) a necessary element in a good life.

The concept of aesthetic value, framed in the terms I propose, presents philosophical problems that I shall have to pass by here. It may even be that the whole attempt to discriminate a particular species of value—that sort of value characteristically and preeminently possessed by works of art—is misguided. But unless we make some distinctions among species of value, or kinds of good, I don't see how our value-seeking, or value-realizing, enterprises can hope to be conducted very reasonably or effectively. Difficult though it is to distinguish a peculiarly aesthetic value from others with which it is intertwined, I do not think the task has been shown to be hopeless or useless. Moreover, there are good reasons to believe that aesthetic value, as a distinct sort, must be one of the general and fundamental categories of value.

Considering a particular society and its "habitat," to borrow a term from A. E. Parr,[3] we can form the concept of the totality of objects (using this term broadly) that belong to that habitat and that possess discernible aesthetic value. They may include natural objects and scenes, articles of use and decoration, and what in some narrower sense are marked off as works of art; they may even include the people themselves, insofar as they are part of each other's environment. This totality of aesthetically valuable objects I call the *aesthetic wealth* of that society.

It may be questioned whether we have here a logically acceptable sort of totality. We can't really count objects as such, but only kinds of objects. Yet objects that are identified by members of a society as individual things will be objects of some kind—stones, trees, hats, beards, songs, dances, or whatever. And within each category we can, in principle, separate the objects that have aesthetic value from those that lack it. Or am I mistaken about this? I can think, offhand, of a lot of things that I would unreflectingly discard from the aesthetic pile: many stones, many buildings, most pigeons, ordinary shoes, old soiled raincoats, etc. I do not say that nothing could be done with these by an artist who set out determinedly to transform them into works of art, but I think that as they stand, in their natural setting, they are for all practical purposes devoid of aesthetic value. Perhaps I am being too hasty; an extremely sensitive and imaginative aesthete, trying very hard, might discern something in the old spilled raincoat—some bit of color-harmony or of visual rhythm—that would raise the aesthetic level of his experience, even though the rest of us are blind to it. I doubt that this is true for every object. But suppose I am mistaken: then everything in the habitat must be listed in an inventory of the society's aesthetic wealth, though some things may add so little to the total as to fall under an aesthetic *de minimis* principle.

Wealth is a potentiality; welfare is its actualization. The *aesthetic welfare* of a society at a given time consists of all the aesthetic levels of the experience of members of the society at a given time. The concept is more useful when framed with respect to a period of time: we then speak of the aesthetic welfare as of a particular day or year. A day on which one has heard a fine performance of Beethoven's D Minor Symphony, or on which one has spent a number of hours exploring a beautiful lake in the mountains, may be said to involve greater aesthetic welfare than a day spent, say, in a subway and in a noisy, cluttered office. The problems of comparison are formidable and may be thought insurmountable. There is no great difficulty in one person's comparing one stretch of his experience with another—he can tell, if he possesses the concept, when the aesthetic level has risen or declined. But does it make sense to sum these levels over a day or a year, to average them, to compare averages interpersonally? If we cannot make sense of these procedures, the concept of aesthetic welfare will remain too amorphous to be manageable, and we shall have to dispense with it. There is no doubt a kind of sense we cannot make until we provide something operationally equivalent to a thermometer, which would enable us to assign numbers to aesthetic levels—even though such magnitudes would be no more extensional and additive than are degrees Fahrenheit. Such a prospect would alarm some of us who are concerned with the arts, but I don't see that it would necessarily do any harm, and I don't see that it would be in principle impossible. Meanwhile, we speak of aesthetic levels as we would of the weather and the climate if we had no thermometers, and we say many things worth saying.

The distinction between wealth and welfare is important to bear in mind, especially in relation to social decisions. Consider, for example, the notorious "deaccessing," as they call it, that has been done in recent years by the trustees of the Metropolitan Museum of Art in New York. Certainly it is up to these trustees to decide when parts of the collection should be sold in order to acquire other works that would increase the total value of the collection—remember, this includes pedagogical value as well as aesthetic value. Moreover, they evidently recognize a duty to preserve the aesthetic wealth of their society, which in this case may justifiably be thought of as a world society. So they find a buyer who will presumably take care of the paintings they have parted with. But I believe they have also a duty (which they apparently do not acknowledge) to preserve the welfare of their society. This would require them to sell only to other museums or institutions that can make the paintings publicly accessible. Selling them to a wealthy buyer to lock up in his vaults or in his private gallery is diminishing aesthetic welfare considerably. The transaction is particularly distressing because the deaccessioning can provide an opportunity to increase aesthetic welfare, if the paintings are spread around where they are most needed. The Metropolitan's clientele may not miss one or two Corots or Constables, but there are many struggling art museums whose visitors would be brightened considerably by having them in the vicinity.

There is something else that the Metropolitan's trustees could have promoted by selling their deaccessioned paintings to smaller art museums—a fairer distribution of aesthetic welfare, or what might be called *aesthetic justice.* I even think that, as custodians of quasi-public works of art, they had a duty to respect this ethical demand. Current movements to take Shakespeare into parks and music into inner-city streets, like the older movement to place sculpture on central-city sites, reflect a recognition of this obligation, though a pitifully small proportion of our social resources has so far been put into such projects. It may be that, as Francis T. Villemain has recently argued,[4] the United States has achieved a state of "aesthetic affluence." But, like other kinds of affluence which we boast, it seems to allow enormous deprivation at the lower end of the scale.

One may question the propriety of dividing distributive justice in general—which applies to all kinds of value or welfare—into distinct species. Why not simply aim at justice per se? But suppose a society succeeded reasonably well in achieving a fair distribution of goods; if they were distributed very one-sidedly (with one person having excellent health but no access to works of art, another having plenty of food but treatment that constantly undermines his self-respect),[5] I think we would have to say that the society fell short of the highest justice. Where we can carve out an identifiable kind of welfare and legitimately consider it basic, we ought to insist that distributive justice be applied within that category as well as across the board.

The problem with justice is to formulate an acceptable criterion, or set of philosophically defensible principles, such that we can say that a society is just to the degree that it lives up to those principles. This profoundly difficult and complex task may be even a little more difficult for aesthetic justice than for other types. We certainly cannot legitimately aim at ensuring equal distribution of aesthetic welfare, since the capacity for aesthetic experience (i.e., for experience with a notable degree of aesthetic quality) is not itself evenly distributed, nor is the motivation to seek it out. We could equalize aesthetic welfare only at a very low level. We can at best frame a principle of equal opportunity (which is not without its own problems), insisting that deviations from it be themselves justifiable in terms of the promotion of aesthetic welfare or greater justice. (For example, why should all those Rembrandts be concentrated in New York, or all those Renoirs in the Barnes Foundation at Merion, Pennsylvania?) Something like the equal opportunity principle must be what the framers of Article 27 of the Universal Declaration of Human Rights had in mind when they stipulated: "Everyone has the right freely to participate in the cultural life of the community, to enjoy the arts and to share in scientific advancement and its benefits."[6] This is something we may well remind ourselves of from time to time.

But the second section of that same article raises one of the hard questions about making a serious effort to attain aesthetic justice: "Everyone has the right to the protection of the moral and material interests resulting from any scientific, literary or artistic production of which he is the author."

The first principle, of equal opportunity, invites us to regard the artistic talents of gifted members of our society as natural resources, to be exploited for the general good. But the second principle is what Kenneth J. Arrow, in a critical discussion of John Rawls's *Theory of Justice,* has called the productivity principle: "that an individual is entitled to what he creates."[7] Of course, these principles are reconcilable, and each contains some ethical truth. I merely point out that there is a problem.

Even if we agree that the concepts of aesthetic welfare and aesthetic justice can be framed satisfactorily and that an increase in both of them is highly desirable, we may still have doubts about the usefulness of these concepts as a practical guide for public policy. Aesthetic welfare seems at once difficult and dangerous to subject to social control.

It is difficult for various reasons. For example, today I was walking down a street in Philadelphia after a rain, and I came across a small puddle with a beautiful patch of oil on it. Here is a bit of accidental aesthetic wealth that is difficult to inventory and no doubt short-lived. I don't know how many other people noticed and enjoyed that oil-slick, and finding out would hardly be worth the cost. Evidently a certain amount of aesthetic welfare would elude the planners and their computers, even if the existing Rembrandts were all carefully catalogued and the forgeries clearly separated from the authentic works. But this is not a fatal difficulty; rough estimates will serve for these marginal items. Changes of taste are more troublesome for a planner. I mean by "a taste" a capacity to derive aesthetic experience from objects of a certain kind (say, from Matisses but not from Braques). A policy of trying to maximize and equalize opportunities for aesthetic welfare will of course aim at variety, recognizing that there are many tastes and that tastes can change. But suppose it is decided that, in view of the great interest in hard-edge abstractionism and the Gospel of St. Matthew set to rock music, the production of such works should be encouraged. It may turn out next season that hard-edge abstractionism has lost out to conceptual art and that the crowds are avoiding such productions as *Godspell, Jesus Christ Superstar,* etc. Such considerations show the limits of aesthetic planning; these are just as well to emphasize, since the last thing we need is a government that decides what kind of art is to be produced.

This is the danger in official aesthetic policy—that is, government efforts to promote aesthetic welfare and justice. The tendency of national administrations in our time to think of everything else in terms of "national security," and to think of national security in terms of minimizing criticism of what they do, does not inspire confidence that United States government, deeply involved in supporting the creation and exhibition of works of art, would keep its hands off suspected political or even aesthetic ideologies. (The cancellation of plans to open the Kennedy Center film festival with the Costa-Gavras film *State of Siege* is a case in point.) But nothing can be accomplished without risks, and little that is worthwhile, it seems, can be accomplished these days without great risks. Without a National Foundation for the Arts, the importance of aesthetic welfare and justice and the need to find them a place among the heavily competing social goals might be wholly lost sight of in official Washington.

So, on the whole, and recognizing the need for various forms of vigilance, I would place among the legitimate objects of public policy the promotion of aesthetic welfare and justice. It must be done in ways that open up, rather than circumscribe, the freedom of artistic expression (by which I mean here only the creation of expressive objects)—which may perhaps be said, by an extension of the First Amendment guarantees of freedom of speech and of the press, to be a constitutional right. It must be done, not by directing that our surroundings shall be altered or supplemented in some specific way, but by releasing creative energies to find their own ways to add to freely accessible aesthetic wealth. It must be done with a constant and lively awareness that fine works of art (though we are not concerned solely with them) are unlikely to be produced according to official formulas, and more often than not carry within themselves aesthetic values that do not meet already felt needs or trigger stock responses, but which will be best understood and enjoyed by citizens of the future. Municipal art commissions, with the power to veto designs for new buildings, have sinned most often in this respect, perhaps—in their fear of artistic experimentation and novelty, not only in their commitment to what is commercially acceptable.

Conflicts must inevitably arise between the aesthetic demands and other goods that cannot be accommodated with them in a given situation (as, for example, the need for more school classroom space, the desire to make an apartment building secure against burglars, the demand for a good return on real estate investments). I know of no defensible universal principle that will tell us simply in all such cases how much weight must be given to the requirements of aesthetic vis-à-vis other values. A minimal requirement is that there be a kind of due process in the proceedings, ensuring that aesthetic considerations are at least taken into account. This might include a provision that the decision-making group include at least some members who, without being committed to a narrow range of tastes, are able to make sensible aesthetic judgments. Minimal standards of aesthetic quality need not rule out the strange or seemingly bizarre; still they would save us from many buildings now going up in Philadelphia, for example, that have nothing at all in the way of proportions, surface texture, rhythmic order, or expressiveness to commend them. Such buildings are not the result of a conflict of tastes, with one side winning the struggle for power; they simply show that nobody really cared much about how the thing would look.

Educational or instructional institutions must play a central role in any undertaking to carry out a public policy of promoting aesthetic welfare and justice. It follows from the nature of these concepts that we can distinguish two fundamentally different educational functions in this role. One is to promote *aesthetic opportunity,* the number and/or quality of available objects with aesthetic value. The other is to promote *aesthetic capability,* the number and/or the ability of persons to take advantage of the opportunities presented.

The phrase "available objects with aesthetic value" refers to the society's accessible aesthetic wealth, to that part of its aesthetic wealth that is, so to speak, in the public domain. The first of the two educational functions itself divides into two subordinate functions, one having to do with the production, and the other having to do with the distribution, of aesthetic wealth.

The first subfunction is to train more and better makers of objects with aesthetic value. This is most basic of all, for even in a society that has inherited great aesthetic wealth, the vitality of its aesthetic life and the vigor of general participation in it will depend on the continuing creation of new sources of aesthetic experience. Under this first subfunction, a further distinction has to be made from an educational point of view. The function of academies of the arts, or of universities serving as academies, is to train professional makers of art objects: those who will devote themselves wholly or primarily to this task and who may accordingly be expected to create the most satisfactory works. But it is also an important educational task (if we wish to promote aesthetic welfare) to develop powers of aesthetic-value creation wherever they may be found. Amateurs may add to the aesthetically valuable objects in the world by growing plants or beards, arranging flowers or hair, designing or assembling clothes, etc. Such activities become significant to the aesthetic economy when widely engaged in.

The second subfunction is to train more and better *aesthetic auxiliaries*—those who, along with professional artistic creators, belong to the "artworld," as Arthur Danto has named it.[8] Their task is to help make works of art accessible by arranging the conditions under which they are most likely to be widely enjoyed: by scheduling dramatic performances and museum exhibitions, publishing poetry, copying scores, restoring damaged paintings, helping sculptors get commissions, etc. The class of occupations comprised under this facilitating or enabling role is extremely varied. Indeed, I'm not sure exactly how to draw its boundaries; the linotyper who sets type for a novel, the agent who sells the manuscript of a short story to a magazine, and the plumber who repairs the heating equipment in the art museum also make their contributions, no doubt. But at some point the contribution becomes separated from aesthetic experience by so many causal stages that we can no doubt exclude it from that set of interconnected roles which make up the institution of the artworld. What is common to those roles is that their performance requires some capacity to have relevant aesthetic experience and some understanding of how aesthetic experience is brought about. (If the museum curator moves the plumber's handiwork to an exhibition gallery and gives it an appropriate label, it enters the artworld—at least according to some philosophers—but I don't know that that makes the plumber an artist.)

We might even envision a broadening role for the aesthetic adviser, so to speak, who is professionally qualified to help institutions with their problems relating to aesthetic welfare and justice. Many institutions now have their health advisers (nurses, public health authorities they can consult) and legal advisers (attorneys on retainer). In time we may see the emergence of ethical advisers for businesses, governmental agencies, and other sorts of institutions—persons whose sensitivity to moral implications and wise judgment of rights and duties might be sought out when tricky questions of moral conflict arise. However, I must confess that current trends in both business and government make this proposal laughably utopian. Similarily, as the best department stores now employ persons with some aesthetic expertise in arranging window displays, and as law offices hire interior decorators to plan their decor (though many of these professional designers are aesthetic quacks), so we might envision a general practice of consulting those who can tell institutions something helpful about the aesthetic aspects of their activities, products, or physical settings.

Of course we would also have to be aware of the danger of letting such advisers become more than consultants. Just as the ethical adviser would not take moral responsibility away from the official who asks his advice, but only try to help him see aspects, implications, and distinctions that have been overlooked (for example, certain civil liberties infringements), so aesthetic advisers could not be allowed to become a guild or academy that sets standards of taste and restricts aesthetic competition. This has happened with certain organizations of architects and sculptors, even in our own time. The solution to the problem of aesthetic quackery is not licensing by some department of the state government that requires everyone to pass an official art appreciation test before being allowed to accept a fee for giving aesthetic advice. Still, some tastes are better than others. Some people are able to discern aesthetic values that others miss or to derive high levels of aesthetic experience from what others can but feebly apprehend. Unless more of this ability gets worked effectively into the decision making that leads to the production of so much of our man-made or man-unmade environment, it does not seem likely that actual aesthetic opportunity will be substantially increased, no matter how many string quartets are composed by Elliott Carter—and I conjure with his works precisely because they have in fact added more than most to our aesthetic wealth, though it may be some time before large numbers of music lovers will be capable of enjoying them fully.

If we put together all the various careers that might fall wholly or partly under the role of promoting aesthetic opportunity or aesthetic capability, we have a diverse group. No less diverse is the set of educational processes involved in preparing people for such careers. But there is a kind of unity here, nevertheless, a central direction in which the activities participate. Ralph Smith's proposed concept of "cultural services"[9] seems to include them nicely and helps us see ways in which they belong together. But I'd like to throw out for discussion a suggestion about the relationship among these concepts which may supplement that proposed by Ralph Smith.

I can't help thinking of the cultural aspect or dimension of a society as including a cognitive as well as an aesthetic component. I'm not thinking of knowledge in a purely formal sense, as one might speak of the number of true propositions stored in our libraries or the memory banks of our computers. I'm thinking of understanding in a way that includes scientific and historical understanding as well as less clearly defined cognitive states and achievements, such as we might more naturally call insight, grasp, or even wisdom. Part of what marks a society as having a high culture, or as being rich in culture, or as giving a high priority to cultural matters, is the state of its cognitive activities as well as its aesthetic activities.

We can distinguish between aesthetic and cognitive interests or values well enough for many purposes, but we often cannot separate the aesthetic from the cognitive, or promote the former without promoting the latter. Part of the educational task in increasing the aesthetic capability of our students is indeed largely independent of their state of knowledge. We want to help them develop greater sensitivity of perception, as in hearing the subtle differences in the way two pianists play a particular passage; we want them to acquire the habit of noticing relationships, for example, the way touches of a certain hue turn up in various parts of a painting; we want them to release their feelings to respond to the lines in a poem. These abilities do not seem to involve cognitive processes or at least very elaborate ones. But to grasp fully the iconological meaning of a painting, the student may have to study social and religious history; to see the difference between early and late stages of a Rembrandt print, he may have to learn something about the technical process of etching; to grasp the richness and complexity of some works of art, he will have to learn the "symbol systems" (using this term in the way Nelson Goodman uses it to make this point)[10] involved in their referential dimension or in their production; systems of representation, conventional gestures in dance or film, musical notation, etc. So a great deal of cognitive activity, of articulate learning and abstract thought, may be indispensable for aesthetic growth. I think this fact helps to support the usefulness of the concept of "cultural services," in which there is a collaboration of aesthetic and cognitive elements.

Considering the importance of aesthetic welfare and the diverse ways in which educational processes can contribute to it, and especially considering the economic weakness of the artworld compared to the great complexes of power in our society, a heavy responsibility for aesthetic welfare falls on educational institutions. Indeed, I believe that promoting aesthetic welfare and justice should be one of the highest aims of such institutions. Here it is tempting to talk in grand terms which may be hard to cash in on specific points. I would consider the fostering of rationality in the broadest sense—that is, developing powers of creative and critical thought—to be the foremost educational goal. Not far behind we should probably place ethical development, taken in an adequately fundamental sense, in which it is kept distinct from indoctrination in conventionally approved rules of conduct but involves concern for others, the perception of ethically significant differences in human actions, judiciousness in judging the stringency of moral obligation, and a serious effort to work out and live up to a personal but defensible scale of values. Not far behind the ethical I would place the promotion of aesthetic welfare, including both the long-range welfare of the student himself and his powers to promote the aesthetic welfare of others.

I don't know whether there are developmental stages of aesthetic growth analogous to those stages that Lawrence Kohlberg, following Piaget, has pointed out in ethical development—though Michael J. Parsons has made some interesting progress in articulating three stages of aesthetic development toward maturity.[11] If there are underlying similar patterns in cognitive growth, ethical growth, and aesthetic growth, this may help to show a basic unity in the whole educational enterprise, though, as we know, one or another of these capabilities often develops faster than another or is blocked at any early stage while others continue to develop. Since we can make the distinctions and observe differential rates, each must be given attention on its own account. What I am arguing for, in the end, is just that if there is such a thing as aesthetic welfare, and such a thing as aesthetic justice, and if they are an important part of a life and of a society worthy of human persons, then aesthetic development must be of very serious concern at all stages of the educational process.

Notes

1. Compare an earlier essay, "Aesthetic Welfare," *Journal of Aesthetic Education* 4, no. 4 (October 1970): 9–20; also in the *Proceedings* of the Seventh International Congress of Aesthetics, Uppsala, 1968.

2. Olgerts Puravs, among others, has emphasized the importance of the individual's "imaginative activity" in the aesthetic encounter. See "Cultural Values, Environment, and the Imagination," *Arts in Society* 9, no. 1 (Spring–Summer 1972): 54–60.

3. "The Happy Habitat," *Journal of Aesthetic Education* 6, no. 3 (July 1972): 25–38.

4. "Aesthetic Education in Social Perspective," *Journal of Aesthetic Education* 4, no. 2 (April 1970): 18.

5. The importance of this primary good, self-respect, has been especially emphasized by John Rawls in *A Theory of Justice* (Cambridge, Mass.: Belknap Press, Harvard University, 1971).

6. I quote this from A. I. Melden, ed., *Human Rights* (Belmont, Calif.: Wadsworth, 1970), p. 148.

7. "Some Ordinalist-Utilitarian Notes on Rawls's Theory of Justice," *Journal of Philosophy* 70, no. 9 (May 10, 1973): 248.

8. See "The Artworld," *Journal of Philosophy* 61, no. 19 (October 15, 1964): 571–84; and the discussion by George Dickie, *Aesthetics: An Introduction* (Indianapolis: Pegasus, 1971), pp. 101ff.

9. I am referring to his (as yet unpublished) essay, "Cultural Services and Educational Policy: Recommendations for Educational Research" [published as

"Cultural Services and Teacher Preparation in the Arts," *Art Education* 26, no. 8 (November 1973): 16–19.—Ed.]

10. See *Languages of Art* (Indianapolis: Bobbs-Merrill, 1968).

11. I am referring to an as yet unpublished essay, "A Concept of Aesthetic Education."

6

Should the Government Subsidize the Arts?

Ernest van den Haag

The government always concerns itself with problems—usually by means of subsidies—when a constituency can be discerned or created. Now there is one for the arts. Hence presidents, congressmen, and senators can acquire cachet and reputations as cultivated and sensitive intellectuals by advocating more federal expenditures on the arts. President Kennedy started much of the rhetoric; President Nixon increased the budgetary appropriations. Ever since, the federal budget for the arts in all forms has grown by leaps and bounds. Although they deplore high taxes and huge benefits, the Congress and the executive branch have been remarkably generous to the arts. The matter raises some questions:

1. What is the role of the arts in American society, and what can it be? What should it be?

2. What is the role of the government in the arts? What should it be? Do Americans want their tax money to be spent for the arts by their representatives? Or, would they prefer to decide individually how much money to spend on works of art and on which works? What would happen without government subsidies?

3. If the arts actually do require a government subsidy, what or who should be subsidized and by what selection procedures?

Although major philosophers such as Plato and Hegel were doubtful about their value, much can be said for the arts. However, it is essential to distinguish arguments for the arts and for their support from arguments for government support of the arts. This essential distinction is seldom made. Yet, whatever can be said for the arts is certainly not sufficient by itself to justify any government subsidies. To be sure, the arts give pleasure to some—a special quality of pleasure or, better, desired experience—and employment to others. But so do whiskey and religion. Hence, an argument for government support of the arts must indicate not only what characteristics make the arts socially (and not just individually) desirable or necessary but also those characteristics that suggest why government subsidies to the arts are justified and needed while they are not for whiskey or religion. It must be shown that private funds are not likely to support the arts to the degree or in the manner justified by their social usefulness, while government subsidies can do so.

The type of argument required is familiar; it is used to argue for public support of parks, or beaches, or police forces: they are needed, useful, and desired but differ from other nice things that may be purchased privately; they benefit not only the individuals willing to spend money for them, but, to a significant extent, the community as a whole, including those who would not volunteer to pay or cannot afford to. An adequate argument for federal support of the arts must show, then, that they yield indivisible collective benefits (as does the police force). If the arts do yield such benefits and they are of sufficient magnitude, the government is justified in compelling individuals to pay taxes, compulsory levies, to pay for the arts, regardless of whether an individual taxpayer feels benefited. Further, the collective benefit yielded by the arts must be shown to exceed the benefits to be expected if every person were to pay for whatever art he wished and could afford to buy. Finally, there must be good reason to believe that the government will not be (much) worse as a patron of art than private individuals are. Note that whatever arguments there are for public support of art probably could be made for subsidies to religion as well. Indeed, religion is subsidized in most European countries. But, for historical-constitutional reasons, no attempt is made to subsidize religion in this country. It has thrived nonetheless—which gives food for thought.

Historical Precedents for Subsidies

The argument for public support of the arts has been convincing since Pericles' time. Sculpture, architecture, music, painting, literature, as well as what today are called the humanities—historiography and scholarship—have been very largely supported by public funds since antiquity. Temples and statues of the gods were erected with public funds. *Mutatis mutandis* public funds were spent for the arts in the Middle Ages. The arts were used to erect monuments to shared beliefs and to celebrate communal feeling; they also celebrated royal houses (literally and symbolically) and the nations, regions, and religions of which they were emblematic.

Public expenditures for the arts have begun to be questioned only since the Industrial Revolution. Until then, public funds were disbursed by religious authorities and by the courts of the nobility; no one was able to question them. The distinction between the prince's (or the bishop's) personal funds and those administered by him was vague. He could dispose of either to foster the arts if it pleased him. His expenditure was accepted as it was in antiquity; tradition indicated that the arts, as did religion, bind together, help make into a cohesive whole, the society in which they flourish. They are an essential part of what civilizes, of the meaning-conferring essence, the soul of the culture of any society—as was the religion the arts used to celebrate. (The word, after all, came from *re-ligare,* to bind strongly.) With the Renaissance the arts became more secular. But the princes—of church or state—who supported them were still regarded as the embodiment of the polity. Their taste and their expenditure were not questioned, and the glorification of their reign through the arts was seen as the glorification of the polity.

Whatever their merit, these arguments scarcely justify tax-paid subsidies for the arts today, particularly in the United States. The arguments are relevant neither to modern art in modern conditions, nor to ancient art in modern conditions, nor to any art in the United States. Aristocracy and church have not been sufficiently dominant in our political history and mixed up with the nation-forming process to justify replacing their support of the arts with a government subsidy. Nor did the arts themselves ever play much of a role in sustaining our national cohesion. They do not now.

Whatever the value of opera (I happen to be a passionate opera lover), it cannot be said, as it may be said in Italy or Austria, that opera has contributed to our national cohesion, history, culture, or consciousness—or that it has any chance of doing so now. Opera was an exotic import of and for the rich who were also willing to pay for it. The educated middle class is getting interested in it now. But it is not clear why those who want opera are entitled to compel others to pay for it—even though these others, in the main, prefer unsubsidized movies or Broadway shows. A subsidy to opera supports or expands our national consciousness as much as a subsidy to the manufacture or the wearing of tails and top hats would.

What is true for opera is as true for classical music, for dance, including ballet, and, by and large, for the great works of art in our museums. They did not play an important role in our history or in forging or celebrating our national bonds—though they did in Europe (which, however, survived their export). We have marvelous things in our museums. But they did not get there through government activities and did not celebrate those activities or our national history, cultural or political. The contents of our museums have nothing to do with our national life, and they have not contributed to our national cohesion or identity. They are politically and socially irrelevant to us (whatever their aesthetic merit).

Tin Pan Alley, jazz, rock, or baseball are more important in the celebration of American values, not only in the working classes and among adolescents, but also in the upper classes and even among educated groups. They need no subsidy.

Subsidizations of Sports and TV

For quite a while, sports (and now TV) have been important elements in our culture and our cohesion, together with the automobile and the lengthening years of instructional and custodial care in schools imposed on the young. But the arts? Certainly not those in museums. Nor the modern artists the government is eager to subsidize. They may or may not be great. But they are at best marginal to American culture. It is not likely that this will change.

If TV or if sports do play the role I have attributed to them, should they be subsidized? They seem to do quite well, thank you, without government subsidy. If the exclusive support of TV by advertisers is regarded as a hindrance to possible informational or aesthetic achievements, there is no reason that TV could not be paid for directly by the viewers, as books or magazines are paid for by those who buy them or are willing to subsidize them. Unsubsidized literature has done well in the United States. The case for public TV is as questionable as the case for government-financed newspapers, magazines, or books, even though the federal and local governments insist on subsidizing public TV and radio.[1]

Unavoidably, public TV is biased. The values presented are not those prevailing among Americans at large, but those of the producers and of the public TV audience, both middle-class liberal. In its more political presentations public TV is definitely "left" of the public that pays for it. (No conspiracy: the people involved find it hard to take seriously values other than their own.) Apart from everything else it seems hard to justify publicly subsidized TV, for it simply amounts to a tax-paid subsidy to upper-middle-class viewers dissatisfied with commercial offerings addressed to the less educated.

To summarize: the arts are not among the activities which contribute enough to social cohesion, national identity, or shared values in the United States to justify support by the government. On the other hand, the activities which would deserve support on these grounds scarcely need it. Sports and TV and rock concerts are doing all right without government subsidy. The schools already are amply supported, and they do incidentally support the arts by supporting artists, writers, and other representatives of the arts directly and indirectly.

So far I have confined myself to denying that there is any justification for government subsidies to the arts under modern American conditions. The tacit assumption was that, whether or not a subsidy could be justified, the government could help the arts to flower by subsidizing them. This assumption must now be questioned: it seems unlikely that the government can help the arts by subsidizing them. Even though it does inflate the quantity of art produced, the government subsidy may actually harm the arts.

The most cogent argument against any form of censorship of art by the government[2] is, very simply, that the government is unlikely to be able to tell bad, worthless (pseudo) art from good. Wherefore, censorship would damage the arts by suppressing "good" as readily as "bad" art. If the government could distinguish valuable from valueless art and would get rid of only the worthless stuff, censorship would make everyone's life easier, as garbage removal does. But no one attributes such powers of discrimination to the government. Indeed, a major part of the general argument for freedom is that we cannot trust any government (democratic or otherwise) to tell vice from virtue, good from bad. If we could, we might not mind if the government subsidized virtue and suppressed vice. As it is, we prefer to leave such decisions to individuals (a few extreme cases excepted), because we have no reason to believe that the government could do better and much reason to believe it would do worse.

Well, if the government cannot be trusted to tell which art is so bad as to deserve suppression, how can it be trusted to tell which art is so good as to deserve subsidization? Either the government can or it cannot tell good from bad art. The answer is that it cannot. This seems to me just as conclusive an argument against government subsidies to art as it is an argument against government censorship of art.[3]

In practice the government's subsidies to art unavoidably become indiscriminate. (This is how the government protects itself against criticism and creates a wide, supportive constituency.) The government cannot actually subsidize art. At best it can and will subsidize a wide range of organizations or persons who claim to be producing art.

Supporting Fool's Gold

Now, a lot of ore has to be mined to get a little gold. One may argue that a lot of subsidy has to be spent on many unworthy artists so that the few worthy artists can be helped. However, there are relevant differences between mining and subsidized art production.

One difference need only be restated. Mining is not subsidized. It pays for itself—the purchasers of the metal pay more than enough for the necessary processes, including the mining of the ore that has to be discarded. Gold mining, thus, is analogous to the private purchase of art or, if you please, the private subsidy given to art producers. It is not analogous to government subsidies. Subsidies suggest that whatever worthwhile art they help produce is not worth enough to the public to persuade it to pay for the whole process, including the worthless art that is being subsidized. Thus, the government compels the taxpayer to do what he does not volunteer to do. I can find no justification for this policy.

There is an even more important difference between mining ore and art production. Payments to the mining industry may lead to more exploration and mining. But they cannot increase the total amount of gold-bearing ore that nature provided. Above all, such payments will not encourage the production of fake or imitation gold since consumers (and even the government) are quite capable of discriminating. Subsidies to art also may lead to more utilization of talent, although they cannot increase the pool of artistic talent provided by nature. But—and this is the decisive difference—a subsidy to art will attract people who would not have become artists without it. Art, unlike gold, is not definable so that the government could exclude subsidies to the untalented. We are forced to subsidize the mining of fool's gold as much as the mining of actual artistic gold, for the government cannot discriminate. The more we subsidize, the larger *the proportion* of fool's gold, of pseudo-art, in the end product being subsidized.

Normally, art production is self-selective. Few people produce art for the sake of money. The main reward is intrinsic—*ars gratia artis.* Artists are willing to risk foregoing income for the sake of self-rewarding achievement however much they hope it will be publicly recognized and become materially rewarding as well. Not that hungry artists are being artists. On the contrary. But the high risk of low income deters those more interested in income than in art and leaves mainly those who are artists for the sake of art, whether or not they are able to produce anything valuable.

Subsidies, however, will increase art production by attracting producers who, without the subsidy, would not have produced—those whose passion for art was not sufficient, without the subsidy, to induce them to risk sacrificing income. Subsidies may actually make it harder for true artists to succeed. Although more money is made available, there also is more competition for it. In this competition, the true artist is likely to be undone by those who, consciously or unconsciously, are interested mainly in money. They will be more worldly wise, better competitors. After all, they are not distracted by artistic concerns and ambitions.

Lacking original talent, the pseudo artist will be more imitative and therefore more easily understood and more appealing—and more eligible for subsidies. A subsidy to something or somebody actually original and valid is harder to justify than a subsidy to something appealing, unoriginal, and therefore more easily understood. Those in charge of subsidization will be safer by going with the fashion, not by helping unknowns who create new things. (This reasoning applies least to those matters which can be demonstrated, for instance, by experiment--and most to the least demonstrable things, foremost art.)

To speak of subsidizing art is, of course, to use a metaphor. One can only buy specific works of art or help specific artists. Since there are no generally accepted qualifications and no agreement on what or who is meritorious, government organizations must subsidize artists who have already been widely recognized—and need the subsidy least—or distribute their bounty so that every claimant supported by regional taste or by the taste of any major social group gets some. (This is, among other things, what Herbert Gans advocates in his *Popular Culture and High Culture.*)[4] Aesthetically this is counterproductive. Bad art, as does bad money, drives out good.

Government subsidies, finally, are biased in favor of the performing arts. Officials feel they can measure quality by the dubious gauge of popularity; this is easier to do with an orchestra than with a composer. The performing arts also involve far more people—performers, support personnel, and the public—than are involved in the lonely act of, say, composing a score or writing a critical essay. Hence, a large constituency. Wherefore, more and more subsidies go to the performing arts. The Metropolitan Opera or the Duluth Philharmonic is subsidized. The further natural bias of subsidies is toward popular performances and expansion of audiences at the expense of quality. It is in this way that political support can be secured.

Much more could be said along these lines. But the idea should be clear by now. (a) There is no good sociopolitical reason for the government to compel taxpayers to subsidize government-selected arts; (b) to do so compels all classes to subsidize the middle class; (c) to do so is more likely to harm than to help in the creation of actual, valuable art.

Subsidies to Museums

What would happen if the government—local and federal—were to cease supporting the arts?[5] What would happen to museums and galleries which have come to depend on subsidies?

Museums acquire, preserve, and display art both of the past and of the present. (They also engage in scholarly and educational activities incidental to their task.) Since much of the acquisition funds of museums now comes from private donations, government subsidies here are unimportant. Even if museums, left without subsidies, ceased to buy art and use acquisition money for maintenance, there would be no damage. The migration of old art from Europe and Asia into the United States and from private into public hands would be slowed. (The prices paid for ancient art would fall.) Since most museums have far more art than they are able to display, no less would be displayed than is now displayed. The egos of museum directors and curators would suffer greatly. But there would be no other damage. Failure to buy modern art would reduce its prices somewhat and its production. Again, no other effects are likely. Art is not produced for museums. Nor should it be. But, let me repeat, most acquisition would continue, since funding for this purpose is supplied by private donations.

Preservation of art, old or new, however acquired, is costly. So is the display of art under reasonable conditions. It is this cost, which museums incur unavoidably, that is largely paid for by public subsidies. There is an arguable social interest in preserving art for future generations; hence, some of the cost of preservation, as distinguished from the cost of display, may well be defrayed out of tax funds. However, there is no reason why those who are currently gratified by viewing art should compel others to pay for their gratification, no reason for museum visitors to contribute as little as they do now to the upkeep of the museums they visit. People are willing to pay, on the average, fifteen to thirty dollars to attend a Broadway show for two hours. There is no reason to pay less to attend a museum. (Preferred, habitual categories of viewers might be offered low subscription rates.) Would museums survive? Churches have survived by voluntary contributions without government subsidies. Museums could charge admission and expect donations. So could opera houses and symphony orchestras. They would survive—although their rate of expansion would be curtailed.

Raising the cost of attendance would thin the ranks of museum visitors (thereby reducing upkeep costs as well as paying a greater proportion of those costs). Lower attendance is regarded as a calamity by pedagogues who feel it necessary to make art available free of charge—even to stuff it down people's throats. Everything else—from bread to concerts—costs money. Why should art be free? There is, of course, no free art any more than there is a free lunch. Museum visits free to the visitor are paid for by taxpayers—largely by people whose incomes are lower than those of most museum visitors. I can see no justification for the shifting of the cost.

Reasonable entrance fees would solve a disturbing problem, deliberately neglected by administrators. Because they like popularity and wide support—which increase their power, their prestige, and their subsidies and salaries—administrators pay no heed to the problems caused by crowding for those who actually come for the sake of seeing art. The treasures of the past are finite; the number of potential viewers is infinite. In each generation only a few can actually see them. But since museums are costless to visitors, they now attract crowds so big as to make it nearly impossible for any individual to contemplate and experience the art they display. Their popularity defeats much of the serious purpose used to justify subsidizing museums. People are herded through galleries—they willingly trot by paintings driven by boredom and by others—so that everybody can satisfy his curiosity and gratify his sense of accomplishment.

If crowds were thinner, as they would be if a visit to the museum were to cost as much as attendance at a Broadway show, those who would still go to a museum would be able to enjoy it. They would find the conditions which make possible the aesthetic experience a museum can help them to achieve.

The absence of subsidies would have similar effects on the performing arts. The price of tickets would rise. Attendance would be reduced. Fewer performances would occur if people would not voluntarily pay for all the performances now subsidized. There would be an additional beneficial effect. The wages now paid performing artists and supporting personnel would decrease with the demand for them. I do not see much reason for a subsidy that leads them to earn far more than those from whom the money is taken. This redistribution is as involuntary as it is undesirable.

Notes

1. New York City, teetering on the edge of bankruptcy, insists on taxing business to support its own radio and TV stations. (The cost is negligible, but why is it needed? As a tourist attraction?)

2. Let me leave aside pornography here.

3. The traditional European subsidies (often combined with censorship) were given by taste-makers, by a cultural elite. Our government does not aspire to that status and we have no tradition of conferring it (*Deo gratias*).

4. Herbert J. Gaus, *Popular Culture and High Culture* (Basic Books, New York, 1974). Gans has a populist point; rather than rely on the government's aesthetic discrimination, we might as well give up aesthetic discrimination, a middle-class prejudice, and replace it by some sort of popular vote.

5. I distinguish tax exemption (not taking money) from support (giving money) and do not oppose the first.

7

A Surfeit of Fine Art

Jacques Barzun

This year, in any year, the budgets of the federal and state agencies that support the arts are to be cut again. Meanwhile, costs in the arts are going up—rent, utilities, printing, and various incidental expenses. Yet one continues to read and hear of one more dance group being formed, yet another chamber orchestra making its debut, newborn theatre companies striving to lure audiences, festivals and exhibits being organized. Each new enterprise is self-assured of prestige, confident of deserving support, and hungry for subsidy from public and private funds.

This disparity between shrinking means and growing supply points to attitudes and assumptions about art that have not been examined for a long time. The most common assumption is that there cannot be too much art, and hence that the public has an obligation to support whatever qualifies under that name. If private funds fall short, let public money make up the difference. But since public money is not an elastic substance, some rethinking is in order, aimed at developing new standards of judgment and response.

The tendency to speak of Art with a capital *A* is the first cause of confusion. Art is not a homogeneous commodity, of which the need and use are self-evident. What the public is offered in the name of art is a multitude of objects and performances that differ in quality and in kind. There is popular art, supplied by entertainers who thrive without any subsidy. They are public heroes and heroines, well supported by worshipful followings. Michael Jackson has never applied for a federal grant, and Barbara Cartland does not need a Guggenheim in order to write her next book.

Another type of art—"high art"—is relatively *un*popular, though it is very popular with its devotees. Auditoriums, museums, and theatres are usually jammed, and by paying customers, but not jammed enough to keep deficits at bay. This type of art, which has traditionally been a source of national pride, is also the cause of perpetual beggary. High art has *never* been profitable.

Today it depends on miscellaneous financing. Individuals and groups rely on the marketplace to provide at least part of their livelihood, but this must usually be supplemented by private patrons or public grants. Our large institutions use their endowments to pay part of their way, but they too require government aid. And then there is the art supported by colleges and universities. This last form of patronage is an innovation of our century and our country, a by-product of the artists' taking refuge in teaching when a widespread passion for culture took hold after the Great Depression. Campus art relies on both private funds (student fees) and public subsidy (state and local grants for higher education). In return, universities offer, free of charge, a wide repertory of plays, music, film, dance, and the visual arts that the market would never venture upon.

Off campus, the old, established institutions are in trouble, and show it: museums and libraries have entered the retail and mail-order business; they sell books, facsimiles of art objects, cuff links, ashtrays, calendars, postcards, and other reproductions of drawings and paintings. The New York Public Library rents out its lobby for dinners and cocktail parties; the Boston Athenaeum, besides running cruises to "art spots," let out its premises for the filming of *The Bostonians.* In Washington, the galleries of the Phillips Collection can be rented for the evening for $5,000.

As for the artists, most of them are periodically in dire straits. Seeing this spectacle, the art lovers are apt to lash out at what they call "our materialistic society"; it should pay for high art more lavishly. This double accusation is without merit. All known societies have been materialistic; human society exists solely for material purposes. Ours is unusual precisely in its generous expenditures for art, education, philanthropy, and other good works. Selfishness and philistinism are hardly our present trouble: some of the most fervent expressions of concern about the arts have come from businessmen and politicians. The former indifference or scorn has been replaced by concern and piety. When the budget cuts come, it is because of other pressing claims—the poor, the sick, the unemployed, the roads, the schools. In short, the trouble is not with the public opinion of art or the public outlay for it; it lies in the distribution of the funds, which has been guided—if the word is applicable—by totally unexamined ideas about "the arts."

Nobody who "cares about the arts" has dared to raise the question of oversupply. We are familiar with the dangers of too much farm produce, too rich a diet, too many births; we should also see too much art as a predicament.

An oversupply of art does not lower prices or cause the artist to go into "another business"; it only augments the need for subsidies. A museum or theatre rarely declares bankruptcy or moves to another town. It struggles on, in deficit and in tears, till rescued—for one short year—by a last-minute gift or a new commercial ploy.

Such is the fated result of an assumption deeply buried in our collective mind. It grew there early in the last century when the artist as a social type came to be glorified as a hero, a seer, a genius. Geniuses must be allowed to do as they please while the rest of mankind gratefully brings its offerings to the altar. We now feel the consequences of this potent myth. Because art generates excitement, because a great many people have some little artistic gift, and because the life of the artist looks wonderfully free, more and more people in each generation decide that they want to be artists. And throughout the land one or another agency is at work to multiply their kind.

Schools watch over every spark of talent and try to fan it into a raging ambition. The finger paintings of two-year-olds are put up on classroom walls and child poetry is publicly recited. This encouragement continues in colleges and in art and drama schools, where scholarships and prizes spur whole classes to proficiency. The résumé of any artist, or would-be artist, shows a string of awards, certificates, and commendations. Mastery of technique and native gift are no longer distinguishing features; they are the norm.

But the next phase is entirely unprovided for: where, how, can these talents find a social use corresponding to their preparation? The competition is intense. Young musicians, actors, and dancers form little groups, get a good notice, and immediately join the scrimmage for support. In painting and writing, the fight is to get into a gallery or a publishing house, only to be told that galleries are overcrowded and that poetry is not commercially publishable. In short, with the best of intentions, we have created a glut. Encouragement has bred expectation, and proliferating expectations have outrun resources.

Consider the glut in Greater New York. According to a report of the Port Authority, in 1985 there were some 117,000 jobs related to the arts in the New York metropolitan area, yielding a total income of $2 billion a year. What is the reality behind the figures? After you have counted the handful of well-known museums and theatres, the opera and ballet troupes performing outdoors and in concert halls, you must add the orchestras, native and visiting; the infestation of chamber music groups; the many libraries, public and semipublic; the almost round-the-clock lectures and poetry readings. In addition, uncounted other "distributors" offer their wares. The churches present plays and Sunday afternoon transcriptions on the organ of works written for orchestra. At the Cathedral of St. John the Divine, one can see a Miskito Indian fertility dance performed at the altar and roller skaters in the aisles enlivening the *Gloria* during the service. In the summer, there is free music in the sunken plaza of Rockefeller Center, Leonard Bernstein goes to Jones Beach to conduct yet another program, and Joseph Papp rewrites Shakespeare for sitters and strollers in the city parks.

One might argue that New York is a world capital, where a concentration of art is to be expected. True, but in many other cities and towns, as well as in "art parks" and converted barns in the open country, the high arts solicit public attention. Regional theatres are on the increase: festivals short and long resound everywhere—Texas alone advertises over two hundred. Art is ubiquitous in our lives: there is a piece of art in the anteroom of many business firms—an image to build up the image. There is art in good hotel and motel rooms, either original works or reproductions, such as the pair of Van Gogh sunflowers I once found, one on each side of a mirror. There is art at conferences and meetings: the sound of a string quartet graces a discussion of Niels Bohr at the American Academy of Arts and Sciences; and the annual report of a faculty club where the food is debatable boasts that in the last fiscal year the club sponsored two evenings of chamber music.

Already in 1840, Balzac noted with dismay that there were two thousand painters in Paris. Degas, fifty years later, said: "We must *dis*courage the arts." But the ever enlarging display of art cannot, of course, be cut or held back. We can pay farmers not to grow crops, but we cannot pay artists to stop making art. Yet something must be done. To lead people on when there is no chance they will ever fulfill their desire is immoral. And our training schools, art councils, endowments, and foundations are doing just that. They flatter the hope and belief that every good work and worker will be recognized and subsidized. When no such thing happens, anger and distress naturally follow.

Nor does the artist's anger refer solely to money. Government grants are awarded by persons (often themselves artists) who assume the role of bureaucrat. Their role cuts them off from the community of applicants. Subsidy, even by a private foundation, is an official act, and on this subject the French experience of three hundred years is conclusive. In France, the academic imitators got the commissions and subsidies; those who produced the works we admire today had to survive as best they could. The term *official art* means art that is competent and safe. As John Sloan said in urging government support: "Then we'll know who our enemy is."

Our current cultural attitudes lead to an oversupply of this competent, enjoyable art, satisfying but seldom great. At the same time, institutions of the highest caliber struggle to keep alive the masterpieces of the past and discover modern works of comparable worth. In the distribution of funds, both the producers and the caretakers are treated alike—and come out the same: disappointed and ill-nourished. Only a change of policy, following a change of attitudes, can put an end to this demoralizing catch-as-catch-can. It would not solve an insoluble problem but might cut half of it away.

The first step would be to accept a distinction between "public art" and all the rest. Over the centuries public money has been provided mainly for public art and public institutions—museums, libraries, opera houses, orchestras, theatres, and dance troupes. All other artistic efforts have been supported by individual patrons and small groups of amateurs, or they have flourished quietly, locally, with no thought of wider recognition. Let us call this activity domestic art, because it corresponds to what people of an earlier age provided for themselves at home. Our mistake, our predicament, is that most of the art now produced is domestic art trying to become public art. There is no reason to neglect or look down on the domestic kind. But there is also no reason to support it with public monies. Its abundance is what creates the fierce competition, which in turn drives the truly public institutions increasingly to become gift shops, bazaars, mail-order houses, and cocktail bars.

No doubt a certain number of those trained by our schools are great painters, composers, poets, playwrights, and performers. If they also have stamina, let them attempt a professional career. They will face a life of solitary toil and repeated disappointment, of problematic reward and fitful success. A few of them will eventually achieve affluence and world renown. In colleges and art schools the young should be taught what "the glorious life of art" is really like. It has not changed in five hundred years; it fills the biographies on our shelves; it is a test of endurance, willpower, and maniacal faith in oneself.

For the less determined, perhaps just as gifted, the practicable goal is to serve a local audience that is willing to provide a simple setting for the artistic activity, whatever it may be. This situation already exists here and there: small groups have been formed which enable composer, poet, singers, and players to come together and play old and new music for the enjoyment of the community, without fanfare, fund-raising, or the compulsion to "go public." The baroque chamber music we play today with so much relish was once exactly this sort of activity, as unassuming as our chess or bridge, which no one proposes to support officially. True, these "private" artists would have to support themselves by means other than art and sacrifice any dreams of world applause. But as things stand, this ambition is sacrificed for them by oversupply. Many of them cannot even find work as teachers; the glut is there too.

With the activities of these artists redirected, regional culture would thrive, and its quality would be enhanced by the contributions of the more talented among them who now vainly try for the highest places. Nor would the denial of public money to such persons and groups be a stingy, meanspirited retrenchment. On the contrary, it would be a cure for the misery of many people, both artists and sponsors. By dropping the whole business of full-scale public exhibition and performance, private artists would no longer have to live the deficit and grant-matching life, struggling with costs of which the greater part goes in fact to stagehands, electricians, printers, landlords, and various profit-making suppliers.

The whole strength of public support—of taxpayers' dollars—would thus be freed to sustain public art, that is, the acknowledged public institutions. In each region these establishments are known to all, open to all, and subject to public criticism when their standards decline. If as a nation we hold the view that high art is a public need, these institutions deserve support on the same footing as police departments and weather bureaus. And I mean *support,* not meager help after periodic anguish and pleading. Public law has already recognized the social worth of these institutions by granting them tax exemption. The rest of their needs should be fully met, so as to free them for their work and take them out of petty commerce.

These suggestions and possibilities have nothing to do with trying to reduce the role of government in society. Nor do they relate to money alone or artistic ambition alone. When I urge this new soberness, I am thinking of high culture as a whole and our relation to it. In the competition for cash, punctuated by elegant ballyhoo, in the overabundance of the offering and the fuss about it in print and on the airwaves, something has happened to the artistic experience itself. Its quality has been lowered by plethora. Great works too often seen or performed, too readily available in bits and pieces, become articles of consumption instead of objects of contemplation. They lose force and depth by being too familiar through too frequent or too hurried use. When I hear of someone's proudly "spending the day at the museum," I wonder at the effect: the intake is surely akin to that of an alcoholic. Music likewise is anesthetic when big doses—symphony after symphony, opera on top of opera—are administered without respite. We should remember the Greeks' practice of exposing themselves to one tragic trilogy and one comedy on but a single day each year. High art is meant for rare festivals, where anticipation is followed by exhilaration and the aftermath is meditation and recollection in tranquility. The glut has made us into gluttons who gorge and do not digest.

Such a condition disables one for judging new art. The eager or dutiful persons who subject themselves to these tidal waves of the classics and the moderns find everything wonderful in an absent-minded way. The wonder washes over them rather than into them, and one of its effects is to make anything shocking or odd suddenly interesting enough to gain a month's celebrity. And so another by-product of our come-one, come-all policy is the tendency to reward cleverness, not art, and to put one more hurdle in the path of the truly original artist.

8

Can Government Funding of the Arts Be Justified Theoretically?

Noel Carroll

The purpose of this article is to explore various avenues for justifying arts funding. Our results are mixed. Some grounds for government arts funding are found, but it is noted that in embracing these justifications untoward consequences may be incurred. Thus, it is urged that we refrain from government funding of the arts because the effects of such funding, when guided by the kinds of justifications available, would be deleterious to the art world. However, the conclusions of this article are provisional; there is no reason to believe that someone may not construct better justifications for government arts funding than those examined here.

The question of whether there are theoretical grounds for government arts funding is unwieldy and needs trimming. First, what does "funding" refer to? Fúnding can be either direct or indirect. One might say that there was government arts funding in this country before 1965 but that it took indirect forms, including land grants, tax exemptions to educational and cultural institutions such as museums, and tax advantages for private donations of art to the public.[1] Concern here is not with indirect funding but with the justification of direct state funding of the arts.

But still the scope is too broad to be manageable, because there are so many different kinds of arts-related activities with which direct state funding may be involved. Much government funding is aimed at what might be thought of as the preservation of culture intact. Other objectives of government funding target community art centers, regional theaters, and school programs. And funding may also be directed to professional artists for the purpose of enabling them to produce new works of art. This latter type of funding is the sort with which this article is concerned. Whereas funding of museums looks to the past of our culture, funding artists is prospective. It is not a matter of preserving culture but of creating culture. The preservation of culture, of course, is involved with education, which appears to be the legitimate realm of state activity. And, furthermore, though even more vaguely, art preservation keeps us aware of who we have been, which knowledge is relevant to us in our practical decision about who we shall become. But it is not so easy to see the way in which prospective funding—i.e., support for the production of contemporary art—can be defended as educational in terms of the state's responsibilities in this arena in the way the preservation might be. Bluntly, contemporary art is not our heritage yet, nor is it clear how much of it will be. So even if funding for the purpose of preservation falls within the state's educational responsibilities, prospective arts funding calls for some other kind of theoretical justification, that is, a justification in terms of the way in which prospective arts funding can be seen as implementing one or more of the proper functions of the state.

Clearly, commissioning arts to design stamps and government buildings is a legitimate government activity. So our question is whether state funding of the production of new art that is not connected to state projects is also legitimate. Admittedly, the great bulk of governmental funding of the arts is not directed to artists. But the question is how even this admittedly small expenditure is to be funded. (Hereafter, "arts funding" refers only to this issue.)

Before proceeding, a word or two about the use of "state" in this discussion is appropriate. Though certain issues particular to the United States will be canvassed, in general our question concerns whether there are theoretical justifications for prospective arts funding in what we broadly think of as modern, pluralistic, democratic states. We should not have in mind the sort of Marxian utopia where we all fish in the morning and write art criticism in the afternoon. That state of affairs would not be blighted by a scarcity of resources or by differences of opinion and, anyway, would not, one presumes, need arts funding (or a state, for that matter). Nor do we have totalitarian regimes in mind; they have no need for justifications. Rather, our question is addressed to pluralistic, democratic states which have fundamental commitments to protecting their citizens from harm—both foreign and domestic—and to securing the welfare of those within their boundaries, i.e., to providing some manner of generally economic assistance to individuals in need, where such needs are connected to the individuals' capacity to maintain a livelihood.[2] Such states are also committed to the protection of the civil institutions upon which democracy rests.

It is important to stress that the viewpoint of this essay is not based on opposition to the idea that states have responsibilities to the welfare of all persons within their borders. For example, the state has responsibilities to the victims of structural unemployment. When someone, through no fault of his or her own, loses the means to a livelihood, the state upholds a system of property distribution that restrains that person from walking onto a local farm and taking whatever she and her family need to live. Since the state thus contributes to the cause of that person's need, it has a responsibility to her.[3] Full acceptance of the principle that the state, in our conception of it, has welfare obligations needs to be emphasized here just because in discussions of arts funding it is often assumed that if one has any doubts about the propriety of arts funding, one must also be skeptical about welfare. Welfare is a legitimate arena of state activity, but it is not clear that all prospective arts funding is.

What does this talk of legitimate arenas of state activity come to? Maybe we can approach this by reviewing one of the more popular defenses of arts funding that recurs in contemporary debates. The point is stated succinctly by Sir William Rees-Mogg, chairman of the Arts Council of Great Britain. He writes, "The Arts Council grant is equal to the interest on the interest on the capital cost of the Trident programme. That is the relative priority the state gives to the enhancement of the human spirit. I am a firm supporter of national defense policies, but just look at the state's priorities—the capital on defense but not even the interest on the interest on the arts."[4]

Many supporters of prospective arts funding will not be so temperate as Rees-Mogg. Appalled at our defense expenditures, many Americans will say it is a scandal that so much is spent on defense and so little on art or that art should not suffer so that defense spending may flourish. Perhaps they will urge that greater bounties for art should be carved out of the gargantuan defense budget. But these remarks miss the point in assuming that defense spending and arts funding are somehow linked. They are not.

Defense is a legitimate function of any state. It is not clear that prospective arts funding is, nor if it is, that it is such a crucial function that it makes sense to tie its destiny in any way to that of so central a function as defense. Undoubtedly our defense spending is extravagant. But it is perfectly compatible to be opposed to the present level of defense spending while also wondering if prospective arts funding is appropriate. For *some* defense spending is recognized as legitimate by nearly everyone, save pacifists and certain types of anarchists, whereas it is not yet apparent that any prospective arts funding is legitimate. The defense spending argument may be politically persuasive, especially for those opposed to the current defense budgeting, but it is not a theoretical justification, for it does not show that prospective arts funding is a proper function of government, whereas defense is.

The discussion of proper state functions may suggest an avenue of justification for prospective arts funding, viz., welfare. If one agrees that the state has a responsibility to secure the welfare of its citizens, then one may be tempted to say that prospective arts funding is a means by which the state secures the welfare of those within its borders. But "welfare," as it applies to state activity, refers to assistance to individuals in need of the basic goods that comprise a livelihood. Is it plausible to suppose that prospective arts funding provides some such goods?

A conclusive answer would require a full theory of needs, which unfortunately we lack. But perhaps we can at least determine whether the products of prospective arts funding sound like the things we ordinarily think of as needs. On one reading, to say that someone needs Z is to say that if she lacks it she will suffer injury, sickness, madness, hunger, or avoidable death.[5] Does the production of contemporary artworks assist individuals in needful situations such as these? Would anyone be harmed, in any literal sense of the term, if prospective arts funding were discontinued? Am I harmed if painter X does not execute the series she would have created had she received a state grant?

Of course, defining basic needs in terms of harms has limitations. But suppose we define welfare needs in terms of the amount of goods and services sufficient to raise an individual from his present state to somewhere above the poverty line.[6] If this is how we conceive of the welfare jurisdiction of the state, then it is difficult to see how prospective arts funding has anything to do with welfare.

Undoubtedly, the picture presented thus far involves thinking of the welfare of nonartists. Our rhetorical questions really ask, "What nonartists will be harmed, in a basic, literal sense, if they do not have the opportunity to see so-and-so's planned series due to a lack of government funding?" Or, even more ridiculously, "What nonartist will fail to be raised above the poverty line should so-and-so's proposed series not be funded?" It may be charged that the case has been rigged. Haven't we forgotten about the welfare responsibilities of the state to artist so-and-so? Isn't it possible that artist so-and-so will fail to rise above the poverty line without funding?

The problem with these new questions, however, is that if artist so-and-so has a legitimate welfare need, then the state will have the responsibility to assist her. That is, if a state is meeting its basic welfare responsibilities to everyone, then there is no reason to propose prospective arts funding as a further aspect of the state's welfare function. Of course, this raises issues about the relation of welfare to the active promotion of employment by the state, and we will come back to that matter.

Some writers who attempt to connect state arts support to the state's welfare function introduce a concept of "aesthetic welfare." Aesthetic welfare, in turn, is defined as "all the aesthetic levels of the experience of members of the society at a given time."[7] It is then suggested that there is a prima facie government duty to preserve the aesthetic wealth of society where that wealth—pictures, plays, and so forth—is what gives rise to aesthetic welfare. It is not certain, however, that this particular notion of aesthetic welfare helps the case for prospective arts funding since it may be that, if there were such a prima facie duty, retrospective arts funding might suffice to discharge it.

Also, one must question whether the connection between "aesthetic welfare" and the concept of welfare relevant to government activity is really unequivocal. First, "aesthetic welfare" doesn't correlate with definable needs, especially basic needs; nor does being below the poverty line imply being aesthetically disadvantaged. And clearly promoting individuals' aesthetic welfare will not raise them over the poverty line. Moreover, the state's welfare responsibility under this conception of aesthetic welfare doesn't seem to be directly connected to individuals but is a matter of ensuring that there will be a large number of aesthetic objects around so that people can have aesthetic experiences if they want them. The state is to ensure the permanent possibility of high levels of what is called aesthetic welfare but might better be called aesthetic well-being. This well-being is to be secured for society at large, construed additively, whereas the state's welfare responsibilities are discharged toward particular persons, viz., anyone in need. Thus the notion of "aesthetic welfare" appears not to refer to welfare of the kind that defines the state's proper domain of activity; it is merely a homonymous term that, though sounding like the concept employed in the discussion of the state's welfare responsibilities, is actually quite separate. Of course, we have not adequately dealt with the notion of aesthetic needs but will turn to it shortly.

In the discussion of welfare, it may be objected that our perspective is too narrow. By speaking of basic needs and poverty lines, we have restricted the compass of the welfare activities of the state to aid in desperate situations and to matters of life support. But must the state's welfare jurisdiction be so constrained? It might be argued that apart from assisting those in need, the state's welfare function also includes benefiting the populace, supplying human goods even to people above the poverty line, thus enabling people to flourish. Were this the case, the defender of prospective arts funding could argue that such a practice would be justified in virtue of the state's responsibilities to benefit the populace, to promote as much good as possible.

First, if the state does have a responsibility to promote human goods over and above the responsibility to prevent harms, it is not obvious that this is best conceived of as part of its welfare responsibility. Perhaps it is rather an obligation to beneficence. Whether the state has such an obligation is an important question which we cannot answer now. Some might argue that the state has such obligations but only after it has discharged all of its welfare obligations—no money for paintings until all the needy are assisted. Personally, I find this viewpoint compelling in our present circumstances.

There are, however, other arguments against state obligations to beneficence that also bear serious consideration. In pluralist societies—such as we envision modern democracies to be—that which constitutes human goods over and above welfare goods is essentially contested. If the state, given conditions of scarce resources, promotes some goods rather than others, it is unjustifiably favoring the proponents of one good over the proponents of a rival good who may, in fact, deny that the good so favored is a good at all. Of course, the problem disappears if we think that the state's obligation to beneficence extends to promoting every human good, every kind of benefit that facilitates human flourishing or that is believed to contribute to human flourishing. But this seems implausible. Even if the state has legitimate obligations of beneficence, there remain questions of the extent of these obligations even where scarce resources are not at issue. Assuming an obligation of beneficience, we may still argue that the state is not obligated to administer every human benefit to its populace. Consider love and affection. These are things that contribute to the flourishing of human life. But we do not think that the state should intervene in human relations to redistribute affection within society so that each receives his fair share. We would not countenance the formation of a new state agency, the Department of Love, whose duty it would be to assist anyone who has fallen below some putative affection line, construed on the model of a poverty line.

The state, even supposing a legitimate function of beneficence, will not be expected to deliver every possible benefit to its citizenry. This observation, of course, is relevant to the question of prospective arts funding, because if the proponent of such funding invokes beneficiaries in defense of it, we shall still want some demonstration that art is the kind of benefit the state has a duty to supply. Is prospective arts funding more analogous to discharging a welfare obligation or to assisting the lovelorn? For a number of reasons, including the degree to which personal preference is involved with both art and love, one suspects that prospective arts funding is more analogous to the imagined administration of affection than it is to the administration of welfare. But that suggests that prospective arts funding cannot be grounded in a putative state responsibility of beneficence.[8]

Of course, the preceding discussion of benefit will dissatisfy those who feel that art is not merely a benefit to human life, but that it satisfies a human need, call it an aesthetic need. Often this belief is advanced through environmentalist metaphors. In the first annual report of the NEA, it was proclaimed that "we need to make our open spaces beautiful again. We must create an environment in which our youth will be encouraged to pursue the discipline and craft of the arts. We must not only support our artistic institutions, both national and local, but we must also make the arts part of our daily life so that they become an essential part of our existence."[9]

The underlying spirit of this plan seems to suggest that just as the government has an obligation to forestall the deterioration of the ecosystem, so there is an obligation to reverse the deterioration of the aesthetic environment. Human animals have aesthetic needs; environments replete with aesthetic and expressive qualities satisfy them. Perhaps it will be argued that environments bereft of such qualities, or possessing them in minuscule degrees, result in some sort of psychic tension, ranging from irritation to alienation. Miles of fast stations, fast-food restaurants, used-car lots, body shops—the strip phenomenon—present an impoverished aesthetic habitat that has unsettling psychic consequences. Similarly, the private sphere, flooded with tawdry, mass-produced consumer goods, is aesthetically deprived in a way that is psychically unnerving. Vigorous arts funding is urged as a countermeasure, including prospective arts funding, which presumably will provide some of the objects we need to restore or perhaps to create the kind of aesthetic environment that promotes our psychic health. Thus, prospective arts funding would be warranted on the grounds that it implements that state's obligations in regard to the health of its citizens.

This argument is not implausible. Of course, it requires "fleshing out." Before it can be accepted, research would have to be undertaken to show that we do indeed have aesthetic needs whose frustration results in some form of psychic discomfort. And if this could not be demonstrated, this particular argument would falter.

But suppose it is the case that there are such aesthetic needs. What would that suggest about prospective arts funding? It would imply that we should do further research in order to determine the kinds of art that satisfy whatever aesthetic needs the earlier research identified. We might then go on to fund the kind of programs and the kind of art that satisfies those needs. But note that this will not imply support for any kind of art whatsoever. It only grounds support for those projects which function to alleviate aesthetic needs or which we predict are probable to alleviate aesthetic needs. Not all art will have this causal capacity. For example, Duchamp's *In Advance of a Broken Arm* as well as much Punk Art will not have this capacity, nor will films like Buñuel's *The Andalusian Dog*. Thus, prospective arts funding of works such as these will not be justified by an aesthetic need argument.

The problem here, of course, involves what is meant by "aesthetic." It is not synonymous with "art." Generally, it is associated with the beautiful and the sublime, or it is associated with the qualitative appearance of things. An aesthetic need, under this reading, would be a need for experiences of the beautiful, the sublime, or for the experience of objects and environments with marked expressive qualities such as warmth, friendliness, or joyfulness. Much art, including, significantly, much contemporary art, is not dedicated to producing aesthetic experience. Indeed, much contemporary art is even avowedly anti-aesthetic. If an artist makes a junkyard piece to portray modern life, it seems curious that he should expect funding on the basis of alleviating aesthetic privations. Nor is it obvious that every expressive quality projectable by a work of art will have the equilibrating effect presumed by the aesthetic need argument. Works marked by turmoil, horror, anguish, and so on are not prima facie defensible under the aesthetic need argument. The point is that even if the aesthetic need argument is acceptable, it will not support prospective arts funding as we know it. It will only support funding of those prospective artworks with high probability of bringing about equilibrating aesthetic experiences. Nonaesthetic, anti-aesthetic, reflexive, and certain darkly expressive artworks will not be defensible in the name of aesthetic experience.

If the aesthetic need argument gives us the means for justifying prospective arts funding, it also seems to have the unfortunate consequence that it only warrants the funding of certain kinds of art—the art of the beautiful, the sublime, and that expressive of psychically equilibrating qualities. If no further justification can be found, the consequence of this is that the state can only fund a certain type of art. Artists pursuing certain nonaesthetic aims cannot be funded by the state. But proponents of art funding, lovers of art, and artists with nonaesthetic projects should be disturbed by this. For if the government places large investments behind one type of art, the evolution of the art world will undoubtedly be affected. Whole avenues of artistic development will appear less viable than the production of aesthetic art. And from the contemporary art world's point of view, this kind of prospective arts funding might be regarded as having a regressive effect overall.

At this point, it may be claimed that the relevant need to consider is not an aesthetic need but a need for art. All societies, it might be said, have artlike practices—i.e., symbolizing practices of some sort—which suggests that art of some type answers a human need. Next, the idea will be advanced that in modern industrial societies, art will disappear if the government does not support it. Thus, without government support the conditions necessary for satisfying our need for art cannot be sustained. Perhaps prospective arts funding can be endorsed as a corollary to this via the claim that the need for art includes a need for new art. And if the state does not fund new art, no one else will.

Of course, this is an empirical claim and a dubious one at that. The arts flourished in democratic societies before the advent of direct public funding; there is no reason to suppose that they will disappear without the direct government funding of new artworks. Where people are interested in art, there will still be an audience to support new work. Were there no audience whatsoever, it would be difficult to determine on what basis the government would justify funding new art. Moreover, in advanced capitalist societies at least, big businesses are attracted to arts patronage because projecting the kind of upwardly mobile profile associated with interest in the arts attracts upwardly mobile investors. One could go on elaborating considerations that count against the disappearance-of-art thesis. But perhaps what is most important to say about it is that, at best, it is not worried about the disappearance of art per se but only of certain types of art, viz., what for want of a better label we call high art. Popular art—movies, TV, pop music—will not disappear if prospective arts funding is discontinued. So it is not the case that our society will be deprived of art, including new art, without prospective arts funding. Hence, if there is a need for art, it will not be frustrated. On the other hand, it is unlikely that there is a human need for our kind of high art. But, in any event, it is also unlikely that our kind of high art is about to disappear if prospective arts funding is halted, though the assumption that it will seems implicit in too many of the arguments of proponents of such funding. Of course, sans funding, high art might be produced at a diminished rate. But here the burden of proof rests with the proponent of funding to show what social evil results from a diminished rate of high art production.

One practical justification for arts funding is that it may function as an economic stimulant, promoting prosperity by, for example, attracting tourists. Insofar as prospective arts funding can be pegged to the state of the economy, it would appear to be a legitimate state operation, since the maintenance of a functioning economy is related to the state's welfare responsibilities. Needless to say, it is often difficult to imagine the way in which grants to individual artists for new works—as opposed to city art centers—can engineer economic well-being, but there is no reason to think that such a connection could not be made in principle. Of course, an economic stimulation argument identifies the value of arts funding not with aesthetic or artistic value but with economic instrumentality.[10] But despite this, the economic stimulation argument seems acceptable, although it can only be mobilized where certain constraints are respected. Where prospective arts funding is employed to stimulate tourism or some other form of economic activity in a given area, the state must be convinced that no alternative form of intervention of comparable cost would yield greater prosperity in that area. Furthermore, where national rather than local stimulation is at issue, the nation state must supply some rationale why it is undertaking to stimulate tourism in one geographical region rather than another. But when these conditions can be met, no obvious barrier to prospective arts funding appears to remain, though it is uncertain how often these criteria can be satisfied.

Connecting prospective arts funding to economic policy suggests another means for justifying state support, viz., employment. If state funding is not forthcoming, then many artists will be unemployed. Unemployment is clearly a matter of concern for the state. The massive unemployment of black inner-city youths is one of the great tragedies of our society, and we must demand that the state do something about it. Many would be in favor of New Deal–type programs to alleviate the program. Can we mount a similar argument in order to show that prospective arts funding can be seen as a way of averting massive unemployment among artists? My inclination is to think not. Artists do not seem to constitute a group that is comparable to black inner-city youths. Questions of justice and equal opportunity do not seem to bear on the issue of artistic unemployment. Moreover, the artistic unemployment we might envision involves artists' unemployment as artists rather than their unemployment simpliciter. That is, I may not be able to support my family as an unemployed poet, but that does not mean that I can't do it in another way, say, as a journalist or a copywriter. It does not seem to me that the state's responsibilities in regard to the unemployed extend to guaranteeing that everyone have the job he or she most desires. The case of artistic unemployment involves people not able to pursue the line of work they most covet, while inner-city unemployment involves people excluded from the work force altogether. Our belief that the state has clear responsibilities in the case of inner-city unemployment cannot ground claims to similar duties in regard to artistic unemployment. If artists are unemployed, the state will have certain duties to them, though it is not clear that those duties include finding them employment as artists.

It may be suggested that a certain conception of fairness can be used to ground government art support. If a given government subsidizes the building of sports arenas, then, in all fairness, arts production should also be supported. If the government facilitates the pursuits of sports fans, then it should, as a matter of treating people equally, also facilitate the pursuits of arts fans, perhaps by means of supporting the creation of new art. Of course, this argument presupposes a context in which some leisure activity, such as sports, is being subsidized. But what, in such a context, justifies that subsidizing of sports? If nothing does, then perhaps what is required is that neither sports nor the arts be subsidized.

Insofar as one objects to sports subsidies, one must forego art subsidies. Of course, a subsidy for a sport might be defended on the grounds that it stimulates the economy of an area, but then arts funding can, in principle, be similarly defended. Again, it does seem correct to say that if a majority, call them sports fans, demand sports funding in the face of opposition by a minority, call them arts lovers, then fairness urges that the leisure activity of the latter group also be supported, though perhaps not to the same extent. The deeper question, however, is whether any leisure activity should be supported. For if any is supported, then all should be in proportion to the allegiance to that leisure activity in the society. And yet this appears extreme. Suppose skateboard racers wanted a national stadium. Does that seem to be something for which the state should pay by levying taxes on the rest of us? Obviously, even wilder examples could be concocted—hopscotch stadia, a coliseum for Bocci Ball, a national gallery of toothpick sculpture. The advancement of the leisure professions may just not be an area the state should enter at all.

One of the earliest arguments in favor of government support of the arts is that the arts perform a moralizing function. During the period of the Second Empire, in nineteenth-century France, the Orpheon, a working-class choral society, was sponsored by Napoleon III's government on the grounds that it would introduce the proletariat to "moral amusements," which would not only cultivate their tastes but "moralize" them.[11] Similarly in this country in the nineteenth century the belief was widespread that through art the populace could be morally improved. These beliefs influenced both school reform and the founding of the great American museums.[12] In the era of state funding of the arts, faith in their potential to make people more moral—faith in the civilizing power of the arts—suggested a line of justification for the prospective funding of art, for surely the maintenance of the moral order in society is a legitimate state concern. Thus, if art can function as a means of improving morality, then the state is justified in supporting it. If art provides moral exemplars or deepens conscience, the state, it would seem, can avail itself of the devices of art to instill moral behavior in its populace.

One aspect of art that is related to its capacity to engender moral improvement is the tendency of certain kinds of art to develop our sympathies for others. Some art enables us to see the world from different points of view, thus promoting not only the acquisition of a formal requirement of morality but also enabling us to grasp vicariously the situations of different classes, races, creeds, and genders. Art, then, can foster greater tolerance within society and thereby bolster the moral order. A strengthened moral order is a goal that the state legitimately pursues, given, among other things, its responsibility to prevent harm from befalling its populace. That is, one way to prevent harm is to prevent people from harming each other by making them more moral. If art can serve the accomplishment of this goal, then the prospective funding of such art seems justified.

But this argument for prospective arts funding does have certain unhappy consequences. The argument assumes that art increases moral sympathies. We have no reason to dispute the contention that some art has this capacity. But it seems unlikely that all art functions this way. If the state is to justify its funding of art on moralizing grounds, then only that art which we can reasonably predict will increase moral sympathies can be funded. This will probably require some empirical research into the moral efficacy of different kinds of art. Art, indeed whole categories of art, that affords no moral uplift cannot be funded on the basis of this argument. Art that works against any increase in moral sympathy will also be problematic. Art devoted, for instance, to outraging the bourgeoisie or politically partisan art is likely to be debarred from funding insofar as it instills divisiveness rather than tolerance. That is, mobilizing this functionalist justification for arts funding, only grounds for certain types of arts funding have been secured. This raises problems like those encountered in our earlier discussion of the aesthetic environment argument. If the state is justified in funding only certain kinds of art and it enters the art world, putting its immense resources behind only moralizing kinds of art, then there is a great danger that the development of the art world will be skewed in certain directions. This violates our intuitions that the realm of art should be pluralist and relatively independent of considerations of social utility. Thus, though the state may be justified in funding certain types of art, we may be loath to have it exercise this prerogative because of the damage it would wreak upon art as we know it. Nor does it seem practicable to meet this objection by saying that the state should fund every type of art in order to fund the kinds of art it is justified to fund. For this will result in a kind of self-defeating schizophrenia: supporting antiaesthetic art in order to support aesthetic art; supporting divisive art in order to support art that expands moral sympathies.

A recent argument in favor of public art support has been advanced by Ronald Dworkin. He draws a distinction between two dimensions of culture. Culture "provides the particular paintings, performances, and novels, designs, sports, and thrillers that we value and take delight in; but it also provides the structural frame that makes aesthetic values of that sort possible and makes them values for us."[13] This structural frame includes a wealth of associations, references, images, and contrasts, which, like language, supply us with the tools with which we forge and map our common life. Dworkin insists that it is better for people to have a complex and multifarious cultural framework and that we owe future generations at least as rich a cultural framework as the one we inherited. Both these values can be achieved by promoting the creation of innovative art. Government support in this area is necessary because it "helps protect the fragile structure of our culture."[14] Admittedly, Dworkin uses this argument to endorse indirect rather than direct arts support by the government. But he does countenance situations in which government support could be direct. And someone other than Dworkin might attempt to use this argument in favor of direct support.

At least two problems, however, beset this approach. First, there is the assumption that the structure of culture is fragile. We have encountered this before. But as an empirical supposition we have argued that its truth is far from obvious. Moreover, when we look at the structure of culture, we note that it comprises many ingredients besides art—social dances, children's games, fashion, sports, religion, indeed the whole gamut of our symbolizing activities. When we think of the twenties, we recall the flapper and the Charleston; perhaps in the future people will think of the eighties in terms of punk haircuts and break-dancing. These images become part and parcel of our ways of thinking; they are the very weave of our common culture. But it seems dubious to consider them to be fit beneficiaries of public funding. Yet if art deserves public funding because of its contribution to our cultural framework, so does anything else that similarly contributes, including, potentially, every sort of symbolizing activity and notably some outlandish ones: hoola-hoops, comic books, Billy Graham, the Watergate break-in, and so on.[15]

One criticism that is apt to be directed at this essay is that we have repeatedly discussed prospective arts funding in terms of things other than art, i.e., in terms of some good consequences which would justify such funding. One may feel that this completely misses the point. Art is good in itself and does not require further validation in virtue of the further consequences it abets.[16] It may be true, though one has one's doubts, that art is intrinsically good. But even if the production of art is intrinsically good, that, in and of itself, would not warrant state funding of the arts. For the state does not and, in some cases, should not be taken to have a role in the production of whatever we conceive to be an intrinsic good or even of whatever is an intrinsic good (if there are such things). State intervention in these matters calls for justification.

In conclusion, there do appear to be theoretical justifications for prospective government funding of art. The two strongest justifications seem to be those concerning the aesthetic environment and the moralizing effects of the arts. However, though these arguments are available, it is not clear that they should be acted upon. For they endorse the funding of only certain types of art. Government support for the arts guided strictly by these arguments may indeed disturb the structure of artistic production and perhaps destroy the art world as we know it.

Notes

1. Edward Banfield, *The Democratic Muse* (New York: Basic Books, 1984), p. 4.

2. Carl Wellman, *Welfare Rights* (Totowa, N.J.: Rowman and Littlefield, 1984), p. 30.

3. Suggested in ibid., pp. 133–34, and by T. Benditt, *Rights* (Totowa, N.J.: Rowman and Littlefield, 1982), pp. 112–16.

4. William Rees-Mogg, "Paying for the Arts: The Political Economy of Art in 1985," *The Economist* 294, no. 7385 (9 March 1985): 94. It should be noted that Rees-Mogg uses this argument only to endorse indirect funding as a way of replacing declines in direct funding. However, I have heard arguments like this in discussions with proponents of direct funding.

5. Joel Feinberg, *Social Philosophy* (Englewood Cliffs, N.J.: Prentice-Hall, 1973), p. 111.

6. Derived from Wellman, *Welfare Rights,* p. 136.

7. Monroe C. Beardsley, "Aesthetic Welfare, Aesthetic Justice, and Educational Policy," in *The Aesthetic Point of View,* ed. M. Wreen and D. Callen (Ithaca, N.Y.: Cornell University Press, 1982), pp. 113–14. Originally published in the *Journal of Aesthetic Education* 7, no. 4 (October 1973): 49–61.

8. My disposition is to see state activity connected to state responsibilities or duties. My inclination is to think that state power is so awesome that, in contested contexts, only things as serious as duties should mobilize it. But others may not share my squeamishness. They will think that in stating the issue above in terms of state obligations to beneficence, I am asking too much. They might suggest that what is really at issue are not state obligations to beneficence but rather a prima facie license to the state to proceed in any area where it can do good or bestow benefit. This construal of the state's relation to beneficence, however, raises the same sort of problems discussed above in terms of an obligation to beneficence. Surely beneficent activity such as arts funding cannot be undertaken until the state has acquired its welfare obligations. And, furthermore, where the benefits in question are contested, it is not clear that the state can implement them over the protests of significant numbers of its skeptical citizens.

9. Quoted in Banfield, *The Democratic Muse,* pp. 68–69.

10. A similar point is emphasized by William J. Baumol in his remarks in "IV. Panel Discussion: Public Support of the Arts," *Art and the Law* 9, no. 2 (1985): 214–28. One kind of economic argument in favor of arts funding concerns the technical notion of a public good. I have not broached this issue directly in the article. Ronald Dworkin has dealt with the epistemological problems involved in considering art in this light in "Can a Liberal State Support Art?" in his *A Matter of Principle* (Cambridge, Mass.: Harvard University Press, 1985), pp. 221–33. (This article is reprinted in *Art and the Law* 9, no. 2, 1985). I agree with Dworkin on this matter; for a differing view, see Baumol, "Public Support of the Arts."

11. Howard Becker, *Art Worlds* (Berkeley: University of California Press, 1982), pp. 181–82.

12. Banfield, *The Democratic Muse,* chaps. 4 and 5.

13. Dworkin, "Can a Liberal State Support Art?" p. 229.

14. Ibid., p. 233.

15. R. Nozick makes a related point in his remarks in *Art and the Law* 9, no. 2 (1985): 162–67.

16. T. Nagel seems to follow this line in his remarks in ibid., pp. 236–39.

9

Democracy and Excellence

Sir Roy Shaw

Underlying some of the most vigorous debates about the arts today are attitudes which are rooted in history or general assumptions which are rarely made explicit.

We are all democrats now—provided you don't ask us to define democracy. In contemporary debates about the arts *elitism* is the most frequently used term of abuse. Significantly, it is regularly misused to denounce any belief in excellence, whereas it properly means the belief that excellence should be kept for the few, the elite. Lord (Kenneth) Clark was being elitist when he rejoiced in his autobiography that a certain architectural gem in Rome was usually empty, showing the huge gap between informed and popular taste. "God forbid," he wrote, "that it should ever be narrowed." This was a strange sentiment for a former chairman of the Arts Council, but fortunately Clark was an inconsistent elitist who used television skillfully to narrow the gap between informed and popular taste.

Democracy, however, has not always been so favorably regarded, especially in discussion of the arts. In the nineteenth century Sir Edmund Gosse (author of the novel *Father and Son*) warned against what he called "the spread of the democratic sentiment." He believed that the traditions of literary taste were being overturned: "Until now, the values in the arts have been determined by the educated classes. Now they are determined by the popular vote. Of late there seem to be certain signs, especially in America, of a revolt of the mob against our literary masters. The revolution against taste, once begun, will land us in irreparable chaos."

That may sound alarmist, but some aspects of contemporary culture seem to justify it. When most people read not literature but daily papers like the *Sun* and the *Mirror,* when most Americans accept a regular diet of television so predominantly awful that visiting Europeans can hardly believe it—then are we not in cultural chaos? As early as 1800, the poet William Wordsworth had discerned the growth of a new popular literature which, by offering "gross and violent stimulants," tended to blunt the discriminating part of the mind. He offered his own poems as a countervailing influence. Thirty years later, the French aristocrat Alexis de Tocqueville visited America to study that burgeoning democracy. What he saw led him to declare (in *Democracy in America*) that "democracy not only infuses a taste for literature among the trading classes, but introduces a trading spirit into literature." What would he have said had he seen today's lurid paperbacks in newsagents' shops or the Mills and Boon novelettes in Woolworth's?

We can, of course, dismiss Tocqueville as an elitist. He *was* an elitist, whose observation of society went no further down than the "trading classes." In our time, however, there are more populists than elitists. As late as 1948, T. S. Eliot may have proclaimed (in *Notes towards the Definition of Culture*) that it was "an essential condition of the preservation of the culture of the minority, that it should continue to be minority culture"; but this comment must be regarded, even by admirers of Eliot (like myself), as an unhappy misjudgment. More characteristic of our time is the view of the American sociologist Herbert Gans (expressed in *High Culture and Popular Culture,* 1975) that the demand made by high culture that everyone should share its standards is not justified in a democratic society. Gans's views have been echoed in Europe by serious writers on the arts. One of these even argues that in a democratic society quantity may have become more important than quality. Tocqueville would have seen this as confirmation of his fears about the incompatibility of democracy and excellence in the arts.

Those fears have been echoed in our time by the philosopher Bertrand Russell. In *A History of Western Philosophy* (1946) he argues that to some extent civilization may be furthered by social injustice: "A stable social system is necessary, but every stable social system hitherto devised has hampered the development of exceptional artistic or intellectual merit. How much murder and anarchy are we prepared to endure for the sake of great achievements such as those of the Renaissance? In the past, a great deal; in our time, much less."

Did Orson Welles read Bertrand Russell? If not, it is a great coincidence that, four years after *A History of Western Philosophy* was published, Welles interpolated into Graham Greene's script of the film *The Third Man* the following now famous words, spoken by Harry Lime: "In Italy, for thirty years they had warfare, terror, murder, bloodshed, but they produced Michelangelo, Leonardo da Vinci, and the Renaissance. In Switzerland they had brotherly love, they had some five hundred years of democracy and peace, and what did they produce? The cuckoo clock."

Must we then conclude that excellence in the arts can only be produced by social injustice and that peace and democracy are indeed incompatible with excellence? I think not; the glories of the Renaissance were produced not because of, but in spite of, the terror and the murder. Their coexistence does not prove a causal connection. Nevertheless, Welles's cuckoo clock is a challenge to anyone who has considered the full range of culture in, say, modern Britain or America, where we see many worse things than cuckoo clocks. For better and for worse the majority of people have been admitted into the general audience for culture. For worse, because the majority have not had the opportunity to develop and improve their knowledge and understanding of the arts—and much else. Hence the rise of cultural industries which make fortunes by exploiting cultural inexperience. Lord Grade, one of the first tycoons of commercial television, once wrote in a newspaper article: "I don't want to change people or lead them. I want to give the public what they want. They don't like things complicated, and neither do I. I like a beginning, a middle, and an end. Most housewives are the same, with the same tastes and desires. I know what the public wants because I am one of them." I regard this as an advocacy not of a "democratic culture" but of a demagogic culture, as a policy of pandering to the lowest or, at best, the least demanding tastes. Lord Grade's fellow television tycoon, Norman Collins, gave the game away when he said that if one gave the public *exactly* what it wanted, "it would be a perfectly appalling service." The real democrat recognizes a duty to meet people's needs as well as their wants and knows, as George Bernard Shaw pointed out, that there is a danger of people coming to want what they get.

Not only do many self-styled democrats put quantity above quality, but for some of them the very word *quality* and its synonyms are dismissed as an elitist category. I recall an amusing but also ominous interchange I had with a local authority member who came to me at the Arts Council to seek a grant for an enterprise run by his authority. I had to tell him that I had been advised that the enterprise was not good enough to warrant a grant. He looked at me sadly and with no sign of irony or conscious humor said: "You know, Sir Roy, the Arts Council is often accused of excellence." *Accused of excellence?* Tocqueville, thou should'st be living at this hour! What has happened not just to our language but to our culture when "excellence" can be used as a pejorative term? Michael Kustow, former director of the Institute of Contemporary Arts and now in charge of arts for Channel 4, has commented on the tendency of some "alternative arts" enthusiasts to dismiss the very idea of quality as authoritarian.

I believe that the task of education, broadcasting organizations, and arts organizations (especially the Arts Council and the Regional Arts Associations) is to make excellence accessible. This is to make the eminently democratic assumption that people deserve the best and need it. It is also to incur the charge of claiming to know better than the public itself what the public should have. However, those who run the arts or the media should not be mere mirrors of existing public tastes but should offer people opportunities to develop and improve their tastes. That, indeed, is the main task prescribed for the Arts Council in its royal charter: "To develop and improve the knowledge, understanding, and practice of the arts." "Developing" and "improving" were explicitly repudiated by Lord Grade in the passage quoted above; he was happy to work for the arrested development of the public mind. There are many like him in the mass culture business.

The prophetic pen of Ortega y Gasset had anticipated Grade's apologia forty years earlier when he wrote: "The characteristic of the hour is that the commonplace mind, knowing itself to be commonplace, has the assurance to proclaim the rights of the commonplace and to impose them wherever it will." Indeed, two thousand years earlier Plato (in *The Republic*) had compared contemporaries who "gave the public what it wants" with a man in charge of a powerful animal whose sole aim is to keep the creature under control by pandering to all its wishes. So he would regard the animal's desires the sole criterion of what is good, being quite blind to any other standard of good and bad. Such a one was the 1960s commercial television executive who said: "We have a very good idea of the intelligence quotient of what we call our 'Nellies,' our typical viewers, and we take that IQ into account in arranging programs and program content." Attitudes like this were effectively denounced in the 1962 report of the Pilkington Committee on broadcasting, a report which exposed the pseudodemocratic pleas of "giving the public what it wants." The committee concluded that the broadcaster could not avoid "giving a lead"—for better or worse. But the contemptuous attitude to the audience continues to be exemplified by performers like Liberace, who knew how to tickle vulgar tastes by tickling the ivories. "My whole trick," he once confessed, "is to keep the tune well out in front. If I play Tchaikovsky, I play his melodies and skip his spiritual struggles. I have to know just how many notes my audience will stand for. If there's time left over, I fill in with lots of runs up and down the keyboard."

"I have to know just how many notes my audience will stand for"—this indicates a clear fear of stretching rudimentary musical knowledge or appreciation in the cause of developing and improving them. The truly democratic policy, in the arts as in politics, is to help people to develop their potential. Thomas Jefferson, author of the American Declaration of Independence, wrote that if the people were not enlightened enough to exercise political power, the remedy was not to take power away from them "but to inform their discretion through education." For many years, the Arts Council did little about its first chartered duty, and it took commercial television some time to live down the Lord Grade philosophy. That it has done so is due to the vision of men like Sir Denis Forman, chairman of Granada Television, Melvyn Bragg of London Weekend Television, and Jeremy Isaacs, head of Channel 4. The BBC had, from its inception over sixty years ago, a broader vision and did a great deal to develop the nation's musical tastes. One of the pioneers of the BBC, Mary Somerville, has written that she and her colleagues were inspired by the ideals of adult education, and Sir William Haley when he was director-general spoke of a pyramid of taste and the duty of broadcasters to help people to climb higher. Unlike Lord Grade, they remembered that both broadcasting organizations are charged with a duty to educate as well as to entertain and inform.

This discussion of democracy and excellence has necessarily led us to look at wider aspects of culture than those with which the Arts Council, regional arts associations, and local authorities are concerned. This is necessary because arts funding takes place in a cultural and intellectual setting which is wider than the arts. But let us return to the specific problem of assessing quality in the process of arts funding. Business sponsors (as I have already mentioned) may spend their money without worrying much about the quality of the arts they sponsor. Like kings or aristocrats in the past, they can please themselves as to what they encourage. A public subsidy organization, however, spends taxpayers' money, not its own, and therefore must discriminate.

Whatever it does, any arts council will (especially in the visual arts area) be accused of "squandering" taxpayers' money on "rubbish," but it must try to avoid that criticism by evaluating the artists and organizations who seek grants. The Arts Council has always spent a great deal of time on evaluation, normally carried out by officers and advisory panels who specialize in particular art forms. Ironically, it has been least successful in evaluating the four national companies (two opera, two drama), which absorb a very large share of the total amount spent by the Council. Traditionally, the music and drama panels did not attempt to evaluate them, though I never discovered why. Sometimes it seemed that the attitude of those who ran the "Big Four" (particularly the two opera house directors) was that their work was not only above reproach but was so obviously excellent that it was beyond assessment. In the early 1980s attempts were made to have the four national companies assessed by the Arts Council's finance committee, on the basis of detailed reports by the specialist directors, but the results were not impressive. Council members on the committee showed little capacity to judge the work of the companies, and the opera company representatives who appeared before them often seemed to regard even minor criticisms as somewhat impertinent. I believe that the term *centers of excellence* is correctly applied to the four national companies, but this does not mean that everything they do is excellent, and some attempt should be made to criticize and even apply financial restrictions on them when they repeatedly fail to achieve high standards, though the best companies may have occasional flops. "The right to fail" is important if the arts are to be adventurous.

In 1975, the Council took steps to improve evaluation by requiring the panels to assess the major companies and by planning to subject all revenue clients to an in-depth appraisal every three to five years, in addition to the "continuous assessment" carried out by officers and advisers. It remains to be seen how this will work. Difficulties in evaluation derive not just from shortcomings in the Council's procedures but from the fact that no unfavorable judgment is ever accepted by a client and its supporters. A decision by the Arts Council's staff and advisers that an individual's or a company's work is poor is always denounced as unfair, stupid, or even politically biased. Successful applicants merely assume that bare justice has been done.

For example, since I left the Council, the grant to John McGrath's 7:84 England drama company has been withdrawn. The company is left wing, hence the withdrawal of the grant was predictably denounced by many, including the arts journalist Joan Bakewell, as political discrimination. McGrath described his company as the victim of Sir William Rees-Mogg's "Tory hit squads." I know that 7:84's grant was terminated because its work was not thought good enough—a judgment made by officers and panel advisers who could by no means be tarred with the same brush as Sir William. Their judgment may have been wrong (I don't think it was), but it was certainly a judgment based on artistic and not political criteria. 7:84 Scotland is better, and it retains its grant.

Much more serious than the understandable inclination of unsuccessful applicants for grants to cry "Unfair!" is a general climate of opinion which holds that value judgments in the arts are purely subjective and have no objective validity. This view is prevalent despite the fact that grant applications include phrases like (to quote two small theater companies) "Our aim is the pursuit of excellence" or "Our policy is to present the highest standard of theater shows." Scepticism about value judgments is usually expressed in common expressions used to terminate a disagreement about the value of a work of art, such as "It's all a matter of opinion" or "That's just *your* opinion." More sophisticated skeptics might call to their aid Hamlet's pronouncement: "For there is nothing either good or bad, but thinking makes it so."

Such generally accepted maxims of conventional folly invoke in support two celebrated philosophers who should have known better. In 1843 Jeremy Bentham wrote, "Prejudice apart, the game of push-pin [a trivial game like tiddly-winks] is of equal value with the arts and sciences of music and poetry." For Bentham, pleasure was the sole criterion of value, hence he continues: "If the game of push-pin furnishes more pleasure, it is more valuable than either. Everybody can play at push-pin; poetry and music are relished only by a few." Lord Grade and his like would certainly agree, but the argument founders on the fact that we must take account not only of the *quantity* of pleasure but also of the *quality* of it. Pleasure itself cannot be the ultimate standard, since common sense acknowledges that some pleasures are not simply greater than others but are actually better. For example, the pleasure of watching cockfighting or video nasties may be considerable for some, but it would generally be held to have not merely a low value but even a disvalue: it is a degrading pleasure.

People who have never read Bentham, or even heard of him, are still his intellectual descendants. Perhaps even more influential, however, has been the legacy of logical positivism, especially A. J. Ayer's book *Language, Truth and Logic,* published in 1935. Over forty years later, Ayer recalled that one of its main theses was that "judgments of value were emotive and not cognitive." This is a harmless sounding philosophical proposition, but it implies that "This is good—or bad" means *nothing more* than "I like it"—or "I don't like it." Taken seriously, this renders meaningless the business of artistic (and indeed moral) discrimination. No wonder a sympathetic observer of the European arts scene in the early 1970s discerned "a phobic caution" about making any attempt to suggest that one work of art might be better than others. Subsequent philosophers may have rejected Ayer's view, but popular versions of it are alive and well.

No wonder, moreover, that in 1977 the Association of Community Theaters "demanded" (rather than asked) of me as secretary-general that I discuss their declaration that their work could not be assessed by "conventional aesthetic standards" but that audience response should now be the main criterion. We did discuss it but with little profit. There seemed no point in telling them that their "new" criterion was as old as the hills—certainly as old as Plato's animal-keeper. These leftish community theaters' views are echoed by the very rightish Kingsley Amis, who proclaims that "public taste may not be the best taste but it is the best available, certainly better than the critic's taste or the expert's taste or the bureaucrat's taste." This echo of Lord Grade comes ill from a former teacher of English literature and is just another manifestation of the prevailing Tory populism. Taken seriously, it would lead us to appoint Pam Ayres as poet laureate and pronounce the *Sun* as far better newspaper than *The Times,* since it obviously accords more with public taste, having a far larger circulation.

Another manifestation of the repudiation of qualitative differences is the egalitarian rejection of any qualitative distinction between the artist of genius and the well-meaning amateur. Many echo, if they do not actually quote, Ananda Coomaraswamy's dictum, made famous in the 1930s by Eric Gill, that "the artist is not a special kind of man, but every man is a special kind of artist." In the same mold are the declarations by one community artist in 1976 that "culture is everything, everyone has culture," and another in 1985 that "everybody can do everything." The second statement is plain nonsense, though its origins can be traced back to Marx and Engels's *The German Ideology* (1846), which declared that one of the aims of communism was to abolish the division of labor and specialization in the arts as elsewhere. The first reminds me of Marcel Duchamp's remark that if everything is art, nothing is art. Even the excellent Gulbenkian report on "The Arts in Schools" (1982) is nervous about acknowledging the existence of "gifted" children, for fear of being accused of elitism. Nevertheless, common sense requires us, when we really know the work of a Mozart or a Turner or a Wordsworth, to say that all people are gifted, but some are more gifted than others. Kenneth Clark put it more emphatically: "The poet and the artist are important precisely because they are not average men; because in sensibility, intelligence, and power of invention they far exceed the average."

Attitudes such as those I have discussed are prevalent not only in society at large but among some egalitarian artists and arts organizations and even among some members of the Arts Council and its staff. It is therefore not surprising that discrimination has not always been effectively exercised. Indeed, the poet Roy Fuller resigned from the Council because he believed it was wasting money on community arts. I had to rebut some of his detailed judgments but could not quarrel with the principle he enunciated: "Public money for the arts cannot properly be dispensed without a strong regard by the dispensing body for standards of excellence and principles of value." I wholly agree, but the Arts Council has to operate in a world where many—perhaps most—do not. The existence of an Arts Council that is not afraid to be "accused of excellence" is one factor, but only one that can help to make our democracy a society in which good art can flourish and be made more widely accessible.

10

American Popular Culture and High Culture in a Changing Class Structure

Herbert J. Gans

America's leisure-time activities (artistic, entertaining, informational, and other) have usually been divided into elite and mass components, high culture and popular culture. However, because leisure-time culture is in part a reflection and an effect of class, a more accurate analysis calls for a set of cultural strata or subcultures parallel with class strata. I proposed such cultural strata in an earlier study (Gans, 1974); the purpose of this paper is to update the previous analysis, describing some recent changes in the American class structure and therefore in American culture.

In the earlier study, I also distinguished between culture and the people who used or practiced it, between taste cultures and taste publics. I made the distinction partly to suggest that cultures do not always satisfy people or meet their needs, but also to indicate that giant mass media such as television networks, film studies, and publishers of mass circulation magazines often seek to, or have to, serve several taste publics with a single cultural product.

I defined taste publics as aggregates of people who make similar choices for similar reasons and therefore have roughly the same tastes and aesthetic standards.[1] Taste cultures were the array of arts, forms of entertainment, and information, as well as consumer goods available to the different taste publics. My feeling was and still is that people's choices in fiction and nonfiction books, films, music, dance, and art, as well as in television programs, cars, sports, hobbies, and so on are related because both their choices and the cultural products they choose reflect and express the same tastes and aesthetic standards. Thus, it is understandable that working-class men who like action dramas on the large and small screens may also participate in active and aggressive sports like football, boxing, and bowling.

My basic idea was a reformulation of Russell Lynes's thoughtful and witty analysis of highbrows, upper middlebrows, lower middlebrows, and lowbrows (Lynes, 1955: chapter 13). I related his conception and categories, without his ironic value judgments, to W. Lloyd Warner's class strata and ideas about symbolic behavior (Warner and Lunt, 1941), updating the former. Ultimately, I outlined five taste publics and cultures, which I called *high culture, upper-middle culture, lower-middle culture, low culture,* and *quasi-folk low culture,* the latter describing the arts, music, literature, and so on of people both too poor to be served by the commercial mass media and much involved still with the folk cultures they had brought with them from overseas or from the American Deep South. What I had in mind can be gleaned from the following capsule descriptions of two major American taste cultures: upper-middle and lower-middle:

> The people who read *Harper's Magazine* or *The New Yorker* are also likely to prefer foreign movies and public television, to listen to classical (but not chamber) music, play tennis, choose contemporary furniture, and eat gourmet foods. Subscribers to the *Reader's Digest,* on the other hand, probably go to the big Hollywood film if they go to the movies at all, watch the family comedies on commercial television, go bowling, choose traditional furniture and representational art, and eat American homestyle cooking. (Gans, 1974:68)

Although class was not the only differentiating criterion in my analysis, its primacy was based in part on the fact that it takes money to buy culture, and people have different incomes. More important, the ability to understand and appreciate some forms of culture implies educational prerequisites, and access to education is regulated by class. The educational prerequisites are particularly important in literature and other "verbal cultures," taste cultures differing therefore by the complexity of their vocabularies as well as their ideas. Other kinds of prerequisites exist in the arts and music, however. Furthermore, many cultural and social institutions discriminate on the basis of class. Museums have traditionally exhibited art and sculpture on the assumption that the visitor has some training in the fine arts, but in the past they also offered strong hints that working-class and even lower-middle-class people were not particularly welcome. Conversely, burlesque houses and working-class bars have used other mechanisms to discourage visits from the people who are welcomed by museums.

In addition, I made the functionalist assumption that all human beings have cultural wants and perhaps even needs, but that partly because of class and class position, they satisfy these in different ways, at least in America. This led to the relativistic hypothesis that all taste cultures are in some respects similar and can be compared because they perform more or less the same functions. For example, some taste publics use rock stars as heroes and heroines or as objects of entertainment and titillation; some prefer movie stars; and the practitioners of high culture use a handful of "serious" but also exhibitionistic novelists, artists, and composers.

The relativist hypothesis is, however, rejected by adherents of high culture, who argue that their culture is inherently different from all others. They believe that high culture's aesthetic standards are universal and must be met by everyone. Resembling in many ways the practitioners of orthodox religions, they conclude therefore that all other taste cultures and standards are aesthetically and otherwise invalid, harmful to both individuals and society.[2]

Finally, my analysis sought to understand how class affects people's cultural choices, but it did not attempt to explain all cultural choice. While class influences the kinds of music people prefer, liking music is not a matter of class. Furthermore, class alone cannot explain why people like specific kinds of music. Country music is probably preferred by lower-middle and low-culture publics, but not all of the people in these publics like country music. Why some people enjoy country music while others with many of the same tastes do not remains to be studied.

Recent Changes in Taste Cultures and Publics

My original five-strata hierarchical model of taste cultures and publics was qualified in several ways, for each taste public was divided into age groups and also into avant-garde, conventional, and traditional factions. Moreover, I visualized it as less static than suggested by my (overly) large number of groups and categories, proposing, for example, that even by the early 1970s the then still emerging "counterculture" was already moving away from its origins as a predominantly but hardly entirely upper-middle avant-garde youth culture. Thanks to the efforts of commercial entrepreneurs, but especially the readiness of young people to move away from their parents' culture, apolitical versions of the counterculture were already becoming popular among lower-middle and working-class adolescents and young adults.

I also noted that post–World War II affluence and the increase in schooling had on the one hand reduced the size of the low-culture public and with it the importance of low culture, but on the other hand they had brought about a drastic expansion of upper-middle culture, partly to serve the large number of new college-educated professionals working in what was even then beginning to be thought of as a postindustrial economy.

Since the early 1970s, the changes both in the American occupational distribution and in the taste cultures and publics in American society have been so dramatic that some cultural observers suggest that the old distinction between high and popular cultures has been erased, forecasting a nearly culturally classless utopia in which all socioeconomic groups would choose from what is a single culture. That people were now free to go to classical and rock concerts without being criticized by classical music audiences as vulgar or by rock devotees as snobbish, that they could be practicing intellectuals but also enjoy TV sports without indulging in "camp" or "slumming"—all inspired the belief that earlier divisions and conflicts over taste had ended. Accordingly, some sociologists have begun to doubt the connection between culture and class, arguing that class position is no longer the best predictor of cultural choice (Peterson, 1983).

Although I will later question this argument and offer some alternative explanations, I shall first describe what seem to be the three most important changes of recent years. One is the now completed transformation of the original counterculture into conventional culture. In the 1980s, long hair on men is no longer a sign of rebelliousness, left-wing politics, or a Bohemian life-style. A second is the widespread change in the commercial culture serving the lower-middle and low-culture taste publics. The mythic Golden Age of the 1950s notwithstanding, commercial television is today far more sophisticated than it was thirty years ago. Words, ideas, and plots are more complicated; the simple Western and crime melodramas with their black-hatted villains are virtually extinct, and so are several of the once invincible religious and sexual taboos that constrained popular entertainment. What is true of commercial culture also applies to many of its lower-middle and working-class customers. Television's Archie Bunker was not only a middle-class caricature but represented an older white working class that has little in common with today's young workers.

The third change is the apparent emergence of a new taste culture that seems in some ways to cut across and blend upper- and lower-middle culture and that, for want of a better term, I will label middle culture. The public associated with the new culture consists mainly of young college graduates who have taken the new professional, technical, and white-collar service jobs that have been created in the U.S. economy over the last several decades—people who in 1984 also became known as "yuppies" (young urban professionals). Some of them will eventually wind up in the upper-middle class and others have already arrived there, but their cultural choices and tastes are different from older members of that class, and the difference is not simply explained by age.

In the absence of good data, the basic characteristics of the new culture can only be guessed at, but its public seems to be more interested in goods than in symbols, more in a set of hobbylike activities than in the traditional arts. As a result, gourmet cooking, eating out, foreign travel, jogging and other kinds of exercise, the acquisition of "collectibles," and the pursuit of fads and fashions take up more time, energy, and money than they have in past leisure cultures. Concurrently, the public's symbolic choices are also different, with people feeling little obligation to offer allegiance to high culture or to participate in its upper-middle culture derivatives.

The outlines of the new culture are most visible in the print media. For example, *Harper's* and *The New Yorker* now share magazine racks with periodicals like *Cuisine, Rolling Stone, Runner,* and *Self,* which offer information, advice, and other features about the variety of hobbylike activities mentioned above. Although their readers are affluent and well educated, the magazines are not as serious by literary standards as the traditional "class" magazines and in effect eschew both literature and politics, suggesting that the new culture is little indebted to high- and upper-middle-culture concerns. A similar pattern exists in book publishing, for the increase in nonfiction titles has involved the same hobbylike topics. The *New York Times,* once a bastion of upper-middle culture, invented five once-a-week, back-of-the-book sections in the mid-1970s which speak partly to the concerns of the new public, while its music pages now include reviews and criticisms of rock and country music.

In the graphic arts, the new culture is less immediately apparent, for the museum and the art gallery, as well as the high and upper-middle art they exhibit, remain dominant. Perhaps the new culture is represented by some kinds of pop art and photographic realism, by the products sold in the burgeoning museum shops, or by the shops themselves. Alternatively, middle-culture art may be found outside the museum, in poster art and in the stores that sell it. As noted earlier, the middle public probably constitutes a major market for "collectibles," but it may also be a constituency for so-called postmodernist architecture. Modern or "international" style design is so severe that it never became accepted anywhere other than in high culture and related circles. The popular hostility and scorn it evoked could not have pleased the corporations that commissioned skyscrapers and factories from world-famous international-style architects in order to demonstrate their good taste and advertise their good will.

This new culture is hardest to discern in television and films because both must serve several publics at once. Perhaps middle culture made its start on the small screen with the first "yuppie" sitcom, "The Mary Tyler Moore Show." But by 1984 it was probably represented by "Cheers," set in a multiclass singles bar, and by "Family Ties," in which a two-career household finds an apolitical but happy medium between the radical protest of the 1960s and the conservative protest of today. Perhaps middle culture is also visible in "Hill Street Blues," a police drama that treats its characters as professionals rather than heroes, and in "General Hospital," an afternoon soap opera about professionals. The prototypical middle-culture movie may be the genre that describes, in seemingly naturalistic fashion, the increasing maturation and sophistication of today's young people, beginning with *American Graffiti.*

I do not want to exaggerate either the distinctiveness or the novelty of middle culture. Also, its most visible current examples are the activities of and the products for young adults. In a way, the validity of the middle-culture hypothesis cannot be tested until later, when it will be possible to see what cultural choices these people will make in middle age, when they are too old for rock music and too overweight for jogging.

Explaining the Changes

The primary explanation of the cultural changes that have taken place since the end of World War II is the long-term transformation of the U.S. economy, its need for well-educated technicians to staff and manage the new manufacturing, service, and communications activities, as well as the new technologies that have been developed in the last several decades. Of course, the economy alone cannot explain the cultural change, but still it provides the jobs that in turn supply money and leisure time to the new taste public. Perhaps the new jobs themselves are also causally significant, creating needs and demands that people then want to satisfy in their spare time.

A second explanation is the general rise in the amount and quality of schooling, for all but the children of the poor, which has come about not only because the economy seeks better-educated workers with high credentials but also because education itself has become a consumer good in great demand. Furthermore, the mass media themselves have supplied schooling, beginning with radio and movies in the pretelevision era, and increasing when the small screen became the basis of everyday spare-time activity. Poorly educated viewers often say they learn from entertainment television, partly, I suspect, because they must do so to keep up. Since advertisers are interested in "upscale" audiences, television programs are increasingly aimed, not at the traditional lowest common denominator, but at the more affluent and better-educated members of the lower-middle public, making it difficult for other viewers to comprehend fully what they see and forcing them to learn.

A third, less often noted explanation is related to a structural change in American mobility patterns, itself partly a function of economic and educational changes. Once upon a time, probably until the 1960s, class position and mobility were intergenerational. The class position of the younger generation was best explained by parental background, mainly because the youthful cohort's occupational and other achievements were significantly influenced by the money, schooling, personal networks, and other advantages that parents were able (or unable) to give their children. As a result, children often moved into the occupations and social worlds of their parents (Blau and Duncan, 1967).

These socioeconomic connections also affected, and indeed required, cultural connections. For example, once upper-middle-class young people had finished college, they were expected to drop their interest in popular music and listen instead to classical or at least semiclassical music, concurrently rejecting the jukebox of that era for the concert hall. Just as young people had to move to the right suburbs, they also had to choose appropriate films, books, and fine arts. In fact, preferences were virtually prescribed for a large array of leisure activities, cultural products, and other consumer goods. Market researchers studied these, advertisers encouraged them, and upwardly mobile households moved "up" from Chevrolets to Buicks and from beer to wine.

The "status attainment" studies of the 1970s showed, however, that in the middle and upper-middle classes at least, class position is now better explained by personal achievement, notably education, and that it can no longer be as easily predicted from parental position. While the older generation's ability to supply children with educational advantages remains important, parental supports as a whole now seem to be less significant, and far more young people are able to attend and succeed in college even if their parents obtained little schooling. In short, sometime during the period of rapid economic growth that began after World War II, many of the intergenerational class connections were broken (Featherman and Hauser, 1978).

The breakup of intergenerational continuity had cultural consequences. Parental as well as school-induced prescriptions for cultural choice lost much of their influence, and young people no longer had to participate in parental culture. For example, upper-middle-class young adults who disliked classical music could continue to develop their adolescent tastes, and if they preferred rock or country music or both, they could pursue these preferences in adulthood without loss of face or prestige, at least among peers.

I do not mean to suggest that either social mobility or cultural choice has become an individual and therefore an asocial process. Indeed, so-called personal achievement is often publicly supported (for instance, by governmental expenditures for higher education). Rather, some intergenerational social processes have been replaced by intragenerational ones, and each cohort is now more on its own.[3] Culturally, age within class now becomes a significant causal factor or indicator.

The new middle culture is further supported by the general decline of intergenerational obligations, for upper-middle-class people can participate in the new culture if they dislike upper-middle culture. So can lower-middle-class people, however. In fact, they may be attracted by the new culture, partly because it has distanced itself from upper-middle and high cultures, but also because it has some lower-middle-culture forebears.

While upper-middle culture has borrowed a good deal from high culture, middle culture does more of its borrowing from lower cultures. Rock, like country and folk music, has some ancestors in the rural and urban slums of America, even if these have been denied as the music moved up the cultural hierarchy. Similar trajectories can be charted for many of the new magazines, which are transformations of old lower-middle homemaker and hobby publications. Pop art borrowed considerably from the commercial art that persuaded earlier middle- and working-class people to buy consumer goods, and many of today's collectibles are the lower-middle- and low-culture consumer goods and knickknacks of the past.

That the new products have often come from below may not be coincidental, for many members of the middle public have come from lower-middle- and even working-class backgrounds. They may therefore not object to drawing culture from the same origins or, for that matter, sharing it to some extent with people who are still in the lower-middle class.

Despite its somewhat more lowly origins, middle culture does not deny people the opportunity to use culture for upward mobility. Although data on how much anyone chooses culture for its substance and how much for its prestige are scarce, given the disrepute attached to "culture vultures," high and upper-middle cultures have always been used for status. Indeed, they may be so used more often in the future, especially if economic conditions reduce occupational mobility. The same opportunities for obtaining prestige through the exercise of taste are available in middle culture, judging by the immense number of how-to books and manuals published for many leisure activities. Besides, $150 jogging shoes and $5,000 stereo systems are obtainable by those who seek prestige through expenditure.

The Declining Power of High Culture

The rise of middle culture has coincided with, and perhaps partly caused, the declining influence of high culture. Although that culture and its public have also grown in numbers since World War II, with attendance at museums, theaters, concerts, dances, and other performances increasing considerably, much of the new audience comes from the upper-middle public, putting further "commercial" pressures on high culture itself. Partly as a result, high culture now seems more marginal than ever, becoming an almost exclusively expert culture increasingly dominated by cultural professionals: creators, critics, and especially academics.[4] Highly educated amateurs can of course still be found in its public, but I suspect that their proportion is smaller than a generation ago. The upper-class "aesthetes," the self-educated socialist working-class intellectuals, and the Central and Eastern European refugees of the 1930s and 1940s are all disappearing. Replacements for them do not seem apparent among the native-born or immigrant population.

High culture is also becoming less influential because of the declining credibility of its claim that its cultural standards are universal. Today's upper-middle and other publics do not stand in quite the same awe of high culture as did earlier generations. Nor do they seem to seek the kind of prestige that high culture can offer or could offer in the past. Partly as a result, the culture is also becoming more isolated: in Manhattan and a few other cities, on Cape Cod and its equivalents, but especially in English and humanities departments on a number of campuses and around "little magazines," most of them also connected to academic institutions. In literature at least, the free-lancer who had to straddle upper-middle culture in order to make a living and thus maintained some contacts outside high culture may be giving way to the academic who, once tenured, need not venture outside again.

Free-lancers have been particularly important because, whether they also served upper-middle culture or not, they have been a major source of innovation in high culture. Moreover, through them, high culture has supplied new themes, ideas, and genres for adaptation by the more commercial cultures, for sometimes what lower-middle culture borrowed from upper-middle culture had initially been borrowed by the latter from high culture. During the 1970s, high culture had lost so much influence in America that some erstwhile literary and arts critics became political analysts for the growing conservative and neoconservative movements, criticizing liberal redistribution and desegregation policies, defending capital punishment, and advocating a military showdown with the Soviet Union.

In the 1980s, however, some of the older critics, aided by new recruits, have gone back to cultural criticism, but the high culture they are now advocating is explicitly political as well. New journals funded by foundations also supporting conservative economic policies are once more fighting old battles among high-culture factions and attacking the perceived deficiencies of other taste cultures. These battles are fought with ideological weapons, the cultural enemies being exposed also as politically liberal or radical.[5]

Middle culture's occasional resemblance to upper-middle and lower-middle culture, as well as its ability to attract both upper-middle- and lower-middle-class people to its publics, helps to explain why some observers believe that the class barriers between cultures have come down. When cultural critics can find explicit political commentary in television sitcoms and can see young professors buying the same rock records as their secretaries, it is possible to conclude that cultural classlessness is on the way. The massiveness, visibility, and vitality of the new culture, as well as its lack of inhibition about borrowing from above or below, can readily suggest that all the classes are now choosing from the same overall culture.

Nonetheless, the majority of class differences in the use of culture remain strong. The low-culture public still reads many of the same newspapers, magazines, and paperback books as it did a generation ago, and its choice of furniture and art has changed little. Vernacular architecture for lower-middle-culture home-buyers remains as soldily wedded to colonial and California ranch styles as before. Tennis continues to be a mostly upper-middle-class sport, its increasing popularity on television notwithstanding; and museum as well as concert audiences are still largely drawn from the same class (DiMaggio and Useem, 1978; Hughes and Peterson, 1983: table 3). The new cultural forms are stratified too: working-class rock enthusiasts lean more to "heavy metal" than do middle-class ones, and paperback romance novels come in enough varieties of character, locale, sexual norms, and class background of heroines, heroes, and villains to satisfy several taste cultures from middle down and various factions with each (Radway, 1984:chapter 1).

Class barriers to the affordability of culture persist as well. Patterns of economic inequality change very slowly. The proportion of Americans earning less than half the median income has remained virtually stable, at about 20 percent of the population from the end of World War II. Since the mid-1970s but particularly since the November 1980 election, the rich have been getting richer again, and the number of poor people has increased, while real income has been declining for almost everyone except the very affluent. Economic patterns have educational implications: the number of high school dropouts appears to be rising again, and the proportion of youngsters graduating from college is declining.

When money is needed to purchase cultural products or education to find and use them, the people who have the money and education can continue to differentiate and segregate themselves from those who have less of both. Moreover, changes in the economy continue to maintain the relation of class and culture. For example, the continuing disappearance of fairly secure manufacturing jobs will eventually reduce both the working-class population and low culture, although in the short run it may increase both escapist and protest themes in that culture. The arrival of a new flood of immigrants, legal and illegal, to take the lower-paying jobs opening up in the economy is once more enlarging quasi-folk low culture.

In comparison to past decades, class barriers between cultures have undoubtedly come down, but mostly inside the middle classes. Some cultural egalitarianism has survived from the 1960s, but some has been spawned by the new middle-class populations, jobs, and cultures described earlier. Perhaps the dominance of television in the leisure diet and the pervasiveness of three-network commercial television fare in that diet have also helped; in that case, the emergence of cable television could stratify the viewer population. So far, however, the viewers have opted for pay television fare that is, in terms of taste, little different from that of the networks, the sizable constituency for R- and X-rated entertainment excepted.

Actually, the correlation of culture with class always has been, and remains, far from perfect. Very expensive products must appeal to several classes, network television being the most prominent example. Culture that is closest to home and family seems to express class position more than does culture that is publicly consumed. Consequently, language habits and home furnishings correlate more strongly with class than do public entertainment choices, other than those chosen with prestige and display in mind. As noted earlier, products with built-in educational prerequisites, notably those requiring a good deal of reading, will show a much higher correlation with class than with culture that can be enjoyed with little or no prior training. Although they may not do so, better-educated people can choose from more taste cultures than can poorly educated people (Wilensky, 1964). The cultural choices of the latter are most constrained by class factors.

The fact is that we know virtually nothing about people and taste, and even the theories and methodologies for acquiring such knowledge are still primitive. Descriptive concepts and measures of cultural choice remain gross. Research on leisure-time budgets shows little in a society in which nearly all the employed spend sixteen hours working and sleeping. Surveys of cultural activities and preferences produce data about general tendencies, which are made more general yet by currently fashionable forms of statistical analysis. The ethnographic and life-history data that can identify fundamental patterns and processes of cultural choice and that are prerequisites to surveys, have not yet been gathered. Class concepts remain primitive as well, and the revival of interest in Marxist concepts of class has helped to produce a virtually complete neglect of the cultural aspects of class. Coleman and Rainwater (1978) is the exception proving the rule.

Future empirical research may show that cultural choice is only weakly related to class, but so far I have seen no evidence that any other variable is more strongly related.[6] True, age is highly significant, and as I suggested earlier, age within class may be becoming more important. Moreover, some cultural products and practices remain segregated by sex. While I am not wedded to describing taste publics and cultures with class labels, it is too early to consider alternatives.[7]

Nor am I prepared to give up the class-based hierarchical or "ladder" model of cultural diversity. As long as economic and educational inequality continues to bar many people from access to jobs requiring verbal and related skills, the model must remain hierarchical. To be sure, the ladder metaphor does not fit perfectly. The high-culture public, being mostly upper-middle class, has never been atop the ladder, and although the upper class still helps to finance high culture, its own tastes run to a traditional upper-middle culture which became known as "preppy" in the early 1980s. Lower-middle- and low-culture publics have never been much impressed by the cultural power or social prestige of high culture. George H. Lewis (1981) has placed the ladder on a horizontal plane in his "multi-nucleated" model, but I would put it on at least a 45-degree incline.

Finally, in the 1980s, the analysis of cultural choice is once more embroiled in ideology, which can only help to stimulate interest in the subject, even if some waters are muddied in the process. Neo-Marxist analysts make fairly direct connections between class and culture, even if they increasingly pay more attention to the role of the state than to that of a capitalist class. Neoconservatives have fastened on the changes in the class-culture relation to proclaim that class per se is no longer very relevant in today's America. Meanwhile, however, the Reagan administration took National Endowment for the Arts and for the Humanities funds away from a variety of small, local, and even folk-culture efforts that its officials thought to be leftist and diverted them to large and powerful upper-middle- and high-culture Establishment institutions. The denial of the relevance of class analysis in combination with schemes that redistribute money from the poorer to the richer is traditional Republican practice, but in the process, new alliances are being forged between the higher cultures and the higher classes. If these persist, they will require new sociological efforts to understand the relations between class and culture.[8]

Notes

An earlier version of this paper was prepared for an international conference on Popular Culture in Europe and America at Cornell University in April 1982. It was also presented at the Tenth World Congress of Sociology in Mexico City in August 1982. I am indebted to Paul DiMaggio for a close reading of that version and for a number of comments that were very helpful in revising it.

A somewhat longer version of the present paper appears in *Prospects* 10, no. 1 (Spring 1985).

1. *Aesthetic* is used very broadly in this essay, for I am discussing standards of what people think is beautiful and good, as well as enjoyable, informative, and inspiring.

2. In my original study, I questioned these beliefs, arguing that because cultural choice is influenced by income and education, people should not be expected to develop tastes or standards that required access to both. I still hold the same view and see no need to update it. Further, I continue to feel that the higher taste cultures are better than the lower in the same way that more money and schooling are better than less.

3. This analysis harks back to David Riesman's emphasis on the rise of peer influence and other-directedness (Riesman, 1950).

4. The central role of professionals is not new, of course, for Paul DiMaggio has discovered that in nineteenth-century Boston, imported professionals from Europe carried out what he calls purification, that is, setting and implementing universal high-culture standards for the Brahmin founders of museums and symphony orchestras who hired them to determine which forms of art and music were to be excluded as vulgar and popular (DiMaggio, 1982).

5. Concurrently, a new defense of high culture has also developed on the Left. Advocated most energetically perhaps by Christopher Lasch (1981), it is as elitist in tone as the defense from the Right and equally critical of the tastes of the lower classes, but it blames these on capitalist exploitation, in much the same way as Dwight Macdonald (1957). Lasch is, however, less interested in socialism than in a return to *Gemeinschaft* through a mixture of preindustrial pastoralism and contemporary decentralism (Gans, 1982). For a current defense closer to the traditional Left position on high culture, see Gitlin (1983).

6. Davis (1982) has reported extensive NORC attitude data which he interprets as questioning the validity of the class-culture concept, but he reports also that education, which is an important class variable, remains the best predictor of attitudinal variation. In addition, answers to standardized opinion-poll attitude questions strike me as poor indicators of culture.

7. I also am not wedded to general concepts such as taste culture and public, which are difficult to operationalize for empirical research. Unfortunately, the study of taste publics or audiences is so expensive that scholars can rarely afford to conduct empirical research and must often depend on secondary analyses of data collected for very different objectives. Market researchers, who for obvious reasons are very much interested in class differences among consumers, have gathered a great deal of data relevant to culture and class, but it is proprietary and not available to scholars. In fact, the Caritas Corporation has developed an analysis of "market clusters," which resembles my notion of taste publics, and analyzes their class by a matchup of postal service ZIP codes with census demographic data (Heller, 1984).

8. A provocative critique of the new upper-class/government/high-culture alliance, from the libertarian Right, has been developed by Banfield (1984).

References Cited

Banfield, Edward C. 1984. *The Democratic Muse: Visual Arts and the Public Interest.* New York: Basic Books.

Blau, Peter M., and Otis D. Duncan. 1967. *The American Occupational Structure.* New York: John Wiley & Sons.

Coleman, Richard P., and Lee Rainwater. 1978. *Social Standing in America.* New York: Basic Books.

Davis, James A. 1982. "Achievement Variables and Class Cultures." *American Sociological Review* 47, no. 5 (October): 569–82.

DiMaggio, Paul. 1982. "Cultural Entrepreneurship in Nineteenth Century Boston." *Media, Culture and Society* 4, no. 1: 33–50.

DiMaggio, Paul, and Michael Useem. 1978. "Social Class and Arts Consumption: The Origins and Consequences of Class Differences in Exposure to the Arts in America." *Theory and Society* 5, no. 1: 41–61.

Featherman, David L., and Robert M. Hauser. 1978. *Opportunity and Change.* New York: Academic Press.

Gans, Herbert J. 1974. *Popular Culture and High Culture: An Analysis and Evaluation of Taste.* New York: Basic Books.

——. 1982. "Culture, Community and Equality." *Democracy* 2, no. 2 (April): 81–87.

Gitlin, Todd. 1983. *Inside Prime Time.* New York: Pantheon Books.

Heller, Karen. 1984. "Hot on the Press." *Washington Journalism Review* 6, no. 3 (April): 26–31.

Hughes, Michael, and Richard A. Peterson. 1983. "Isolating Cultural Choice Patterns in the U.S. Population." *American Behavioral Scientist* 26, no. 4 (March–April): 459–78.

Lasch, Christopher. 1981. "Mass Culture Reconsidered." *Democracy* 1, no. 4 (October): 7–22.

Lewis, George H. 1981. "Taste Cultures and Their Composition: Toward a New Theoretical Perspective." In *Mass Media and Social Change,* ed. Elihu Katz and Tamas Szecsko, 201–18. Beverly Hills, Calif.: Sage Publications.

Lynes, Russell. 1955. *The Tastemakers.* New York: Harper and Brothers.

Macdonald, Dwight. 1957. "A Theory of Culture." In *Mass Culture: The Popular Arts in America,* ed. Bernard Rosenberg and David M. White, 59–73. Glencoe, Ill.: The Free Press.

Peterson, Richard A. 1983. "Patterns of Cultural Choice: A Prolegomenon." *American Behavioral Scientist* 26, no. 4 (March–April): 422–38.

Radway, Janice A. 1984. *Reading the Romance: Women, Patriarchy and Popular Literature.* Chapel Hill: University of North Carolina Press.

Riesman, David, with Nathan Glazer and Reuel Denney. 1950. *The Lonely Crowd.* New Haven, Conn.: Yale University Press.

Warner, W. Lloyd, and Paul S. Lunt. 1941. *The Social Life of a Modern Community.* New Haven, Conn.: Yale University Press.

Wilensky, Harold L. 1964. "Mass Society and Mass Culture: Interdependence or Dependence." *American Sociological Review* 29, no. 2: 173–97.

11

Art versus the Arts

Ronald Berman

Because the National Endowment for the Arts has such a good press, and because it serves such a large and conscious public, it is often assumed that the Humanities Endowment also should be both visible and popular. And it is often assumed that the work of the Humanities Endowment should be very like that of NEA; that is, today it should constitute highly practical things which amuse, entertain, and benefit the public. But it may be useful momentarily to be theoretical, to question certain ideas and definitions about what art—or the arts—are and what the humanities do.

I think it is crucial to begin with the matter of defining art in order to understand the humanities. What, we may ask, is the position of art in our culture? Why should it be supported, and what does its support accomplish?

I think it is a truism that art is now defined in terms of middle-class values and aspirations: it is the pursuit of the majority. Current dogma, selected almost at random from media or from publications of NEA, assumes that art is quintessentially socially useful. And that dogma asserts that art should be universally accessible. It argues that distinctions of quality are invidious, a theme which makes possible the current relationship between art and politics. In the view of many who support government patronage, art serves a mass electorate. It provides "experience" and "activity" for that electorate.

But if art has become bourgeois, the artist has not. The artist thinks of himself as a political revolutionary. The function of his art is to express a position on public issues and to serve ideas, to embody a particular kind of alienation, and to show that the aesthetic object is less important than the personality shaping it. The two sets of ideas are contradictory but not exclusive: the most established of museums will exhibit the blank canvas or empty frame that is a calculated insult to its own existence. By so doing, the institution exhibits its social responsibility (or responsiveness) and the artist his revolutionism. None of the values involved seems to have much to do with the practice of art.

The belief that art is a form of permanent revolution is probably as useless as the idea that it serves external ideas, and the object of art comes to represent something other than itself.

That art represents the General Will is a credo of public relations. But it is taken seriously enough and has effects on artistic thought and activity which are serious enough to change their definition. One of the better sources for the argument that art is a public utility is the Congressional Record. Congressional debate on the National Endowment for the Arts has been conducted in a variety of moods since 1965, the year the Endowment was founded, but its common theme has been the public value of institutionalized creativity. Perhaps the most crucial of congressional debates were the authorization hearings held in both House and Senate in 1973, for it was then that support for the arts first decisively defeated its opposition. It was a matter not simply of the roll-call but of the thrust and conclusion of argument: here for the first time adherents of publicly supported art made a case which overwhelmed their opponents. That case was both ideological and political. To support federal patronage was no longer a matter of apologizing for high ideals. The tactics used were no longer those of smuggling in cultural support among other and higher proceedings. At this point in our cultural history a number of things, as in a chemical precipitation, became instantly plain.

Institutionalized art had by the seventies become economically important. That fact was indicated by the heavy representation of municipal lobbies in the wings. Perhaps more important, a cultural shift of major proportions had occurred. It was no longer necessary at hearings or on the floor of the House and Senate to defend art as a minority interest but rather as the vocation of a large and formidable constituency. Two other things were suggested by the tenor of congressional debate: that art had become identified with values previously confined to education or religion, and that art (or the arts, which are very different) had taken on bureaucratic shape and political identity.

In opening the debate in the House of Representatives, John Brademas invoked President Nixon's statement that the arts provided us with "the intangible but essential qualities of grace, beauty, and spiritual fulfillment." The interpretation of that rubric by Congress turned out to be a paradigm of a larger cultural process. On the floor of the House, congressmen summarized countless arguments and affirmations provided by local and national lobbies for the arts. The main argument was that government should extend its social and educational programs and that support of the arts and humanities was part of domestic support in general. Contingent arguments were intended to show that, as far as the arts were concerned, there was a direct connection between the appropriation of funds and the resolution of one or more social problems. And nothing could indicate better that art was a political commodity than the recognition that its support pleased important constituencies.

The argument for the support of the arts had little to do with the actual creation of aesthetic objects and even less with scholarship, criticism, or training. Art was what federal funds supported. Art assisted hospitals, urban ghettos, rural regions, community centers, and various agencies of welfare.

The social functions of art were emphasized in their variety, the debates suggesting that art displaced adolescent violence and anomie, encouraged craftsmanship, discouraged crime, and offered new opportunities for employment. Art was an alternative to drug addiction, an auxiliary to prison rehabilitation, and a solution to the problems of old age. Exposure to art might relieve inner-city tensions and possibly improve the tone of the adversary culture. Most appreciated of all was the effect of art—or the distribution of funds in its name—on regionalism. Hundreds of associations had sprung up under the influence of federal support of the arts, and they were necessarily connected to the economic life of congressional districts.

It was not mentioned but it was generally understood that these associations were composed of two new important groups. The first was made up of traditional patrons of the arts and those who aspired to patronage. They had found that organization into public corporations relieved them of the personal responsibility to contribute funds while it maximized their influence on government policy. Since this group tended to be affluent, educated, and socially conscious, it was involved also in traditional political activities: the trustee of an association sponsoring the art would typically have a previous connection with fund-raising. He would have experience and weight in civic affairs. But now, instead of taking on the burden of solicitation or of personal contribution, it was possible to exert leverage on the operations of government. To be a member of a state council on the arts was to receive substantial amounts of federal funds and to have a voice in their distribution. Local sponsorship and patronage were extended into the mutual relationship of Congress and a constituency.

The second group was bureaucratic, composed of men and women who found new administrative careers created by the distribution of public funds. The expertise required is not entirely artistic: Dick Netzer, in *The Subsidized Muse,* states that lobbying for additional funds is a primary function of state council staff. Both groups, the members and the staff, lobby in another sense, which is to identify the regional support of art with direct social service. As they define what they do, art takes on the shape of domestic assistance to selected constituencies.

During the debate, the language of congressional discourse concentrated on numbers and participation. "Thousands of people and whole communities" were the object of federal subvention. It was consistently stated that the benefits of art were in fact social and that their civic effect was nowhere better shown than in the diffusion of money and programs among the young, the disadvantaged, and minorities. The remarks of one congressman which I have cited give an exceptionally useful sense of art as a social activity. It is a local service directed at an important constituency:

> Iowa has one of the highest percentages of population aged 65 or older. It is therefore particularly fitting that the Iowa Arts Council this year provided assistance to the Iowa State Commission on the Aging for a senior citizen arts festival, an event which proved highly successful and which I hope will be repeated yearly. We have an immense reservoir of training, experience, and talent in older Americans—upon retirement they have increased time to devote to these talents, to their crafts and hobbies. The federal, state, and local programs in the arts should take particular cognizance of their needs and their potentialities.

It was a representative statement; others claimed the same kind of benefit and made the same assumptions about the ends and means of artistic activity and support.

Political discourse needs to be discounted because it always implies social benefits. But in speeches like the one above there are two things that ought not to be explained away as the normal exaggeration of congressional salesmanship. The first is the tactical end of distributing funds to constituencies in the name of art. The second, less political, is more important: it is the redefinition of artistic activity. That redefinition was provided by the various lobbies for art upon which congressional committees rely almost absolutely. The bureaucracy of art—members and staff of state councils, the National Endowment for the Arts, and House and Senate committees—believe that the primary purpose of the support of art is the distribution of funds. They believe in programs rather than grants. A grant is specifically designed to produce a particular effect; a program means only to be an instrument of equity. Most people prefer programs because stipulated amounts annually are conveyed to all interested parties, which eliminates application, competition, and uncertainty.

The debates summed up issues connected not only to the support of art but to its practice and definition. The language of social piety tends to disguise a profound problem of interpretation. It is plain that artistic activity is no longer thought of as professional activity. It has in fact become the opposite, a form of middle-class relaxation. The "democratic" assumption is that we are all artists, while the populist assumption underlying it is that activity is its own end. This has a superficial resemblance to the Victorian idea that art exists for its own sake, but it is very different. The implication of activity being its own end is that standards are superfluous: art is anything with creative intentions.

I think that at least part of the new definition of art becomes clear through its new political identity. It is indispensable to begin consideration of that identity with the difference between art and a concept that has come to displace it: the arts. *Art* means creativity and refers itself to the history of achieved things from Altamira to the present. *The arts,* a term which has become an essential part of the vocabulary of policy, is used generally to imply creativity while promoting the ideas of the congressional debate that I have described and the subsidy of associations, bureaucracies, and institutions. It means the distribution of funds for purposes felt to be artistic.

Some of the most praiseworthy efforts of the National Endowment for the Arts have gone into the maintenance of institutions. But a certain moral—and artistic—cost has been involved. I am not speaking simply of the diversion of funds for lobbying or other aspects of political reality. In the fourteen years since the inception of this agency, and after the expenditure of the better part of a billion dollars, we are hard put to name a single work of art worth recollecting that it has made possible. Nor can we associate its support with a productive idea affecting the understanding of art either by artists or their audience.

The NEA represents "the arts" rather than art, which is understandable given the fact that it reflects the will of its constituency. And the arts stand for the distribution of funds rather than specific accomplishments, the subsidy of associations promoting themselves as well as their purposes, the relationship of the private sector of patronage to government, the use of art for social purposes, and the satisfaction of particular constituencies.

Those constituencies are larger than one might think. There are 25,000 members of Actor's Equity and about 15,000 amateur theaters. The Bureau of the Census states that there are now about a million people who identify themselves as artists by occupation. Artistic identity is having something of a boom. Without being simplistic, one can say that is probably because many vocations, like teaching, have been devalued, especially those dealing with cultural affairs. Competing institutions of culture have declined—religion, for example. And, as social status has become a matter of self-ascription, artistic character has become enormously popular. The use of the word *creative* has changed in an interesting way: it has been removed from the realm of achievement and applied to another realm entirely. What it means now is an attitude about the self, and it belongs not to aesthetics but to pop psychology.

There has been a natural overflow from the promotion of "the arts." More or less without a stop we are informed by the new class of government patrons that art is a universal good. One of the few activities of government not criticized by the media is its cultural subvention. And, of course, the availability of funds always draws into existence those able to benefit from them.

Yet, actual creativity is hard to find. I have asked a deputy chairman of the National Endowment for the Arts why that agency risked so much resentment by refusing to give more than 2 or 3 percent of its annual budget to individual artists. This policy has made it easy to attack NEA for its subservience to institutions and for its plodding subsidy of production and performance. The reply was that there are not enough good artists in the United States to justify giving them more than 3 percent of NEA's annual funds. The million citizens characterizing themselves as artists for the census—joined by many more than a million to whom the arts are less than a vocation but more than a diversion—have creative intentions. But they cannot paint.

The politics of "the arts" is clearly a cycle; funds are distributed to organizations created by the distribution of funds. Netzer's *The Subsidized Muse,* which is the best study of the economics of government patronage, states flatly that state arts councils "may be regarded as costly sops for congressmen determined to spread federal largesse widely and thinly, and as a means of creating a nationwide corps of lobbyists for NEA." There are of course other social purposes: in a piece in *Commentary,* Samuel Lipman observed that "arts funding is seen by politically and socially activist groups as providing the means of increased visibility for their causes." Other benefits have been the prestige conferred by artistic purpose, significant numbers of administrative jobs, and the connection more firmly established between the arts and good causes.

Support of the social theory of art derives not from the congressional imagination but from the influences shaping it. If art means middle-class associations like state councils and ceaseless promotion of activity, then Congress will support that. If art means the diversion of funds to the young, the old, or minorities, then Congress will find that acceptable too. The arts constituency determines finally what the definition of art or of "the arts" will be. And that constituency has in the most determined way exempted artistic activity from critical standards. Art is whatever is done, whether crafts, hobbies, or simply the display of intentions. It is an ennobled form of middle-class entertainment.

Modern art has long been noted for the strenuous attempts of artists to offend the bourgeois imagination. But art now behaves as if it were anything but the culmination of the modernist movement. It is a radical product consumed by a distinctly unradical class. An enormous amount of artistic activity has now been concentrated into performance, production, and other middle-class modes. The models are the Kennedy Center and Wolf Trap Farm, large establishments heavily supported by government, corporations, and foundations and offering a combination of mass-audience programs and enough adversary culture to stay ahead of the media. The sixties may have radicalized art and its discourse, but the seventies and eighties have given it back to the middle class. It is difficult to talk about contemporary art as if it still had anything to do with modernism. Music, drama, dance, and exhibition are now the major modes, while the art of ideas matters far less than it used to. Poetry, for example, is now limited to the academic audience, although in the earlier part of the century it had a much more formative role. The performing arts now dominate, and they represent the new role of social art: an auxiliary to daily life provided by the mutual operations of large institutions.

It makes no sense to be ungrateful for performance and production or for the fortunate survival of civic benevolence. But subsidized events for large audiences tend inevitably to become a kind of cultural welfare. They are designed for the largest common denominator and frequently translate art into another idiom.

The nervous attitude of art critics toward corporate support of performance is based upon suspicion of the profit motive. There is no denying that the sponsors of mass-audience culture have their own interests in mind. Texaco has stated that its support of the Metropolitan Opera broadcasts is based upon economic facts: the opera audience is loyal and buys Texaco products; a significant proportion of the 400,000 shareholders in the company own stock because of their interest in its cultural activities; the opera audience is "upscale" or composed of those with discretionary income; and the audience is politically sophisticated, receptive to the corporation's side of controversy involving energy, taxation, and regulation. But it is a truism that sponsorship is a matter of self-interest. What is more significant is the relationship between corporate and public and public ideas about culture.

The most interesting thing about corporate support for the arts is not the profit motive but something that might be called the cultural imperative. A survey of corporate backing of the performing arts in *Advertising Age* claims that "corporate involvement in social, civic, and cultural activities" is now routine. This support is not related directly to sales; corporations too have visions of social mobility and derive the same benefits from patronage as traditionally accrue to individuals.

Corporations have perforce a sense of their place in society and within culture. As we frequently see in televised commercials, corporations no longer exclusively try to make sales. They present interminable displays of their social conscience, of the love and loyalty and services they live to confer. The usual perception is that corporations are trying to sell themselves instead of a product. But even that is not really accurate. Corporations may be trying to sell themselves—and to buy respect—but they are even more insistently trying to articulate what they believe are common values. Their nervous affirmations of clean water for good fishing or new forests for the next generation rest on the understanding that democratic institutions are involuntary social arbiters. If they do not affirm certain ideas, they may be accused of opposing them. Corporations undertake to support whatever ideas are popular, vaguely moral, and untroublesome. They may even believe some of these ideas. They can certainly interpret the zeitgeist as well as art critics.

It is necessary to observe, if only parenthetically, that corporations are now at the stage of structural development implying cultural support on a large scale. They employ many people in offices of public affairs, which are subordinated to ideas about public relations. There is a good deal of ready money available because the tax code exempts 5 percent of profits for charitable donations. Corporations have come to resemble state councils on the arts, maintaining bureaucracies devoted to the distribution of tax-free funds. They are vulnerable to local pressures, especially in metropolitan areas: corporate officers maintain the same position and must perform the same largesse as entrepreneurs did before them. But they can only live up to social expectations by dispensing tax-free corporate donations.

The managerial class has the same mind-set as those who define cultural values in utilitarian terms. Art as a diffuse social activity fits the corporate idea about its own place in democratic society. That kind of art is universal and uncontroversial. It begins with a head start since intellectuals and the media find it difficult to quarrel with support of "the arts." There are more than political benefits, for executives are assured that they exist culturally. In an age in which cultural issues matter as much as political issues, that is an advantage.

There is an especially revealing passage in the survey of *Advertising Age:* "There is no doubt, as former CBS president Frank Stanton pointed out to the 25th anniversary conference of the Public Relations Society of America, that the essential values of the public 'are most clearly evident, and in some instances evident only, in the arts—in music, the drama, and the dance, in the architecture and design and in the literature of the people and of the times.'" When critics of corporate patronage hunt for the profit motive, they overlook what Stanton calls "values" and what others have described, according to *Advertising Age,* as the "community" or even the "communion" that the corporation pursues with its customs. The corporation goes so far as to hope for "involvement with a customer as a total human being" —which is somewhere, one supposes, between a theological and a matrimonial relationship. The corporation believes, probably rightly, that the educated middle class has a morally positivist understanding of culture. Art, in that understanding, reflects the orderliness and intelligibility of life. It celebrates social beliefs and reinforces individual self-esteem. And, since it is just about the only aspect of industrial democratic life to have retained ritualistic, mystical, and even holy elements in its character, it is beyond criticism.

Performance is seen by its sponsors as an occasion of social solidarity. It is superego art. We can never be sufficiently reminded that it brings people together, is accessible to every mind and sensibility, has moral and therapeutic benefits, and implies the common taste of a mass middle class.

Within the social definition of "the arts," distinctions are invidious: Warhol matters as long as he is a celebrity; the same can be said of Rubens. Not since the happy ending of *King Lear,* provided by Nahum Tate for the Enlightenment, has the interest of the audience been so solicited. The age of reason preferred a world without tragedy—and so it got philosophy. At the end of Tate's version of *King Lear,* Kent, Gloucester, and the king retire to a monastery and Edgar marries Cordelia. It is a triumph of poetic justice. The implications for us are fairly clear. When production and performance are tailored to a theory of what the public taste demands, good art will not necessarily be rejected, but bad art will certainly become accepted.

The consumption of bad art has been made easier by its sponsors, its production by other factors. There have been a number of theories for artistic decline, especially in painting. The most visible attack on painting recently has been Tom Wolfe's *The Painted Word,* and in that book the blame is put pretty squarely on the devil's work done by criticism. In Wolfe's view—and although the book is outrageously funny, its message is serious—movement or minimovements like Op and Pop art follow the temptations of ideas. An idea is broached by a critic, and a market is created on the spot as artists try to embody it, sell it, and live up to its philosophy. But if anything, the critics of contemporary art (like those of the movies) seem to be better than their material. It is not that ideas are bad, but contemporary art seems to be dominated by ideas which are second-rate. It might even be said of much of our art that it works without ideas, that it has become technique without a motive.

One of the most interesting of cultural facts to be recognized by government is the separation of art not only from a theory but from the discourse of other disciplines. In splitting its patronage between arts and humanities, the federal government has acknowledged the preferences of opposed constituencies. One endowment deals with books and ideas, with scholarship and research, with the theory and criticism of art—and that is the Humanities Endowment. The Arts Endowment deals only with what is left. What is left includes a good deal, about twenty different activities from dance to folk crafts. It ranges from the subsidy of the housewife who played the piccolo in Leadville, Colorado, immortalized by a House Committee on Appropriations as the ultimate object of federal patronage, to the subsidy of the Metropolitan Opera. But what is left needs to be measured against what has been left out.

At least in government, which is not a bad indicator of social preference, the disciplines of thought have been removed from those of "activity." The arts are perceived—and legislatively defined—as the realm of "experience" or of sensation, as a form of entertainment, and as a diffuse activity which is its own end. Government is sometimes all too good an indicator: it reflects in this case the separation of art from sustaining thought, a separation as important as that which has been discerned between science and its opposing cultures.

Within the world of art itself there has been a separation of word and act. Scholarship takes place in universities and deals with the dead. The criticism of art takes place in the media and is practiced there by those who believe that art and its social context are identical. If there is a universal theme to media coverage of the arts it is that the amount of money distributed to constituencies, institutions, and approved social causes defines ideal "support." As for the practice of the arts, that has become our largest amateur activity.

For about a century and a half the professional artist has viewed himself (sometimes rightly) as untutored genius, social critic, political savant, existential philosopher, and in half a dozen other roles. These have set him off from the rest of bourgeois society and made him its greatest critic. But the quality of enabling ideas has fallen off since Shelley said that poets were the unacknowledged legislators of mankind. Modernism arose, in part, because of artistic hostility to bourgeois values and because of the hostility of those values to art. But the world depicted in the novels of Sinclair Lewis no longer exists. The middle class has long since put up the white flag and embraced the creed of its conquerors. Art is the most honored of all civic activities, and "creativity" is the most honored of all motivations.

The desire of modernism to offend the middle class was subordinate to the production of work which meant more, and contained more, than the reflection of what it hated. Oscar Wilde wrote that only bad artists had ideas or "character": the good ones "exist simply in what they make, and consequently are perfectly uninteresting in what they are." The moral for us is somewhat ambiguous, for it suggests that artists express feelings about bourgeois society in lieu of actual creativity. By now artistic alienation should have run its course, like all other inspirations. But our world is still being addressed by art as if it were Victorian; either the sins of the father are being visited upon the third generation, or those of the artist upon his audience.

The visual and dramatic arts have in the last two decades accomplished something self-defeating. They reflect social ends and political arguments so perfectly as to become what they represent. It has often been observed that Dickens invented some of the most stupendous bores in literature. But his description of them was never boring. In fact, his bores are fascinating. The paradox of art is that it must recognize some difference between the model and the work. If it didn't, then there would not need to be any work, only a model. By refusing to distance itself or complete an act of interpretation, art becomes what it loathes. If it remains a pilot-fish of the bourgeoisie, then its movements are restricted to the path of the beast it feeds on.

Resentment, ugliness, and absurdity are major motifs of contemporary art. But it is after all self-defeating for painting and drama to have become resentful, ugly, and absurd.

Jacques Barzun in *The Use and Abuse of Art* describes the exhibition of works molded in human excrement, the artist who exhibited himself, framed by plastic testicles, as he reclined in a coffin, and a man who "cut off pieces of his own flesh and photographed them." Daniel Bell, in *The Cultural Contradictions of Capitalism,* describes the transformation of drama from rhetorical to visual art: "In the 'Destruction of Art' symposium held in the Judson Church in New York in 1968, one of the participants suspended a live white chicken from the ceiling, swung it back and forth, and then snipped off its head with a pair of hedge-clippers. He then placed the severed head between his legs, inside his unzippered fly, and proceeded to hammer the insides of a piano with the carcass. At the Cinematheque in 1968, the German artist Herman Nitsch disemboweled a sheep on stage, poured the entrails and blood over a young girl, and nailed the carcass of the animal to a cross." Aristotle, who saw a good deal of drama and said that spectacle was the weakest part of performance, evidently didn't know the half of it.

The late Harold Rosenberg wrote of the German arts festival Documenta 5 that it was momentarily captivated by the current prestige of mental illness. Since madness has been adopted by therapy as a more authentic condition than sanity, it has become a recurrent theme in painting. The theme of "self-expression" at Documenta 5 took the idea of the self to be that of pop psychology, i.e., a dramatization of ascribed feelings: "Genuine schizophrenia shaded off into 'artistic' or drug-induced imitations in galleries of photographic horrors involving fish heads, genitalia, evisceration, blood-stained religious vestments, and crude crucifixes, plus photographic portraits of the artist gagged, gashed, and split in two." Art shares in the general illiteracy of intellectuals, and ideas generated by the social disciplines articulate its resentment. To some extent the motives are political: not simply to attack bourgeois taste but to reject and devalue those standards which imply the existence of a legitimate social order. But there is a particular vulnerability in the visual arts that cannot be explained entirely in terms of political beliefs or social resentment.

The explosion of cultural criticism from Ezra Pound to Lionel Trilling left the visual arts untouched. But the effects on the arts of literacy were profound. Malraux suggests in *The Voices of Silence* that the paintings of the past three centuries cannot compare with what was done before that time; and it might be said, with less exaggeration, that nothing before 1920 can compare with the criticism after it. The number of poets in that period who were intellectually significant for culture at large as well as within their vocation was extremely large. That number included Pound, Eliot, John Crowe Ransom, Robert Penn Warren, and Robert Lowell. As men of letters their only competition can come from the greatest of the Romantic poets. Poetry either resisted ideology, as in the case of W. H. Auden, or transcended it.

From 1920 on, it has been characteristic that critics like Trilling could work in fiction and that poets like Auden could master criticism. But the visual arts and too much of drama have separated out from the unified movement of modernism and treated technique and politics as if they were ideas.

The story of the arts is that of two decades. Painters were in the thirties no more inherently vulnerable to the Popular Front than were poets or novelists, but they did not resist it as well. They were bemused by the high status of official culture under communism and have indeed never recovered from the attractions of that notion. Artists became identified with the cause, and art was understood to be a technique expressing political belief. Writers had begun to circulate nationally, to infiltrate universities, and to work out their independence, but artists concentrated into a single and much smaller society in which it was difficult to be different. There were no Orwells in the visual arts.

The sixties completed what the thirties had begun. The political failure of radicalism led it to a sustained and successful attack on the cultural realm. There was a cross-fertilization of political righteousness and "creativity." It was in the sixties that radicalism confused its style with its accomplishment and artists confused themselves with the work of art—and, of course, a lot of people confused themselves with artists.

It has been said that modernism contained the seeds of its own destruction, which seems probable enough. But the definition of art as a political ideology or a social attitude was a product not of modernism but of the sixties. The modernists attacked the middle class because art stood for values which the latter seemed not to understand; the burgeoning of artists who hate art derives from other motives. If, as *Advertising Age* reminds us, even corporations realize that "the essential values of the public" are "most clearly evident, and in some cases evident only," in art, then the war on aesthetics becomes politically understandable.

In defense of the artist's resentment of art the claim is routinely made that freedom finally does imply an end not only to objective standards but to moral or imaginative constraints. Perhaps. But Harold Rosenberg describes an instance which puts that conclusion in some doubt. Jean Toche, who defines his own artistic genre as the composition of manifestos and protests, has accused the Museum of Modern Art of vandalism because it removed an inscription spray-painted over another "artist," on the *Guernica* of Picasso. Toche was supported in this gesture by over a hundred teachers, critics, and curators who denounced the museum, which leads one to reflect that it may be difficult to decide which is the Mona Lisa of this art form: the sledge-hammering of the Pieta or the explosion of the Parthenon.

Unfortunately for all of us, the visual arts insist on defining themselves in terms which are derivative. Giant excavations or earthworks become a "statement" about the landscape; miles of white sheets strung across the countryside imply the "labor" of all involved in the enterprise. With every step that art takes toward "dialogue" with the times, it moves closer to a position abandoned with great indignation more than a century ago. "Dialogue" is, after all, a kind of synonym for the "communion" which the corporation seeks so passionately and so advisedly with its clientele. It makes no difference that it is recommended to us by the current avant-garde. As a matter of fact, in *Artculture,* Douglas Davis reviews the moribund argument that the "dialogue" of artist and society is essential. We are back to the idea, already old in Plato's *Republic* and even there unconvincing, that art ought to be socially responsible. Its new responsibility is predictable: "The 70's," Davis said, "are a decade in which appalling truths have finally become clear to large masses of people, from the poisonous quality of the air we breathe to the stupendous revelations of corruption that accompanied Nixon's resignation." The function of art is said to be to interpret those truths to us. That seems to be exactly what modernism was trying to kill off when it declared its social independence. By labyrinthine ways a century of frantic contemporaneity has found itself back at square one. The artist thinks of himself as a revolutionary but addresses himself to approved social truths. The business of painting is, evidently, to hate Nixon.

Government has defined the arts as nonintellectual activity for the majority. Sponsors from the private sector think of art as a repository for social values. And artists are guided by ideas or subideas which fit rather nicely alongside these definitions. It is not only that a common danger is posed by the attack on quality and standards: government betraying its impatience with any obstacle to majority participation and artists asserting that standards are relics of a dead past. The sum of attitudes from opposing sides is that art has no particular value in itself.

12

Arts Education as a Political Issue: The Federal Legacy

Laura Chapman

When Congress established the National Endowment for the Arts in 1965, there was no nationally organized arts constituency. This is no longer the case. Indeed, what has emerged from more than fifteen years of federal activity in the arts is a new arts bureaucracy, consisting of state and local arts councils and various groups established for the purpose of influencing public policies bearing on the arts. What kind of arts education has been endorsed and promoted by the new arts establishment? In federal policies and programs, in the recommendations for arts education issued by blue-ribbon panels, and in the promotional activities of various arts advocates, we find elements of a national policy aimed at "de-schooling" arts education.

The Emergent National Policy for Arts Education

Recommendations for the de-schooling of arts education have emerged in piecemeal fashion over a period of time. This policy position, articulated in full form during the late 1970s, reflects how the new arts establishment—those who have political and economic power in the art world—envision arts education for American youth. Equally, the recommendations bear the imprint of decisions made within federal agencies having some responsibility for arts education, particularly (but not exclusively) the National Endowment for the Arts.

Before tracing the origin and the implications of this viewpoint, let me outline the major themes which define it. The main ingredients of the policy position are as follows:

> Arts education means education in all the arts, not only music and the visual arts, but also dance, theater, and creative writing. Education in the arts means making art—performing as a musician, dancer, actor, sculptor, and so on. Arts education also means being exposed to the making of

art—seeing actors, painters, musicians, and so on do their work firsthand. Of far less importance is studying art from an historical or cultural perspective, acquiring an understanding of artistic traditions, or gaining an intellectual understanding of art.

Arts education, thus conceived, should be de-schooled to a substantial degree. In other words it should be delegated to artists and to arts or social service agencies within the community. In addition, schools should be free to employ artists and other noncertified personnel to deliver arts services to children and youth within the schools.

Citizens should approach the problem of improving arts education as they would approach any other civic effort that involves (1) fund-raising for special projects or (2) fund-raising to provide community services for a special population. In effect, arts education is a special social service which citizens need not expect their schools to provide. Programs might be planned and implemented through arts councils or independent committees. The school is merely one of many agencies through which arts education might be delivered. Just as arts services might be delivered through agencies other than the school and persons other than certified teachers, so too might the instructional program within the school be financed by sources other than the regular school budget. Funds for arts education might come from corporate and private foundations, labor unions, fund-raising campaigns, as well as creative use of federal or state funds earmarked for special programs (arts for the handicapped, arts for the talented).

Given that much instruction could occur outside of school, the residual program of in-school arts instruction should be redesigned so that the arts are interrelated (as the sciences and social studies are said to be). In addition, the arts should be used as tools for learning other subjects, especially reading and mathematics, and integrated into the regular curriculum. Another important function of the in-school program is to make the school more interesting to children, thus reducing truancy and vandalism and improving the general conduct of children.

Present and future arts teachers should be trained as "arts generalists" and have administrative skills. The arts generalist would be employed to (1) manage the arts services offered by individual artists and community agencies and (2) monitor or teach the residual in-school program.

While the arts establishment might well have used its growing influence to urge the reform of in-school programs, it has, I believe, put a stamp of approval on the very ideas which have served to weaken arts education.

And in emphasizing the cost of employing artists and "delivering" arts education to youth, the arts establishment has fostered an attitude that may persuade citizens and school administrators to judge that instruction in the arts is an expensive frill, beyond the expectations we should have for school.

How have these recommendations surfaced as the key features of a national policy? In order to answer this question, we must understand something about the channels through which the recommendations have been forged and promoted and some of the reasoning behind them. Most of them are the legacy of an arts-in-education movement spanning about fifteen years and encompassing a variety of interconnected programs, many of them federally supported. The concepts behind this movement have been widely disseminated and have been incorporated into the operations of advocacy groups and agencies whose work in arts education is not dependent upon federal funds.

Grand Visions of Curriculum Reform

The U.S. Office of Education Seminars

The stage for the arts-in-education movement was set in the mid-1960s through a series of seminars, as well as a short-term research program, conducted under the auspices of the Arts and Humanities Branch of the U.S. Office of Education and directed by Kathryn Bloom from 1963 to 1968.[1]

These Office of Education conferences stimulated discussions which set three major precedents. The first was the opportunity for art and music educators to think about the reform of school curricula on a fairly grand scale. Major centers for research and curriculum development were just being established with federal funds, and there was hope that one or more of these centers might address art and music. A second precedent was the direction of thinking taken by many professionals in education at that time. Following the example of the new mathematics and science curriculum projects, arts educators called upon artists and scholars in the arts to identify the "key concepts" and "methods of inquiry" they employed in their work. Their insights were to be used as source material for designing arts curricula that would be up-to-date and authoritative.

The Office of Education seminars also renewed interest in the idea that artists, in particular, might be brought directly into classrooms to demonstrate their methods of inquiry, strengthening the performance-based studio curriculum in most schools and protecting the arts from becoming a "packaged" curriculum.[2] Although it was clearly impractical to employ artists to reach over 30 million school-aged young people, these discussions foreshadowed and gave credibility to a later program known as Artists-in-Schools, sponsored by the National Endowment for the Arts and initially supported by the U.S. Office of Education as well.

A third precedent was established through these exploratory seminars. Arts and music educators were informed that any major curriculum projects undertaken with federal funds must include all of the arts, in order to avoid the potential problem of favoring one art form over another. A report from one of the first seminars, held at the Pennsylvania State University in 1965, foreshadowed the requirements that would soon be placed on almost all federal programs for education in the arts.

Harlan Hoffa, then on the Arts and Humanities staff of the U.S. Office of Education, articulated the problem for visual arts educators: "It is unlikely that an R&D [research and development] center would be established for [visual] art education alone. However, I think it is perfectly conceivable that a center could be structured around the concept of arts education . . . including the visual, performing, and literary arts, or around perceptual education, or around *aesthetic education* or any other related construct. . . . It could encompass . . . *interdisciplinary* activity between all of the various arts" (italics mine).[3]

In response to these conditions, music educators and visual arts educators who were interested in fairly ambitious research and curriculum projects had the choice of bringing along "all of the arts" or receiving no federal funds. This early federal position left an imprint on later programs and helps to explain, in part, why arts educators were urged to reexamine various methods of relating the arts, integrating and correlating the arts to other subjects, and setting up interdisciplinary programs. This "all the arts" requirement also seemed to provide a means of strengthening instruction in dance and theater, which few schools offered.

The CEMREL Aesthetic Education Program

Beginning in 1967, the federal interest in arts education was channeled almost exclusively into a single curriculum development effort, the Aesthetic Education Program, located at one of the new regional educational laboratories established by the U.S. Office of Education, CEMREL, the Central Midwestern Regional Educational Laboratory in St. Louis. As coauthor of the planning proposal for the Aesthetic Education Program in 1967, I can attest to the fact that some of us objected to the scholarly and somewhat alien title for the program, yet all who were initially involved in this venture thought it wise to take advantage of the opportunity for a major curriculum development effort, comparable to earlier mathematics and science projects.[4] Not until the early 1970s did it become apparent that the "new" mathematics and science curricula were far from perfect and that the cost of an arts version of those curricula would be dear—not just in dollars for the production of instructional materials in the arts, but in the effect of those allocations on other federal activity in arts education.

The CEMREL Aesthetic Education Program was intended to address both the creative and appreciative dimensions of music, dance, theater, literature, and the visual arts. The curriculum, designed for use in grades one through six, would be presented through sets of instructional materials which had been thoroughly tried out in schools, then published and marketed. A teacher education program was also planned.

The Aesthetic Education Program was bound to be either a spectacular success or a gigantic failure. The federal gamble was that one well-supported program could deliver the goods. Although some federal support was given to two other centers for arts curriculum development, the CEMREL program was by far the most ambitious.

Questions about the effectiveness of the Aesthetic Education Program can best be answered by examining its status since it was officially terminated in 1978, ten years, and about $12 million, after it began. Of the forty-four sets of instructional materials developed to the stage of publication, only twelve had been published by 1982.[5] Publishers had little interest in the project, primarily because the entire curriculum was costly and difficult to market to administrators whose primary concerns seemed to be the three R's and for whom the phrase "aesthetic education" had no meaning or an elitist connotation. In the absence of a complete and marketable set of curriculum materials, the supporting teacher education program was also severely handicapped.

One can hardly judge that the initial aims of the Aesthetic Education Program were achieved, but through related activities the CEMREL program had an indirect influence on arts education well beyond its major mission. In addition to a host of scholarly documents produced for the project,[6] the CEMREL materials developed for classrooms (though limited in number) became an ingredient in a number of pilot programs which were sponsored by other agencies. CEMREL also conducted the first tryout and evaluation of the program later known as Artists-in-Schools.[7]

A Mixed Bag of Other Federal Programs

During the years that the CEMREL Aesthetic Education Program was in full swing, its financial requirements preempted almost all other federal support directed exclusively to arts education. Other projects in arts education were financed, but through federal programs within the U.S. Office of Education that were not officially designated for the arts. Thus, the arts were tied to programs to forward school desegregation, to enhance reading performance, or to reach specific groups such as the talented, the handicapped, or ethnic groups.[8] The opportunity for the arts and humanities staff in the U.S. Office of Education to actively shape a more coherent program of research, teacher education, and curriculum development was also greatly reduced by several staff cutbacks and various reorganizations of the Office.

The mixed bag of projects supported by the Office of Education helps to explain, in part, why discussions of arts education have been shaped in a way that emphasizes the arts as means to promote better racial and ethnic understanding, as means to reduce truancy and dropping out of school, and as means to improve the reading or cognitive skills of children. Arts education was featured in a number of pilot programs having these missions and became instrumental to achieving them. What children were learning about the arts was not the point of these programs and was not evaluated as systematically as other outcomes.[9]

So fragmented were federal programs bearing on arts education that in 1976 an effort was made to identify the scope of all arts education activity supported with federal funds and to develop a coherent federal policy for the future.[10] If it had not been obvious before, it became clear at that time that the interests of the National Endowment for the Arts had begun to dominate discussions of arts education and would continue to do so. Since the Office of Education was handicapped in addressing critical needs—for improved in-service education for teachers, systematic evaluation of school programs, and other approaches to curriculum development and research—the Arts Endowment offered its own solutions to at least some of these problems, all of them keyed to the Artists-in-Schools Program.

Grand Visions of Artists in Schools

Although the National Endowment for the Arts (NEA)[11] might seem to be the logical agency to strengthen arts education in schools, the primary missions of the NEA were to expand employment opportunities for artists and to make the arts more accessible to all regions and sections of the American population.

Early in the history of the Arts Endowment, a policy was established that the NEA would not support projects that "actively and purposefully teach."[12] This policy seemed to be based on two major considerations. First, the original legislation which established the Endowment for the Arts and the Endowment for the Humanities made a distinction between the practice of the arts and the study of the humanities. Thus, the Arts Endowment was slated to emphasize the making or performing of art, not the study of art. The study of art, especially art history, was to be supported by the Humanities Endowment. To complicate matters, the Office of Education was responsible for programs addressed to elementary and secondary schools and teacher education. Nobody was clearly in charge of a school program that might include the study of art through studio practice as well as art history. By virtue of its title, the Arts Endowment seemed to have responsibility for all proposals dealing with the arts, including arts education in schools.

The Artists-in-Schools Program

These territorial problems among federal agencies contributed to the formation of a national direction for arts education in which the interests of the Arts Endowment and its constituency were well represented. Within the Office of Education and in the Humanities Endowment, arts education was only one of many topics to be addressed. Increasingly pressed to answer questions on arts education, the Arts Endowment responded to most questions by placing an emphasis on amateur or professional training in the practice of art, as well as exposure to the arts through concerts, exhibitions, and so on. There was much less emphasis on formal programs to build an appreciation of the arts through the study of art history.

Through a pilot Artists-in-Schools program in 1969, the NEA discovered that artists could be employed in schools if several conditions were met.[13] The artists could not be identified as teachers, since that would cause problems with teacher certification standards. The school placement had to be attractive to artists—allow them time to work at their art, offer them a studio with decent equipment, and provide a better salary than they might receive with other part-time work. But this was a costly arrangement, and the program could not be advertised as "educational." In effect, schools were to become patrons of the arts. The Artists-in-Schools Program (renamed, in 1980, the "Artists in Education Program") became the showcase through which the Arts Endowment and arts councils could demonstrate an interest in arts education, employ artists, and win political points by demonstrating that children were being exposed to the arts.

The growth in state appropriations for arts councils has provided a channel for each state to fund variations on the Artists-in-Schools Program. Even if federal funding were withdrawn, state and local arts councils are likely to pursue the employment of artists in schools, and perhaps more vigorously, for the services offered to children are useful in generating public support for all of the operations of an arts council. Moreover, because school funds can be diverted to arts councils for the services they deliver to youth, schools can assist arts councils in financing the employment of artists. For example, a study of financial support for the Charlotte Symphony Orchestra (North Carolina) suggests that school programs accounted for "most of the increase in the orchestra's total budget from $101,000 in 1970–71 to $428,000 in 1974–75," primarily from local government support and funds from the county school board.[14]

Although the NEA did not officially call the Artists-in-Schools Program "educational," it sought to demonstrate that the program had educational value. Under pressure from arts educators who questioned the program, the Arts Endowment commissioned a study of it. However, the agency selected to do the study was heavily dependent on funding from the Arts Endowment for other aspects of its operation, and the report that it produced buried all negative results. Indeed, the final report was issued as a publicity package for the Artists-in-Schools Program (complete with a poster). The failure of the NEA to secure an impartial evaluation of this program was regrettable, to say the least.[15]

In spite of a number of criticisms of the program—including charges of a lack of solid documentation of the duration and amount of time artists spent with students, or of the cost of such contacts in each of the arts, or of the measured educational benefits—the Artists-in-Schools budget grew from $145,000 in 1969 to a projected $5.9 million for 1982, making it the largest federal arts program for school-aged youth.[16] In the meantime, regular school arts program and supervisory staff in the arts were being eliminated in many of the nation's schools. About this trend the NEA had little constructive to say. The general concept of employing artists in schools was to become a central theme in other reforms promoted by the Arts Endowment and to a lesser extent by the U.S. Office of Education.

Through the Arts Endowment and its various lobbies, the idea of placing artists in schools was elaborated into recommendations that artists not only be employed in schools but also be engaged in curriculum design, teacher education, and other dimensions of policymaking for schools. In the movement to de-school arts education, one also finds suggestions that the arts education offered to youth might be planned and implemented by arts councils or other "independent" agencies. By the mid-1970s, almost all of these ideas had been charted through pilot programs and promoted through a number of channels.

The JDR 3rd Fund Arts in Education Program

One of the most important of these channels, particularly in regard to pilot or demonstration projects, was the Arts in Education Program of the JDR 3rd Fund, directed by Kathryn Bloom from 1968 to 1979. Among the guiding premises of this private foundation program were (1) that all of the arts would be considered in the projects it would undertake, (2) that artists and community agencies would be considered as "major resources for teaching and learning about the arts," and (3) that the arts should contribute to the general education of children—be infused into the total curriculum of schools.[17]

During the eleven-year history of the Arts in Education Program of the JDR 3rd Fund, approximately $500,000 per year was invested in pilot projects (about $3 million in all). Because the program emphasized the use of artists and community agencies as "resources" for teaching, many of the Arts in Education projects served as the testing ground for the Artists-in-Schools concept, as well as the involvement of community arts councils in arts education planning. In the initial years of the Arts in Education Program, the focus was on pilot projects at the scale of a single school or small school district and, in many cases, involved the use of the CEMREL curriculum materials. The resources of the JDR 3rd Fund were a stimulus for the school district to enhance its arts program and become better prepared to carry arts education forward after these special funds were withdrawn (usually after two to three years).

This early work of the Fund provided "case" material about the procedures for designing programs based on a school-community "partnership" —the hallmark of the JDR 3rd Fund projects. Following the pilot work in schools, grants were made to stimulate change in large school districts, as well as state departments of education and arts councils. Among the final activities of the Arts in Education Program were the development of two national networks to initiate change and a strategy to place arts education on the agenda for discussion as a national policy issue.[18]

The first advocacy network directed its efforts toward state departments of education. The campaign strategy reflected its political intent and the experience of the Fund's work with the Pennsylvania State Department of Education.[19] Representatives from arts councils, professional associations of arts educators, and other civic and business groups were called together in each state to form an informal lobby and develop a plan for arts education within the state, based on an analysis of needs and resources. This process was carried out under the auspices of the Alliance for Arts Education (AAE), a program jointly sponsored by the U.S. Department of Education and the John F. Kennedy Center for the Performing Arts.

The general strategy, developed in consultation with the JDR 3rd Fund staff,[20] called for each state AAE committee to develop a "comprehensive statewide plan for arts education." The AAE committee was to urge the state department of education to (1) identify the arts as eligible for support within programs earmarked for minorities, the talented, handicapped, and others, and (2) encourage schools to use community resources for arts education. States that participated in this comprehensive planning process became eligible to compete for grants to support demonstration programs in schools. The criteria for the pilot projects were similar to those for the statewide planning process. Representatives from local arts agencies, parents, and civic and business leaders were to be involved in designing the arts education program and implementing it. The model for change, in short, was essentially the same as that which had been employed in the JDR 3rd Fund Projects: a school-community partnership.[21]

A second network established by the JDR 3rd Fund's staff was the League of Cities for the Arts in Education. The main advocacy channels for this program were the American Council of the Arts and the Association of Junior Leagues. The mission of this network was to urge civic groups or arts councils to initiate a comprehensive plan for arts education within their communities.

The suggested model for change called for the arts council or civic group, in consultation with school officials, to establish a comprehensive plan, identify resources for schools, and set up a coordinating "hub" —administrative center—for the delivery of arts services to school-aged youth. In addition to coordinating the use of arts resources in schools, the hub was intended to serve as a fund-raising agency for special projects. In the initial years of its operation, the hub might be supported by a mixture of funds from civic and business groups, the arts council, foundations, and special grants from participating school districts. However, since the community agencies were to provide services in response to requests from schools, responsibility for most or all of the budget eventually would be assumed by schools.

Within this scheme, the initiative for planning arts education programs rests with the community, and so does the administration of the budget. Schools are urged to plan programs around available services—performances by members of the local symphony or opera company, dance groups, or exhibitions and demonstrations by local artists, poetry or storytelling sessions, puppet shows, and the like. Ultimately, these services are intended to become an integral part of the arts curriculum, so "infused" into the school program that the district would be expected to pay for those services.[22]

The Blue-Ribbon Treatment for Arts Education

Overlapping these two networking activities, and bringing the philosophy behind them into a position of national prominence, are the reports of several blue-ribbon panels. In the tradition of influencing national policy through the establishment of blue-ribbon panels to study issues and make recommendations to Congress or federal agencies, several panels were established to address arts education during the 1970s.

Without question, the most influential of these panels was the Arts,

Education and Americans Panel, chaired by David Rockefeller, Jr., and including such distinguished citizens as author James Michener, Nobel physicist Glenn Seaborg, former CBS president Frank Stanton, and Francis Keppel, former U.S. Commissioner of Education, among others. The two-year effort of the panel was supported by a consortium of private foundations, as well as by the National Endowment for the Arts and the U.S. Office of Education. The project was initiated in 1974 at the suggestion of Nancy Hanks, then chairperson for the NEA, and Kathryn Bloom, among others.

The panel report, entitled *Coming to Our Senses: The Significance of the Arts for American Education,* offered ninety-eight recommendations for arts education, in a form and manner clearly intended to shape national policies.[23] The recommendations reflected the interests of the NEA, state and local arts councils, and, most important, the constituencies that these agencies represent—namely, artists and patrons of the arts.

The report calls for increased involvement of artists and arts councils in the education of children. Education is to be tied to "making art" and "exposure to art." Within the report, many of the case studies and reasons for teaching art which were promulgated during the first decade of the arts-in-education movement are reiterated. The arts are portrayed as tools for learning and as a means of reducing truancy, improving reading, and pursuing similar goals. The report recommends that schools be free to employ noncertified personnel—artists—to work in schools. Although the report might seem to represent the views of arts educators, especially in its emphasis on making art, it was issued and presented to members of Congress without benefit of prior review by representatives from the four professional associations representing educators in music, the visual arts, dance, and theater, which have about two hundred thousand members in all.[24]

In order to sustain the momentum created by all of these activities and to implement the recommendations in *Coming to Our Senses,* a follow-up advocacy group called The Arts, Education, and Americans, Inc. was formed by David Rockefeller, Jr. In October 1979, this group established the National Advocacy Program for Arts-in-Education. Still in operation today, the program sponsors conferences, offers a speakers bureau, has initiated a national publicity campaign through the print and broadcast media, provides consultation services, and operates a publications program. In 1980 and 1981, a series of monographs addressed to "support groups" for arts education was issued. Four of the first ten monographs are addressed to planning and financing arts education for schools through techniques commonly used in fund-raising for united appeal campaigns or other civic projects.[25] The monographs describe a planning and a budgeting process for arts education that would permit schools, if they wished, to do little more than serve as advisors to the program, publicly endorse it, and assist in fund-raising, but otherwise leave the administration of arts education to an independent agency. That agency, most likely an arts council, would have the power to hire (and fire) persons who worked in or through the schools to deliver arts services to youth.[26]

A variation on the theme of de-schooling arts education was offered by a blue-ribbon panel of school administrators appointed by the U.S. Commissioner of Education in 1972 to study and develop recommendations on high school and adolescent education. The final report of this panel, published in 1976, recommends that education in the arts be provided to adolescents through new "Participatory Education" programs to be offered by "community arts centers closely associated with the high school." The panel suggests that such centers would be governed by "a community council for the arts [and] would provide facilities and support for all the arts and crafts for which sustaining interest was forthcoming." Opportunities would be provided for "joint participation of adolescents and other interested and qualified adults in the community . . . to learn by doing." The panel envisions such centers as operating day and night with amateurs, volunteers, paid staff, and professionals competing for program space and, of course, for clients.[27]

The panel on adolescent education apparently had no reservations about the quality of education that might be received in a community arts recreation center where the popularity of a class would be criterion for offering it, nor did this panel envision art as much more than a hobby. If these recommendations were taken seriously, art instruction in secondary schools might well be disbanded altogether, and school-aged youths would be free to determine what art activities they might wish to pursue. All of this adds up to another expression of the belief held within the educational establishment that making art is a recreational activity and little more.

Similar themes are found in the report of a task force appointed by the National Endowment for the Arts to make recommendations on the "Education, Training, and Development of Professional Artists and Arts Educators." Throughout the task force report issued in December 1978, one is struck again by the emphasis placed on the training of talented students outside of schools or through special schools; the use of artists as teachers of children and of educators; and the retraining of arts specialists as arts generalists who can help to administer the services delivered by artists and community agencies, teach related arts or interdisciplinary programs, and demonstrate the use of art to enhance learning in other subjects. This task force claims not to have addressed the issue of an appropriate curriculum for elementary and secondary schools, but assumes that whatever the curriculum is, the artist will, by definition, assure a program of high quality.[28]

What is significant about these reports is the willingness of highly influential groups—outside of the profession of arts education—to assume that the school is not, in some fundamental sense, responsible for transmitting knowledge about art to young people; nor is it the most logical agency for doing so. It is as if the professional arts community, with the consent of the educational establishment, has determined that arts education is analogous to athletics. Like the professional sports community, everyone seems to be satisfied with scouting future talent and building fans for the arts by employing living artists as "coaches" and "stars" for children to see and emulate. Just as physical education has been reduced in many schools to competitive sports activities and athletics, art education too is portrayed as if it were a form of spectacle—an arena for the display of talent, a spectator sport in which the scheduling and financing of arts events is a major problem.

I believe that the emphasis being placed on the living artist as the star performer—agent of reform in education and highest example of "knowing about art"—reflects, in part, our general fascination with stardom, action, and spectacle in American culture. But it also reflects the dominance of the performing arts in the formation of national policies on the arts and arts education.[29] Unlike most of the visual and literary arts, the performing arts usually occur through a collaborative effort. The performance and performer are inseparable. The artistry in a concert, dance, or play is fashioned at the moment of encounter, and if the encounter is "live," so much the better. In addition to this tradition of collaboration, many performing artists (about four hundred thousand) are represented by trade unions whose officers are both skilled and authorized to speak on behalf of their interests in the councils where decisions about policy are made.[30]

The visual and literary arts are usually created and appreciated under more solitary, private circumstances and are identified with the creation and sale of art products. Most people who are trained in the visual and literary arts pursue their art as individuals. In the development of careers in the visual arts, being unique, creative, and innovative has taken precedence over efforts based on shared concerns. There are no powerful trade unions or well-organized support groups for the artist who works alone.[31] These and other differences in the structure of political and economic power within the art world have helped to produce recommendations for school programs that favor the employment of artists as performers, whose art is to be created in the presence of a young audience. Apart from the exposure of children to living artists, one finds little concern for the kind or amount of arts education regularly offered in the school curriculum.

Public Policy for Arts Education: Some Basic Issues

Federal programs, the thrust of statements being issued by arts advocates, and many of the policy recommendations offered by various blue-ribbon panels reflect a profound distrust of the school as an agency for art education, a skepticism about formal education in art (except for the talented), a lack of esteem for programs that transmit knowledge about art in ways other than through firsthand encounters with living artists or making art, and a willingness to use the arts as a means to ends other than learning about art. A number of issues are presented by these and other recommendations from the arts establishment.

The first issue is justice. At present, access to instruction in schools is so restricted that most young people have little more than a brief exposure to art. Because the majority of them are denied sound and continuous instruction in schools, intellectual access to art is restricted to youngsters whose parents already value art and can afford to provide their children with special opportunities for the study and enjoyment of art. The balance of influence in the adult world of art is kept in place through this privilege of birth and the special advantage of one's parents' education.

The second issue is trustworthy knowledge and its transmission. We are quick to bemoan the lack of public understanding of art, but in our schools we treat art as if it had no content worthy of study in its own right, as if art had no history, no context of meaning beyond that which one can discover oneself through making art or through exposure to individuals whose knowledge of art is presumed to be trustworthy because they are called artists. The ethical question is whether we believe that the self-proclaimed truths of artists are an adequate basis for education. This issue is particularly important in the visual arts, where, in their desire to be regarded as innovative and creative, artists not only may endeavor to insulate themselves from historical and other "outside" influences but advocate that students of art do the same.

In almost every subject, we express concern about the accuracy and scope of knowledge being transmitted, the purpose and efficiency of the education children are receiving. In the arts, however, either we allow classroom teachers who have little or no grasp of art to teach it or we act as if the personal enthusiasms of artists solved all problems of the quality of instruction —its appropriateness to children and their general education, its efficiency, and so on. If useful and reliable knowledge about art is thought to consist solely in the individual opinions, preferences, and personal discoveries of the teacher (or the artist), then we must be prepared to define art as something so idiosyncratic, so free of social, cultural, and historical influence, that teaching it really is pointless. Reasonable people know otherwise.

A third and related issue is power. The idea that knowledge is power is taken for granted in teaching reading, writing, arithmetic, and the so-called basic subjects. In our schools, art is treated almost exclusively as a manipulative activity. The ethical question is whether, in fact, we are setting low expectations for children in our schools—letting children of the working class use their hands, but not really expecting them to be capable of much more. The current insistence that school programs focus on "hands-on" manipulative activities is an effective way to restrict opportunities for children to discover that art can be perceptually and intellectually challenging even if one has little interest or skill in creating art. It is an effective way to restrict the growth of children's appreciations—especially of art forms that do require study and a background of knowledge beyond that which children may acquire by making art. Thus, while seeming to provide an equal opportunity for all to "participate" in art, our schools expect little more than engagement with art as a manual task, a skill, or a craft. Equal opportunity is not provided for young people to be engaged with art in a manner that broadens their horizons.

The fourth issue is freedom of choice. One of the arguments for de-schooling arts education is that the schools should not have a monopoly on arts education. The premise is false. If anything, it is the absence of school programs that contributes to the virtual monopoly on the arts now exercised by a particular social class. The majority of our citizens depend on our schools to transmit knowledge that would not normally be provided in the home or community. And citizens rightly expect that knowledge acquired in school will open doors for youth, extending their sense of human potential and accomplishment and giving them an opportunity to make informed choices.

As we consider the increased use of public funds to support the arts, the issue of freedom of choice in the arts is no longer just a matter of interest in the personal development of children. It becomes a matter of public interest to ask who will benefit from such funds and who will have a voice in how they are used. Clearly, those who are educated in the arts are best poised to speak on such matters and to benefit most from the arts which are supported. If, as a matter of national policy, we intend to support the production of art with public funds but, in effect, restrict the circulation of knowledge about art to the college-educated, to the affluent and their children, let us at least be candid about what we are doing.

The fifth issue is priorities. Informed decisions about the future of art education must be made. To the credit of the arts establishment and the arts-in-education movement, some discussion has been stimulated beyond the professional field of art education. But this discussion has not been guided by a sensitivity to the larger social issues, to differences among the arts, or to the role of formal education in the appreciation and production of art.

Many educators and citizens who influence school policies are not well informed about the arts and easily conclude that art is being "taken care of" if there is the slightest bit of any of the arts in a school. Too rarely are questions asked about what is taught, to whom, how often, and toward what ends. Many parents likewise believe that art is being taught if there is evidence that children are permitted, now and then, to use art materials.

Art educators, too, have contributed to the problems in our schools, chiefly through a failure of vision and intellectual leadership within professional associations and at the university level. But as a professional group, we in art education have a disposition to be grateful for crumbs and leftovers; we have an affinity for the casual, improvised teaching situation; and we are, I believe, more tolerant of shabby teaching than we ought to be.

Within most of our schools, we find that something called art is allowed to happen but on such a haphazard basis that we are not doing much service to children or to art. As a nation we have reached a point where a choice must consciously be made to offer in our schools sound programs of basic instruction in art or perhaps to exclude art education altogether.

Because current instruction in our schools is so meager and so concentrated on making art, we already know a good deal about the consequences of the very programs and policies that are now being advocated at the national level—and advertised as if they were brand-new. We have not, on a national scale, tried the other alternative—namely, offering in our schools sound, balanced, and continuous instruction in art and requiring the study of art as part of the basic education of all our children.

Notes

1. C. Fowler, ed., *An Arts in Education Source Book: A View from the JDR 3rd Fund* (New York: JDR 3rd Fund, 1980), pp. ix, 203–5. For a review of the research programs, see J. Murphy and L. Jones, "Research in Arts Education: A Federal Chapter," Report 76-02000, mimeographed (Washington, D.C.: Office of Education, 1978).

2. H. Conant, ed., *Seminar on Elementary and Secondary School Education in the Visual Arts* (New York: New York University, 1965).

3. E. L. Mattil, ed., *A Seminar in Art Education for Research and Curriculum Development* (University Park: Pennsylvania State University, 1966), p. 399.

4. M. Barkan and L. H. Chapman, "Report on the Planning Phase: Aesthetic

Education Program," mimeographed (Columbus: Ohio State University, Department of Art Education, 1967).

5. *CEMREL Newsletter* (1980): 7. Each unit contains materials for the teacher and six students. Through a telephone call to the Publications Department of CEMREL (in April 1982), I was informed that eleven units could be purchased for $704.00. One unit was no longer available.

6. For a listing of these, see S. S. Madeja and S. Onuska, *Through the Arts to the Aesthetic: The CEMREL Aesthetic Education Curriculum* (St. Louis: Central Midwestern Regional Educational Laboratory, 1977), pp. 137–41.

7. S. S. Madeja, ed., *The Artist in the School: A Report on the Artist-in-Residence Project* (St. Louis: Central Midwestern Regional Educational Laboratory, 1970).

8. For examples, see L. Jones, "The Arts and the U.S. Department of Education: A List of Funded Projects and Activities," mimeographed (Washington, D.C.: U.S. Department of Education, 1979).

9. M. Snow, "Arts in Education Evaluation, A Report to the Pennsylvania State Department of Education," mimeographed (Harrisburg: Pennsylvania State Department of Education, Bureau of Curriculum Services, 1979).

10. J. Eddy, "Toward Coordinated Federal Policies for Support of Arts Education," mimeographed (Washington, D.C.: Alliance for Arts Education, John F. Kennedy Center for the Performing Arts, 1977).

11. I have used the terms *Arts Endowment, National Endowment for the Arts,* and *NEA* interchangeably.

12. Quoted in J. Eddy, *Arts Education 1977—In Prose and Print: An Overview of Nine Significant Publications Affecting the Arts in American Education* (Washington, D.C.: U.S. Office of Education, Arts and Humanities Program, 1977. GPO Publication no. 260-934-2044), pp. 27–28.

13. Madeja, ed., *Artist in the School.*

14. D. Netzer, *The Subsidized Muse: Public Support for the Arts in the United States* (Cambridge, England: Cambridge University Press, 1978), pp. 114–17, 186.

15. E. W. Eisner, "Is the Artist in the School Program Effective?" *Art Education* 27 (1974). 19–24; Western States Arts Foundation, "A Study of the Poetry and Visual Arts Components of the Artists-in-Schools Program," Technical Report (Denver: Western States Arts Foundation, 1976); R. A. Smith, ed., "Artists-in-Schools: Analysis and Criticism," mimeographed (Champaign: University of Illinois, Bureau of Educational Research, 1978).

16. Allocations of funds are cited from "Capital Comments," *Artspace* 4 (1981): 2.

17. Fowler, ed., *Source Book,* p. 7.

18. Ibid., pp. 203–5.

19. Ibid., pp. 153–79.

20. Ibid., pp. 215–26.

21. G. C. Wenner, "Comprehensive State Planning for the Arts in Education," mimeographed (New York: JDR 3rd Fund, 1976); U.S. Office of Education, "Arts Education Program: Regulations," F. R. Doc. 76-11946 (Washington, D.C.: U.S. Office of Education, 1976).

22. Fowler, ed., *Source Book,* pp. 215–27; N. Shuker, ed., *Arts in Education Partners: Schools and Their Communities* (New York: JDR 3rd Fund, 1977), p. 20.

23. Arts, Education and Americans Panel, *Coming to Our Senses: The Significance of the Arts for American Education* (New York: McGraw-Hill, 1977).

24. R. Klotman, "Statement on Behalf of the Music Educators National Conference, National Dance Association, and National Art Education Association," mimeographed (Washington, D.C.: Music Educators National Conference, 25 May 1977).

25. Arts, Education, and Americans, Inc., report no. 4, *Ideas and Money for Expanding School Arts Programs;* report no. 5, *Method and the Muse: Planning a School Arts Program;* report no. 6, *Developing Financial Resources for School Arts Programs;* report no. 9, *Creative Collaborations: Artists, Teachers, and Students* (New York: Arts, Education, and Americans, Inc., 1980–81).

26. Arts, Education, and Americans, Inc., *Method and Muse,* pp. 22–23.

27. U.S. Office of Education, *The Education of Adolescents: The Final Report and Recommendations of the National Panel on High School and Adolescent Education* (Washington, D.C.: U.S. Department of Education, 1976), pp. 12–14. Available from U.S. Government Printing Office, no. OE-76-00004 (1976).

28. National Endowment for the Arts, *Report of the Task Force on the Education, Training and Development of Professional Artists and Arts Educators* (Washington, D.C.: National Endowment for the Arts, 1978), pp. 27–35.

29. Netzer, *Subsidized Muse,* p. 187.

30. L. Kreisberg, ed., *Local Government and the Arts* (New York: American Council for the Arts, 1979), p. 116.

31. For a comparison, see Rockefeller Panel, *The Performing Arts: Problems and Prospects* (New York: McGraw-Hill, 1965).

13

Policy for Arts Education: Whither the Schools, Whither the Public and Private Sectors?

Ralph A. Smith

An exception to the rule that the relations of the arts, culture, and education are rarely well articulated is Samuel Lipman's recent analysis of American culture and cultural policy in which Lipman not only advocates a strengthening of the link between the arts and education but also assigns a predominantly educational role to the National Endowment for the Arts. According to Lipman, the foremost government agency with responsibility for cultural policy would discharge its obligations to the greatest benefit of society and culture if it would accept and take seriously the task of educating the public about the arts. As educator, the Endowment should concern itself primarily "with communicating to our citizens the particular kind of knowledge about ourselves, our world, and most especially the civilized heritage that art enshrines."[1] Such a commitment to teaching implies that the agency would not only emphasize the substance and content of its programs over such considerations as the size of audiences reached or the amounts of money generated but also encourage the presentation of less popular and contemporary art as an extension of the well-known repertoire. It would do this, moreover, by stressing not the revolutionary character of new art but its evolution from the past. Toward these ends, the Endowment should enlist the cooperation of the educational establishment and make greater use than it has of teachers and artists. The Endowment's mission, in other words, is too important to be left to cultural administrators.

Lipman's suggestion of a predominantly educational role for the Endowment implies a reordering of priorities and a new agenda. His recommendations can also be read as an expression of regret that the agency has not realized its earlier promise and that government support for the arts has reaped but meager results or results of the wrong kind. This assessment is supported by Ronald Berman, who in 1979 stated that after the expenditure of more than a billion dollars it was difficult to associate the Endowment either with any notable idea in training, appreciation, or learning in the arts or with any artistic achievement of outstanding quality that would constitute a notable increment to the cultural heritage.[2]

Both Lipman and Berman point out that the current state of affairs in cultural policy is the consequence of both unavoidable trends and deliberate policy decisions. The Endowment could not have gone untouched by the tendency toward centralization of decision making and the bureaucratization of modern institutions, which in the Endowment's case has produced a new class of cultural officials increasingly preoccupied with political considerations and administrative procedure. Cultural officials were nonetheless free to some extent to choose the policies that would serve culture, but, as the record of the past two decades demonstrates, they have increasingly elected not to support individual artists or artistic creation but to provide cultural services in the form of "arts experiences" that get "delivered" by cultural organizations that perceive their primary function as the obtainment of government grants to help provide the experiences in question. Thus it happened that the National Endowment for the Arts, the agency founded as the champion and protector of the arts, came to be looked on, and appealed to, mainly as a dispenser of funds to cultural organizations. Whenever public monies are available for disbursement, however, numerous groups surface to demand their share. This means that a good deal of the agency's time and energy must be spent trying to satisfy contending interests.

Contributing to the politicization of cultural policymaking is a pervasive welfare state mentality. Berman notes that during the seventies in particular, cultural services were in effect justified by assimilating them to social services and expecting them to accomplish similar ends, that is, the melioration of social problems. The arts became one more weapon in the government's arsenal to fight poverty, crime, alienation, and racial segregation. In a social-welfare conception of culture, however, beliefs that art is worth having for its distinctive values, that its creation requires genuine talent and creativity, and that it has left a legacy of admirable achievement worthy of preservation tend to be obscured. Concern for quality and standards, in other words, gets deemphasized.

Other factors mentioned by Lipman that have influenced culture and cultural policy today are the use of the arts to help restore the legitimacy of modern governments; the importance the arts have assumed in a secular age as a source of spiritual values; the devastating blow dealt to the life of culture, art, and learning during the sixties; and the insufficient attention given in justifying support for the arts to public benefits in contrast to private pleasures. More later about the last of these. Problems and disappointments notwithstanding, Lipman thinks there is considerable good will toward the arts in society and that a public well educated about the nature of high culture and the government's proper role in supporting it would welcome a truly educational Arts Endowment.

For the moment, I defer my estimate of the Endowment's capacity to function effectively as educator and will conclude these introductory remarks by noting two reasons why an educator should feel encouraged by Lipman's essay: his unequivocal avowal of the importance of education to the life of the arts and culture and his essentially humanistic conception of the arts. When art is understood not only as a source of enjoyable experience but also as the communicator of values and knowledge, it can be accommodated to the purposes of traditional liberal education, to humanistic education in the best sense of the term. Liberal education has always had its defenders, but because of his stature as performing artist, critic, and publisher, Lipman is in a position to argue the values of humanistic education with an authority denied to many members of the educational establishment.

The Arts as a Humanity

Regarding the question of policy for arts education, I will distinguish my views from most existing policies by speaking of an excellence curriculum for arts education at the secondary level (grades 7–12). This in turn calls for a definition of excellence in art, about which all I can say here is that I believe it to consist in the capacity of works of art at their best to induce worthwhile experiences in those properly disposed. I cannot present a formal analysis of worthwhile experience here, although Lipman has caught its essence in the remarks I have quoted. By saying that works of art not only have the capacity to provide personal enjoyment and gratification but are also sources of humanistic knowledge, Lipman in effect subsumes the arts under the humanities, even if he does not proceed to the next logical step. I take this step and suggest that the arts be regarded as a humanity and taught as such in the schools.

But how shall we regard the humanities? We can hardly do better than to adopt Albert William Levi's definition of the humanities as the arts of continuity (or history), the arts of communication (or languages and literature, and in the instance at hand the special languages of the arts), and the arts of criticism (or philosophy in its critical dimension.)[3] Without following Levi in all details, I think we can understand the study of the arts under each of his rubrics, such that, in rough outline, an excellence curriculum, at least for secondary arts education, might look something like the following.

The historical dimension of arts instruction is satisfied when we can say with Levi that students have learned to walk proudly with their cultural heritage and appreciate how the art of any period, including their own, has evolved from the art of the past. In this respect, we do well to remind ourselves of what the late Lord Kenneth Clark once pointed out: great works of art reveal the re-creation of traditional forms that express the artist's own epoch while also retaining a relationship with tradition.[4] Even when artists self-consciously attempt to shun history, it is impossible to understand what they are trying to do without a sense of previous artistic accomplishment. By helping students acquire an *art-historical framework,* an arts education program aligns itself with the arts of continuity.

Historical knowledge of the arts is not an end in itself. It is instrumental to understanding the nature of *aesthetic communication.* The ability to place an artwork in historical and cultural contexts readies students for that kind of participating awareness that provides access to a work's peculiar power and meaning. We move, that is, from speaking about art in general and works of art in historical succession to an emphasis on the individual classic, masterpiece, or touchstone. Students must spend considerable time with works of art which Clark has described as having the qualities of inspired virtuosity, supreme compositional power, intensity of feeling, masterful design, uncompromising artistic integrity, imaginative power, originality of vision, and a profound sense of human values. Only by examining works in depth can students begin to appreciate the distinctive human accomplishment we call art. Only by attending closely to the qualities of each masterpiece will students be able to apprehend what great art has to say to them. Thus do students participate in what Levi terms the arts of communication.

We mislead students, however, if we stress only the messages communicated by works of art. The overall power and meaning of a complex work of art are manifest only as the result of an accurate and skilled perception of its manifold of qualities, as the consummation of an aesthetic experience. While I will not present a formal analysis of aesthetic experience here, what I do *not* have in mind is the casual use of the term *art experience* that disfigures so much policy rhetoric—as in "all students should be provided with an art experience"—but rather the quality of experience afforded by excellent art to informed percipients. The value of such experience has been asserted by numerous philosophers and theorists; by John Dewey in his classic *Art as Experience,*[5] Harold Osborne in *The Art of Appreciation,*[6] Monroe C. Beardsley in *The Aesthetic Point of View,*[7] and E. F. Kaelin in *Art and Existence,*[8] among others. The significance of aesthetic experience is also what Hilton Kramer seems to be defending in his critical forays against varieties of postmodernist art and criticism.[9] Moreover, as quite recent publications indicate, the topic continues to interest theorists.[10] Whatever else may be said about aesthetic experience, it extends in an important way the grasp of the perceptual powers while providing feelings of keen alertness, vitality, and exhilaration. Most important, such experience is preconditional to any estimate of a work's aesthetic value.

The activities identified by the third term in Levi's definition of the humanities, the arts of criticism, follow naturally from efforts to understand the nature of aesthetic communication. It is not possible to teach students to appreciate excellence in art without conveying principles of value. Students learn the rudiments of aesthetic judgment, first, implictly through the decisions made in selecting classics and masterpieces for study and, second, deliberately when teachers defend their choices with critical reasons and invite students to justify their own assessments. In this way an excellence curriculum for arts education develops in students the ability for *critical reflection.* Considerable effort should be spent on the development of this capacity since it is precisely what is lacking in today's audiences for the arts. Having equipped the young with the skills and attitudes needed for critical reflection, we will also have set them on the road to self-sufficiency in the realm of art. We will have inured them to at least some degree against the seductiveness of the meretricious in the aesthetic realm.

To sum up, an arts education program of the kind in question would view art as one of the humanities and be offered as a part of a curriculum of liberal or general education. It would aim at cultivating in students historical understanding, aesthetic appreciation, and critical reflection. Stated somewhat differently, the principal goal of teaching art is the development of the disposition to interpret artworks properly and to appreciate artistic excellence. In the exercise of such a disposition, relevant knowledge must be brought to bear on the matter at hand. This knowledge derives principally from the history and theory of art. The general purpose of arts education then is not only to introduce the young to the world of art but also to build in them a sense of art that will inform their future commerce with art objects.[11] A sense of art is simply another name for the conceptual frameworks and perspectives that people bring to their experience of art.

An Excellence Curriculum for Secondary Education

Significant humanistic objectives for arts education cannot be attained in a term, in a year, or even, for that matter, in two years. I suggest that six years are needed to complete an excellence curriculum in the arts.[12] Such a program would be composed of eleven units of study consisting of core and elective courses. Work should begin with a core introductory course of one unit that would familiarize students with clear-cut instances of visual art, music, and literature. This course would be followed by two more units devoted to the history of the arts, the principal purpose of which would be to build a historical framework and to convey the wisdom that the history of any subject provides: events do not occur in a vacuum, continuous evolution rather than abrupt change is the rule, and many things seemingly new have precedents.

When students begin the detailed examination of carefully chosen classics and masterpieces, some options regarding period style may be permitted, but each student would be required to study a number of classics in each of the major arts. Three units of such study should be sufficient. Once more, the central objective is to learn how to appreciate excellence in art, and this can be accomplished only by studying a limited number of works in depth.

The objectives of familiarization, historical awareness, and aesthetic appreciation might seem enough for teachers and students to handle. Still, the recommended six years of study might make it possible to offer two units of seminars designed to probe a number of puzzling topics and problems which arise in our thinking about art and the art world. In these seminars students would have an opportunity to fashion elements of their own philosophy of art.[13] At appropriate levels of analysis, seminars could concentrate on some of the numerous antinomies, dualisms, and paradoxes in art. How, for example, can art be both purposeful and purposeless? How can it be both work and play? Why are disputes about taste claimed to be impossible when tastes are constantly being disputed? How can art be defined when it keeps changing?

Yet another group of questions arises when we reflect on the consequences of art's infiltration of, and in turn its infiltration by, other spheres of society. What happens, for example, when high culture enters the mass media system of communication,[14] when government decides to support culture and learning,[15] when city planners either undervalue or overvalue aesthetic considerations in their designs for construction projects and urban renewal?[16] In each case, what are the gains and losses? The discussion of such problems should not be deferred until the college years.

As a change of pace and context, another core unit might consist of a service requirement in order to give students a sense of the institutional realities of the art world. I borrow the suggestion of a service unit from the Carnegie Foundation report on the high school.[17]

As for creative and performing activities, they are not, I think, indispensable to a humanistic curriculum of arts education. We have been reminded that one can learn a great deal about a subject without knowing the details of its craft and that it is the professional's fallacy to think otherwise.[18] Yet a number of thoughtful people believe that creative and performing activities are relevant to aesthetic learning, so I will not argue the matter. A good reason can, in fact, be adduced for requiring students to take perhaps two units in such areas as painting and graphics, instrumental and vocal music, or photography and filmmaking. We can justify practice in composing or performing the media of the various arts on the basis that the elements of the apperceptive mass that function when persons perceive artworks are derived from practical experience as well as from conceptual learning. A feel for design, expressiveness, and style may well be refined through efforts to create compositions of one's own or through attempts to make a personal statement. In a humanities conception of arts education, however, these activities remain subsidiary; things are clearly slanted toward historical, appreciative, and critical studies.[19]

So much for some of the particulars of a secondary school arts education curriculum that has as its principal objective the building of a disposition to appreciate excellence in art by involving students in introductory, historical, appreciative, creative, and institutional contexts during a course of study spanning six years that consists of an arts sequence of core and elective units. Such a curriculum is, of course, an ideal or prototype, something to be striven for and perhaps never to be completely realized. For although the idea of teaching the humanities through the arts is not novel, I am not aware of any program in today's secondary schools that could be said to exemplify the prototype in question. But I will not be dissuaded by those who might say the model is unrealistic. Rather, I would hope that the plan would be entertained as a truly humanistic conception of arts education, a vision of what teaching the arts could be like, and a spur to action. Once more, that action would have to amount to more than mere tinkering, for, as John Goodlad[20] tells us in his impressive study of schooling, what little arts education one can find today is largely in disarray. Though unfortunate for high school students who are denied sustained encounters with the arts, this state of affairs presents a propitious moment for a new initiative. Yet the moment cannot be seized unless we can find and train teachers capable of working in humanistically oriented arts programs. A few remarks on teacher preparation are thus in order.

The Preparation of Humanities Teachers of the Arts

An excellence curriculum consolidates departments of art, music, and literature at the secondary level into humanities departments with responsibility for teaching the arts. Teachers who have been educated in the humanities are best qualified to work in these departments. In general terms, this means that the preparation of arts teachers should take place in an atmosphere in which commitment to scholarly standards and artistic excellence is taken for granted, an atmosphere in which it is not necessary constantly to defend the values of high culture and in which it is assumed that the best that has been thought and created constitutes the most fitting object of study. One would prefer that this atmosphere pervade both sites at which arts teachers currently receive their training: colleges of education and fine arts as well as colleges of liberal arts and sciences. My recommendation does not imply deprofessionalizing teacher preparation or the abandoning of a role for colleges of education. It is simply an acknowledgment that colleges of education generally do a poor job of preparing subject-matter specialists. Accordingly, I endorse an evolving pattern that assigns to academic departments the major responsibility for providing teachers with the knowledge they need to teach their subjects competently.

Colleges of education can continue to provide work in the history, psychology, and philosophy of education and ensure that prospective teachers learn their craft and have opportunities for supervised practice of their pedagogical skills. To realize that distinctively educational studies can be as substantive as courses in the humanistic disciplines, we need only recall that rational philosophy itself had its origin in speculations about the proper education of the young and that from Plato to Dewey most of our respected thinkers have addressed educational problems.

Although I have sketched an ideal, certain realities must be faced. I said that colleges of education do not train subject-matter specialists very well. There are those who say that colleges of education do not do anything well and should therefore be abolished. Such critics, however, do not face up to certain facts. True, a commitment to high academic standards is often lacking in today's colleges of education, and the love of learning and knowledge for their own sakes is not vigorously emphasized. One also observes sentimental attitudes toward the young and a heavy investment in programs that either are politically popular or set minimal criteria of achievement. But this is not all due to the anti-intellectualism of educators. Accorded a low priority and drained of funds by their university administrations, colleges of education have little choice but to concentrate on certain areas—for example, programs for special populations, vocational and bilingual education, reading research, and so forth—in which grants are readily available. Improving teacher education implies rehabilitating colleges of education and giving them the support that the importance of their task deserves.

Regarding the contempt expressed in academia for educators, something might be done about it if we recognize it for what it is. Harry Judge,[21] an Oxford don and British observer of American education, characterizes the attitude of academics toward educators as one of the persistent snobberies of higher education in the United States. "Who," writes Judge, "wants to become a member of a profession that is constantly sniffed at and spat upon?" What is more, low esteem and low pay make it difficult for the entire education profession—in the public schools as well as in colleges of education and college arts education departments—to attract and retain qualified young people. For the good of all, things must be turned around. Lipman recommends that the Arts Endowment make its peace with the educational establishment. Would that others heard and heeded his call—especially those who are on shaky ground when they excoriate colleges of education.

But how justified are we in thinking that future humanities teachers of the arts would receive a solid foundation of knowledge in colleges of liberal arts? Has not the current state of higher education in general occasioned alarm? Over the past three decades, anti-intellectualism, dilution of standards, and waywardness have not been confined to colleges of education but have infected all of academia and perhaps the humanistic fields most severely. In particular, we have witnessed submission to the demands of the youth culture in the sixties, acquiescence in the devaluing of general studies in favor of specialized training in the seventies, and now, in the eighties, a revulsion against Western values in favor of cultural pluralism and near capitulation to Marxism and derivative ideologies. These conditions have prompted a number of critics to call for the remoralization of higher learning.[22] Since the preparation of teachers for an excellence curriculum in the arts depends on the health of various segments of higher education, such remoralization must occur if there is to be any hope that education can help raise the level of learning and culture in society. Otherwise, American civilization will continue to decline.

The Public and Private Sectors

In saying that culpability for the current state of affairs in American life, culture, and learning should be distributed among numerous groups and agencies in the society and in requesting understanding of the difficulties faced by colleges of education, I do not intend to exonerate the arts education establishment from past misadventures or exempt it from bearing the major responsibility for charting a new course for the field. Arts educators remain the only group with a long-range commitment to the teaching of the arts. And if we accept the proposition that the reinvigoration of art and cultural life depends to a significant degree on the quality of the arts education future citizens receive, then the public schools with their encompassing reach are clearly the foremost institutions to undertake the task of arts education. Still further, when liberal education that includes a humanistically conceived arts education program is offered to the entire secondary-school population and not just to those planning to attend college, the objection that an excellence curriculum in the arts is maleficently elitist is patently absurd.[23] But is the arts education establishment adequate to the task?

The record of the arts education establishment over the last two decades is not encouraging. The afflictions that have beset all levels of schooling have had especially adverse effects on arts education. Sensing its own weakness and hoping to strengthen its threatened existence, the arts education establishment tends to be inordinately influenced by the educational ideas of prestigious organizations or agencies. Recently, however, the field has begun to show signs of independent judgment. It has developed a capacity for serious conceptualization of its purposes and for the criticism of ideas inimical to aesthetic learning. Anyone who takes the time to review the theoretical literature that has accumulated over the past twenty years, particularly in visual arts education, will be impressed with its substance.[24] Few, of course, have done this, and so the old stereotypes continue to hold sway. But even if the arts education establishment took the initiative and the public schools adopted humanities programs in the arts, the public and private sectors would probably still try to influence arts education. What form should such influence take?

First of all, I agree that we should not distinguish too sharply between the public and private sectors. We do better to adopt John Dewey's definition of a public as consisting of all those who organize on behalf of an interest that society has devalued and that henceforth will be looked after and promoted by elected officials representing the interest in question.[25] That seems a fairly good description of the influential arts constituency we have today, the members of which come from both public and private groups. This said, I will nonetheless examine a few institutions separately.

I will begin with the Arts Endowment, for which Lipman envisions a primarily educational role. I think that the Endowment's most important educational function should be that of setting an example. If we hope to engender an appreciation of excellence in art, then an Endowment that unwaveringly espouses the importance of high culture would perform an invaluable service to both arts education and the public. Attempts on the part of the Endowment to support arts education programs for the schools directly are another matter. Minimally, such support requires that the Endowment learn to think educationally and not confuse patronage, revenue sharing, and entertainment with teaching and learning. The record of the Endowment in this regard, however, is not encouraging. But attitudes seem to be changing.[26] Frank Hodsoll is talking about the importance of excellence in art and recognizes the necessity to work closely with the education establishment, a recommendation also made by Lipman. Yet such efforts will be handicapped by policies that rely too much on state art agencies and cultural organizations to accomplish educational tasks that are better undertaken by teacher-training institutions, state departments of education, and the schools. And so I am somewhat dubious about this direction the Endowment has taken. On the other hand, the funding of regional centers of research in arts education holds promise so long as the research conducted therein is closely tied to curriculum design, implementation, assessment, and teacher education. In short, while I applaud Lipman's recommendations and am cognizant of changes in attitude in the agency, the test of it all lies in the future. But overall I am inclined to be less critical than in the past, in large part because I think some lessons have been learned.

I further venture the opinion that the Humanities Endowment is a more appropriate agency to advance Lipman's and my conception of arts education than the Arts Endowment. By practically every indication the Humanities Endowment holds greater promise for encouraging truly humanistic approaches to aesthetic learning. Once interests have become institutionalized, however, arrangements are hard to change, and thus the Arts Endowment will probably not relinquish its educational programs. One might also say matters should be referred to the Department of Education, but it simply has too many things to worry about to give arts education the attention it deserves. So we shall just have to hope for the best from the new policy formation complex of which Samuel Hope speaks.[27]

Museums—cultural institutions that overlap both private and public domains—must be mentioned if only because of the educational programs most of them have and the educational language they often use to justify their activities. Following a period of unplanned growth and adventurism, museum officials too appear to have entered a period of reflection and reordering of priorities.[28] Whether museums will eventually retreat from trendiness and accommodation to special interests remains to be seen. Two things, however, are obvious. Museums are merely adjuncts to arts education programs in the schools and not a substitute. They serve arts education best by honoring their basic functions: the conservation and exhibition of the cultural wealth of the society.

In speaking of private-sector forays into arts education, I refer to efforts mounted over the last twenty-five years by highly regarded foundations with the advice and support of a fair number of public officials. In assessing these ventures it is necessary to discriminate between an initial period of activity that lasted from the early sixties until the late seventies—the first wave, so to speak—and a second, more recent wave funded from a different source and directed by different officials that began to gather strength a few years ago and is now beginning to show some results. Lipman's judgment that the private sector has lost its integrity and independence of judgment and by so doing has weakened the very cornerstone of its existence receives support from earlier private-sector interventions into arts education. I have recorded my critical observations on these developments elsewhere and will say here only that their basic mistake was to confuse humane intentions and good will with substance and excellence.[29]

Through some of its more recent efforts, the private sector has signaled an intention to redress past mistakes. Instead of dreams about the arts sparking educational reform, we find realism regarding the prospects for sweeping change. The new breed of private-sector representative emphasizes that art should be taught as a demanding subject in a curriculum of general education that aims at cultivating educated commerce with art.[30] It is realized that to achieve this objective, substantive content from art history, art criticism, and the philosophy of art must be incorporated into both teacher preparation and art education programs. The private-sector officials I have in mind are also aware of the need for cooperation with the arts education establishment, and good working relations are developing apace. More than that, arts educators and academic scholars are being brought together for the common purpose of improving aesthetic learning. To the virtues of seriousness and good faith has also been added that of patience. The lesson has been learned that if private-sector efforts are to have lasting impact, fundamental tasks must be attended to first. In short, this new venture may leave a significan legacy *if* (and it is an important qualification) it can abjure mere proceduralism, an inordinate emphasis on public relations, and projects of dubious value. It must also eventually center its attention on the secondary grades. If it can do all this, it will have restored some integrity to the private sector.

Conclusion

Reservations about the government's capacity to perform the role of educator notwithstanding, I share the belief that it is in a society's interest to maintain a high level of culture, an accomplishment that implies an important role for the public schools. Yet this belief has come under strong attack. Edward Banfield[31] puts the matter starkly when he claims that art is inherently incapable of serving the public interest because whatever meaning or value art has is appropriated in aesthetic experiences that by their nature are private and subjective. Certainly he believes that, within severe limits, the arts are not important enough to pull public funds away from other areas of need and study.

Banfield has stimulated some interesting discussion about the government's role in supporting culture and the justifiability of teaching the arts in the schools. He has, moreover, marshaled some interesting evidence in behalf of his argument, evidence of the sort, incidentally, often cited by the political Left and not only the Right. In this respect the conservative Banfield often beats ultraliberals at their own game. Art, however, is both a private and a public good. When people confront great masterpieces of art or attend cultural performances—very few of which, we should remember, would be accessible at all if some government or quasi-public body had not provided for their preservation and presentation—they are, it might be said, not private citizens so much as members of a public sharing the civilized values epitomized by the work in question. If we may think of a public in this way, as the totality of persons who when experiencing works of high culture feel their membership in civilization reaffirmed, then government spending on the arts can be defended as being in the public interest because civilized values are in the public interest. Accordingly, public school instruction in the arts becomes justifiable because it contributes to the quality of both individual and social life.

Works of art further constitute a major part of a nation's cultural heritage. When of high artistic quality this heritage can become, as Stuart Hampshire has pointed out,[32] a principal source of glory and pride for any city or nation and a continual reminder of its history. So long as it is kept from deteriorating into mere chauvinism, civic pride is in urgent need of encouragement at a time when the values of Western civilization are under heavy assault. It is only those who have never been educated in these values who can say that attempts to transmit the cultural heritage are fraudulent and irrelevant to the majority of people today. Such cant can be refuted only by ensuring that schools induct the young into their civilized heritage.

Support for a thriving cultural life can also be in a democratic society's political interest. The freedom of expression we find in the arts of democratic societies provides an important contrast to conditions of artistic creation in totalitarian states. Citizens should be reminded by their government more often than they are that their freedom to participate in the arts in all their complexity and variety is a privilege denied to most people around the globe.[33] The full exercise of this particular freedom may also provide, as Lionel Trilling had hoped the appreciation of literature might do, an antidote to ideological thinking.

Exhortation to appreciate the nation's artistic heritage is, of course, meaningless unless persons have been prepared for their role as participants in and, to some extent, shapers of their culture. The objective of teaching art should be to set students on the path toward independent judgment and choice in the domain of art. Through their assessments and choices they will influence that domain; if their preferences are enlightened, that influence will be for the good. The role of the government in the area of the arts can also gradually change. Inordinate advocacy will not be necessary because the importance of the arts will be assumed.

In concluding, I repeat that I am in complete accord with Lipman's opinion that the problem of raising the level of culture is basically an educational one. All sectors of society will benefit from an improved educational system. Attempts to ignore this basic truth or the failure to address its implications directly only delay the results we all want. Lipman says it is time to start teaching. I contribute the recommendation that we concentrate efforts at the secondary level and relax the grip that images of elementary arts education have on our thinking. It is after all at the secondary level that schools begin systematically to induct the young into adult society. The early years must unquestionably lay good foundations, but it is only during the later years that the arts can be studied in any depth or complexity. And so I conclude with the advice of that extraordinary nineteenth-century apostle of culture, Matthew Arnold: organize your secondary education.

Notes

1. Samuel Lipman, "Cultural Policy: Whither America, Whither Government?" *New Criterion* 3 (November 1984): 14.

2. Ronald Berman, "Art vs. the Arts," *Commentary* 68 (November 1979): 46–52. Reprinted in Berman, *Culture and Politics* (New York: University Press of America, 1984), chap. 11.

3. Albert William Levi, *The Humanities Today* (Bloomington: Indiana University Press, 1970). Also see Levi's "Literature as a Humanity," *Journal of Aesthetic Education* 10, nos. 3–4 (July–October 1976): 45–60.

4. Kenneth Clark, *What Is a Masterpiece?* (New York: Thames and Hudson, 1979), 10–11.

5. John Dewey, *Art as Experience* (1934; New York: Capricorn Books, 1958), especially chap. 3. Cf. vol. 10 of *John Dewey, The Later Works, 1925–1953,* ed. Jo Ann Boydston, with an introduction by Abraham Kaplan (Carbondale and Edwardsville: Southern Illinois University Press, 1987).

6. Harold Osborne, *The Art of Appreciation* (New York: Oxford University Press, 1970), especially chap. 2.

7. Monroe C. Beardsley, *The Aesthetic Point of View: Selected Essays,* ed. Michael S. Wreen and Donald M. Callen (Ithaca: Cornell University Press, 1982), especially chap. 16.

8. Eugene F. Kaelin, *Art and Existence: A Phenomenological Analysis* (Lewisburg: Bucknell University Press, 1970), especially chap. 6.

9. For example, in the *New York Times,* 31 December 1978, Kramer states that it is the responsibility of criticism to estimate not only the social significance of art

events but also the quality of aesthetic experience they afford. In "T. J. Clark and the Marxist Critique of Modern Painting," *New Criterion* 3 (March 1985): 8, he criticizes the tendency of ideological writing "to discredit the idea of *aesthetic* achievement in art and replace it with scenarios claiming to represent an authentic *social* history of art." And in "The Met's 20th-Century Folly," *New Criterion* 5 (March 1987): 2, he writes that the design of the Met's new galleries of twentieth-century art ensures that "the dignity of aesthetic experience will not be the uppermost consideration."

10. See, for example, Michael H. Mitias, ed., *Possibility of the Aesthetic Experience* (Boston: Martinus Nijhoff, 1986).

11. The notion of a sense of art was suggested by Arthur Danto's *The Transfiguration of the Commonplace* (Cambridge: Harvard University Press, 1981). Particularly suggestive is his belief that "to see something as art at all demands nothing less than . . . an atmosphere of artistic theory, a knowledge of the history of art" (p. 135).

12. For a more detailed discussion, see Ralph A. Smith, *Excellence in Art Education: Ideas and Initiatives* (Reston, Va.: National Art Education Association, 1987), chap. 3.

13. Such seminars would lend themselves to the Socratic method of teaching, suggestions for the use of which may be found in Mortimer Adler, ed., *The Paideia Program: An Educational Syllabus* (New York: Macmillan, 1980).

14. This question is discussed in Harold Rosenberg's "Art and Its Double" in his *Artworks and Packages* (New York: Horizon Press, 1969).

15. Berman, *Culture and Politics,* note 2 above. Cf. Dick Netzer, *The Subsidized Muse* (New York: Cambridge University Press, 1978).

16. Jane Jacobs, *The Death and Life of Great American Cities* (New York: Random House, 1961).

17. Ernest L. Boyer, *High School: A Report on Secondary Education in America* (New York: Harper and Row, 1983), chap. 12.

18. Jacques Barzun, *The House of Intellect* (New York: Harper and Brothers, 1959), 12.

19. Some tips about how to combine practical activities with a humanities approach to the study of the arts may be found in the perception keys in F. David Martin and Lee A. Jacobus, *The Humanities through the Arts,* 3d ed. (New York: McGraw-Hill, 1983).

20. John I. Goodlad, *A Place Called School* (New York: McGraw-Hill, 1984), 218–20.

21. Harry Judge, *American Graduate Schools of Education: A View from Abroad* (New York: Ford Foundation, 1982).

22. Allan Bloom's *The Closing of the American Mind* (New York: Simon and Schuster, 1987) is only the latest upbraiding of higher education for its lost sense of mission. Cf. Harry S. Broudy, *Truth and Credibility: The Citizen's Dilemma* (New York: Longman, 1981).

23. For my views on elitism, see "The Question of Elitism," in Smith, *Excellence in Art Education,* note 12 above, chap. 4; reprinted in *Design for Arts in Education* 87 (May–June 1986): 34–42.

24. This became apparent to me when I reviewed the serious writing in the field of visual art education since approximately midcentury. See Ralph A. Smith, "The

Changing Image of Art Education: Theoretical Antecedents of Discipline-based Art Education," *Journal of Aesthetic Education* 21 (Summer 1987): 3–34.

25. John Dewey, *The Public and Its Problems* (New York: Henry Holt, 1927).

26. Frank Hodsoll, "Some Thoughts on Art Education," *Studies in Art Education* 26 (Summer 1985): 247–56.

27. Samuel Hope, "Strategic Issues in American Arts Education," *Journal of Aesthetic Education* 21 (Winter 1987): 25–40.

28. See, for example, *Museums for a New Century* (Washington, D.C.: American Association of Museums, 1984); "Art Museums and Education," a special issue of the *Journal of Aesthetic Education* 19 (Summer 1985); and Elliott W. Eisner and Stephen M. Dobbs, *The Uncertain Profession: Observation on the State of Museum Education in Twenty American Art Museums* (Los Angeles: Getty Center for Education in the Arts, 1986).

29. See my review of the Arts, Education, and Americans panel report, *Coming to Our Senses* (New York: McGraw-Hill, 1977), in the *Teachers College Record* 79 (February 1978).

30. I have in mind the efforts of the Getty Center for Education in the Arts under the directorship of Leilani L. Duke. For an initial sense of its approach, see *Beyond Creating: The Place for Art in America's Schools* (Los Angeles: Getty Center for Education in the Arts, 1985). For subsequent discussion of the center's efforts, see the literature of arts education since 1985, namely, *Studies in Arts Education* 28 (Winter, Summer 1987); *Art Education* 40 (September 1987); and the *Journal of Aesthetic Education* 21 (Summer 1987). The latter is a 259-page special issue devoted to the antecedents, meaning, and disciplines of DBAE. Writings about DBAE are quite uneven, ranging from uncritical advocacy and mere opinion, pro and con, to critical analysis.

31. Edward Banfield, *The Democratic Muse: Visual Arts and the Public Interest* (New York: Basic Books, 1984). For a view that aesthetic experience is compatible with the public interest, see Monroe C. Beardsley, "Aesthetic Welfare, Aesthetic Justice, and Educational Policy," *Journal of Aesthetic Education* 7 (October 1973): 49–61. Since Beardsley's writings figured so prominently in Banfield's argument against federal subsidy of the arts, it is surprising that Banfield should have overlooked this essay. Beardsley's essay is reprinted in his *Aesthetic Point of View.*

32. Stuart Hampshire, "Private Pleasures and the Public Purse," *Times Literary Supplement,* 13 May 1977, a review of Janet Minahan's *The Nationalization of Culture* (New York University Press, 1977), a study of state subsidies to the arts in Great Britain.

33. In this respect, I recall some remarks by the editors in the inaugural issue of *The New Criterion.* We read that "capitalism, for all its many flaws, has proved to be the greatest safeguard of democratic institutions and the best guarantee of intellectual and artistic freedom . . . that the modern world has given us" (1 [September 1982]: 4).

14

The Role of the National Endowment for the Arts [Today]

Excerpted from
Toward Civilization: A Report on Arts Education by the National Endowment for the Arts *(1988)*

The Arts in Education Program

The goal of the National Endowment for the Arts in the area of education is to advance comprehensive and sequential education in the arts as a part of basic education in the schools. The Endowment pursues this goal primarily through its Arts in Education Program. Many of its arts discipline programs also fund educational projects both in and outside the schools. The Endowment's current work is described and evaluated in this chapter.

We also consider the educational role of the National Endowment for the Humanities and the National Science Foundation, our federal equivalents for the other two branches of education, as well as the work of the U.S. Department of Education (see Appendixes A, B, and C, respectively).

The Endowment's arts education effort began in 1966 as the Arts and Education three-year Laboratory Theater Project. The project was established in cooperation with the U.S. Office of Education (USOE) and state and local school boards to "develop new audiences of all ages and to improve the quality of secondary school instruction in dramatic literature by making live professional theater productions an integral part of high school curricula."

The Endowment then funded an Academy of American Poets program in which established poets gave readings for teachers to stimulate their interest in poetry and in which younger, lesser-known poets read and discussed their poetry in high school classrooms. By the 1967–68 school year, these programs had reached cities in Arizona, California, Illinois, Minnesota, and New Mexico.

The Artists-in-Schools Program (AIS) was established in 1969 through a transfer of $100,000 from USOE to the Arts Endowment. It placed visual artists in residence in six school districts throughout the country. The project was administered by the Central Midwestern Regional Educational Laboratories (CEMREL).

An additional $900,000 was later transferred by USOE to the Endowment to expand the program to other states and to include the disciplines of dance, music, and theater. In 1971, USOE funds were replaced by $750,000 in Endowment funding, and by 1979 this amount was increased to $4.86 million. By the 1973–74 school year, AIS programs had been initiated in all fifty states and two of the six special jurisdictions.

In 1980, the program, renamed the Artists in Education Program, was expanded to provide for artist residencies in educational settings beyond schools and school systems. A Special Projects category was established to support projects to "demonstrate and further the knowledge of the value of the arts and artists in the education process."

In 1986, after extensive field consultation, research, and consideration by the National Council on the Arts, and with the encouragement of Congress during the Endowment's 1985 reauthorization, the program was refocused to encourage states and localities to make the arts a basic and sequential component of the school curriculum, from kindergarten through high school, while continuing support for artist residencies. The program was renamed the Arts in Education Program (AIE).

The Fiscal Year 1988 AIE program budget is $5.5 million for three funding categories:

1. State Arts in Education Grants (SAEG) ($3.4 million) are awarded to state arts agencies to support the placement of practicing artists of professional excellence in a wide variety of educational settings. Funds may also be used to support projects which make the arts a more basic and sequential part of education, including teacher in-service workshops, advocacy efforts, institutional collaborations, and development of sequential arts curricula.

   In the 1986–87 school year, the Arts in Education Program funded 7,851 artists in residence in 11,187 sites in all fifty states and five special jurisdictions, reaching 3.5 million students and more than 116,000 teachers. Despite these efforts, it is estimated that artist residencies reach only approximately 10 percent of schools and are not for the most part integrated with curriculum instruction. But they have given many young people a chance to meet "real live" professional artists who can convey to them a sense of the creative process and give them a rare contact with original art. As several state arts agency representatives have pointed out, residencies have been a "foot in the door" for development of school support for regular instruction in the arts.

An artist residency program can have multiple effects. For example, in Fiscal Year 1986, the Endowment provided $163,900 to the Ohio Arts Council to support its artist residency program for the 1986–87 school year; the state matched this sum with $850,900. The program involved 127 artists, 51,355 students and other participants, and 1,688 teachers and administrators at 107 sites. Residencies were both long-term (five to twelve months) and short-term (two to three weeks). These residencies involved teachers and school administrators in in-service workshops. The Ohio program also has a Special Projects component to assist collaborations among schools and universities, museums, and community arts organizations. It funds twelve fellowships for arts teachers to pursue summer projects that enhance their artistic development.

2. Arts in Schools Basic Education Grants (AISBEG) ($1 million) are awarded to state arts agencies on a competitive basis. These grants encourage their collaboration with state and local education agencies in planning and developing a practical commitment to make the arts a basic and sequential part of education K–12. The AISBEG grants include a first phase of planning grants (up to $50,000 a year for two to three years) to assist in making the arts education planning (developed with the help of the planning grants) operational.

Sixteen of the forty-two states which applied in Fiscal Year 1987 received planning grants, and eight more are being funded in Fiscal Year 1988. Many of the Fiscal Year 1987 applicants that did not receive Endowment grants nevertheless proceeded with statewide planning in arts education. We expect more states to participate in this category in coming years.

The Maine State Commission on the Arts used its Fiscal Year 1987 grant to assist planning for the development in Maine of high-quality, comprehensive, and sequential arts education programs using the state's arts resources. Working with the state education agency and the Maine Alliance for Arts Education, the commission is identifying model arts education programs and disseminating information about them to school administrators and teachers. It is also seeking funding and other resources to help schools and cultural organizations meet recently enacted state curriculum requirements making the arts both a high school graduation requirement and part of the basic course of study at the elementary level.

The Endowment's AISBEG planning support of $20,000 was matched with $63,000 in cash. To put its long-range plan into practice, the Maine Arts Commission is eligible in Fiscal Year 1988 for an implementation grant of up to $150,000 for three years.

3. *Special Projects Grants* ($1.1 million) are available to a wide variety of not-for-profit organizations such as educational institutions, arts institutions, and local arts agencies. They support projects which advance arts teaching as a basic part of education K–12 and provide for Endowment leadership initiatives. Twenty-eight Special Projects grants in Fiscal Year 1987 were awarded for activities such as curriculum and teaching guide development and for teacher education.

In Fiscal Year 1987, this category also funded a joint initiative with the U.S. Department of Education to establish an Arts Education Research Center and a Center for the Learning and Teaching of Literature. First-year funding in a three-year plan is $807,000 for the Arts Education Center and $500,000 for the Literature Center. The centers will undertake research and disseminate information and analysis concerning specific elements which should be part of the learning, teaching, and assessment of arts and literature education. They will work closely with the newly established Elementary Subjects Center, also funded by the U.S. Department of Education. The information developed by the centers will be made available to school districts and schools, universities, arts organizations, and parent and professional organizations.

Discipline Programs

Although the Arts Endowment has funded arts education initiatives largely through the Arts in Education Program, the educational activities of arts organizations are also eligible for support from the Endowment's discipline programs. The extent of funding has been determined by individual program priorities and by the quality of applications received. The following examples represent the kind of work funded.

Through its Media Arts Program, the Endowment has entered into an agreement with the J. Paul Getty Trust's Center for Education in the Arts to produce a television series on the arts for young people aged eight to ten for home viewing, with instructional materials for use in schools. Pilot programs are now being produced and tested. A decision is expected in 1988 about proceeding with a full series. The Endowment has invested approximately $1.9 million to date on this effort, with funding coming primarily from the Media Arts Program.

The Folk Arts Program has funded projects to educate students about America's multiethnic traditions. The Expansion Arts Program has funded organizations such as Urban Gateways, which trains professional artists in all disciplines to work in schools in the eight-county metropolitan area of Chicago, and Concerned Musicians of Houston, which sponsors a "Jazz and Poetry" series in the public schools.

The Museum Program, under the Utilization of Museum Resources category, has funded a variety of educational projects. Examples are the Fiscal Year 1986 grant, in cooperation with the J. Paul Getty Trust Grant Program, to the Denver Art Museum to develop new labels, printed material, and audiovisual instructions for students, and a Fiscal Year 1987 grant to the International Center for Photography to compile a primer on photography for students aged eight to fifteen. In addition, many visual artists' organizations supported by the Endowment have outreach programs in neighborhood schools.

The Design Arts Program has supported a number of arts education projects including a kit compiled by the Boston Children's Museum to teach graphic design to young people, a Pittsburgh Architects Workshop to produce a workbook on design for high school students, and a project in Oakland, California, to teach elementary pupils about urban planning.

The Inter-Arts Program supports a number of presenting organizations involved in education such as the Los Angeles Music Center and the Clearwater, Florida, Performing Arts Center and Theater, as well as two festivals specifically aimed at children in Philadelphia and Pittsburgh. The Dance Program supports dance companies, many of which have outreach programs in schools or mount special children's performances.

The Opera-Musical Theater Program supports companies like Opera/Omaha and the Midwest Opera Theatre and School in St. Paul, Minnesota, which take touring productions to the schools. It also helps the Michigan Opera Theatre-in-Residence program, which offers communities a full week of in-school performances, lecture demonstrations, master classes, and workshops.

According to the American Symphony Orchestra League, 79 percent of America's orchestras, many of which are supported through the Music Program, spend an estimated 11 percent of their budgets for young people's concerts, reaching an estimated 10 million students annually An unusual example is the work of Strings for Schools, an arts organization which reaches some 62,000 children in rural southeastern Pennsylvania with chamber music concerts accompanied by commentary and slides. Affiliate Artists, Inc., based in New York, also receives Endowment funding to support its artist-residency program. Affiliate Artists brings singers and instrumentalists who are in the early stages of their careers into schools.

Regional theaters supported by the Theater Program often stage special performances for school groups, and many also provide special instructional materials to enhance the experience. Perhaps the most acclaimed student performance series are the "Discovery" program of the Trinity Repertory Theater in Providence, Rhode Island, and the New York Shakespeare

Festival's "Shakespeare on Broadway," which stages Shakespeare presentations for schools in a rented Broadway theater.

Media Art Centers supported by the Media Arts Program have also brought outreach programs to schools in their vicinities. Multimedia, Inc., brings Chicago school children to its center for film viewings and discussion, and Film in the Cities, which has a similar program in Minneapolis–St. Paul, is currently developing a K–12 media arts curriculum.

The Literature Program has made awards to such notable writers' organizations as the Teachers and Writers Collaborative, which sends poets to public school classrooms all over New York City. It has also helped fund the Collaborative's *Whole World Catalogue,* a handbook for teachers of creative writing, which has been used since 1977 as a major national resource for writing teachers.

The Challenge Program

Since 1977 the Arts Endowment's Challenge Program has awarded more than $193 million in three-to-one "matching" grants to outstanding American institutions. Some of these have an educational focus. For example, a 1987 award of $150,000 will be used to establish an endowment fund for New York's Studio in a School, a unique visual arts program which enlists students, parents, and teachers to work in public elementary schools that have no formal arts programs. Earlier grants have included $100,000 to Boston's Cultural Education Collaborative, $200,000 to Young Audiences, Inc., and a major award of $650,000 to the Exploratorium in San Francisco.

In 1987, the Endowment created a new Challenge Program, Challenge III. One of its four components is to foster arts appreciation. The first awards under the new guidelines will be announced in October 1988. The specific targeting of appreciation projects—those seeking to develop "deeper and broader education in and appreciation of the arts"—creates a significant new opportunity for Endowment support of arts education. The program is open to a wide range of educational institutions, systems, or consortia, as well as arts organizations. Grants will range from $50,000 to $1 million and must be matched three to one. To serve the needs of organizations which are not yet competitive at Challenge Program levels, the Endowment's Advancement Program will also be opened to arts education for the first time in Fiscal Year 1990.

Evaluation of Endowment Efforts

Concern for arts education has always existed at the Arts Endowment, and the Endowment's efforts have been helpful in placing artists in schools and stimulating outreach on the part of arts institutions. But Endowment-supported projects relating to arts education were primarily conceived as helping artists and arts institutions rather than educating K–12 students. Until recently, they had not addressed the central issues involved in making the arts a basic and sequential part of the K–12 curriculum.

In 1978, the National Council on the Arts published a report on Endowment efforts in arts education. The general conclusion was that outside of AIE-funded artist residencies, the Endowment's efforts in education should be confined to assisting professional training in those fields where this was considered a priority.

But the Endowment's 1982 survey of its public participation in the arts caused this conclusion to be reappraised. According to this study, 61 percent of American adults had not in the preceding twelve months attended a single live performance of jazz or classical music, opera or musical theater, or ballet, nor visited a museum or gallery. The inference from this 1982 study was that the artistic efforts supported by the Endowment were not benefiting the majority of Americans. This led the Endowment to reevaluate its position on arts education and begin to consider activities which could over time make the artistic activities which it supported more a part of the lives of all Americans.

The initial efforts in this direction included consultation with representatives of the arts and education sectors across the country. On the basis of that consultation, a new AIE program was developed. While many of the state arts agencies which had been beneficiaries of Endowment funding of artist residencies were initially skeptical, the new program quickly became popular with the vast majority of states. For the first time, the Arts Endowment was able to enlist support from many elements in the education sector, particularly the associations which represent arts teachers.

The thrust of the new program is, first, to encourage collaboration among state and local arts and education organizations and agencies in making arts education integral to the school curriculum and, second, to make the case to the governance and education sectors that basic and sequential arts education K–12 is not only in their interest but, most important, in the interest of the students and the nation.

This evolution of Endowment thinking, which began in 1983, was joined in 1984–85 by congressional concern for arts education. A hearing on the subject was held by the full Committee on Education and Labor in February 1984, and arts education was an important part of the Endowment's reauthorization hearings in 1985. The result of this congressional concern was twofold: the inclusion by Congress in the Endowment's basic purpose of a special provision regarding arts education in schools, and the congressional request for this report.

Although arts education is now receiving increased attention from the Endowment, it remains true that the Arts Endowment spends less time and money, as a proportion of its overall activities, on arts education than do its counterpart agencies, the National Endowment for the Humanities and the National Science Foundation, on K–12 humanities and science education. Only 3.3 percent of Arts Endowment funding is currently budgeted for support of education programs, compared with 12.8 percent of Humanities Endowment funding for humanities education and just over 5 percent of National Science Foundation funding for science education.

These differences derive from the fact that the Arts Endowment has traditionally focused on professional arts creation, production, presentation, exhibition, and preservation, rather than education. The Humanities Endowment and the National Science Foundation have, on the other hand, from their beginnings considered education as one of their principal priorities. These differences may stem in part from the perception that education in the humanities and sciences is necessary to understand, appreciate, and use them, while the "serious" arts, like entertainment, can be experienced without knowing anything about them.

Similarly, in the schools themselves, arts education has been primarily production and performance oriented. The emphasis has been on providing it to talented students rather than all students, on the implicit assumption that the general student can appreciate the arts simply by experiencing them. Education in the humanities and sciences, on the other hand, has always been considered necessary.

The very limited U.S. Department of Education funds for assisting development of the content of arts education have been devoted primarily to performance and production through support of such activities as the Kennedy Center's education programs. It should be noted, however, that when William Bennett became secretary of education, the department's focus on the arts as a part of education changed. The department now considers the arts to be a basic part of education, and it has joined the Arts Endowment in funding through the Office of Educational Research and Improvement a variety of efforts to assist the process of making them so.

In sum, the Arts Endowment from its beginnings in the 1960s has through both its Arts in Education and discipline programs funded a number of projects to provide arts resources for schools. But not until very recently has it attempted to change the attitudes of the schools and the general public toward the arts as educational essentials.

The Endowment's new efforts build on its earlier programs, but now seek, first, to change basic attitudes about the arts in education and, second, to provide information and models for the schools to use in moving forward with arts education as a basic and sequential part of the K–12 curriculum. While the Arts Endowment's traditional efforts on behalf of arts education were useful, they were also limited and did not address the basic difficulties confronting arts education in schools. The new Endowment efforts do address these difficulties, but their potential for effectively addressing them remains to be seen.

It is the conclusion of this report that Endowment resources for arts education, both staff and money, need to be enhanced and continued over a period of at least ten years in order to gain a true sense of the effectiveness of this basic endeavor. The results of the Arts in Education Program's encouragement of collaboration, planning, and implementation of model programs in schools can be assessed only after a generation of students have benefited from them. Even if a particular school district were to implement Endowment-funded state and local planning with a series of curricular programs in 1989, it would be thirteen years before the first student passed through all the grades containing those programs.

It is therefore this report's general recommendation that the current direction of the Arts in Education Program be continued and strengthened over the next decade, and that in preparation for reauthorization in the mid-1990s a second arts education report to the Congress be prepared. On this basis, the President and the Congress could evaluate progress.

The National Endowment for the Arts has an important and timely opportunity to influence the course of arts education. While it is not an education agency, the Endowment should pursue current initiatives and, to some degree, operate in the arts education area as do the National Endowment for the Humanities and the National Science Foundation in humanities and science education. Such a role would not necessarily require substantial additional funds for the Arts in Education Program, but it would require changing the way in which the Endowment functions vis-à-vis the other sectors of arts education.

It should be remembered that the National Endowment for the Arts is not an education agency and that decisions on learning goals, curricula, resources, and testing and evaluation are, and should be, ultimately made at the state and school-district levels. Nonetheless, the Endowment believes that it can and should exercise a leadership role in encouraging, in collaboration with state and local arts agencies and state and local education authorities, a more basic and sequential approach to arts education.

It cannot be stressed too much that reform in arts education must be undertaken on a long-term basis and measured in decades, not years. We know at this stage of no school district in the country that has included the arts in the curriculum systematically, comprehensively, and sequentially from kindergarten through twelfth grade. The task of restructuring and reforming arts education is therefore more difficult than for subjects traditionally included in the core curriculum.

Recommendations

The National Endowment for the Arts, which is to arts education what the National Science Foundation is to science education, should (1) make the case for arts education, (2) facilitate collaboration among the four sectors concerned with arts education (governance, education, arts, business-producer) to make it a basic and sequential part of school instruction, and (3) assist development and distribution of curricular, instructional, and assessment models for the benefit of state and local education authorities. To this end:

a. The policies and resources (staff and money) of the Endowment for arts education should be continued and strengthened over a period of at least ten years in order to allow implementation of present policies and of the recommendations in this report to bear fruit. The Fiscal Year 1989 budget request for the Endowment's Arts in Education Program provides for such strengthening in that year.

b. The Endowment should provide the president and the Congress a report on progress in arts education in preparation for the Endowment's reauthorization in the mid-1990s (the reauthorization which follows anticipated reauthorization in 1990).

c. The Endowment should advocate the development of higher standards for state and local arts curriculum guides, courses, and curriculum materials. It should provide limited funding to assist state/local curriculum development. It should, in cooperation with the U.S. Department of Education, convene a meeting of experts to review curricular materials (including the work on curricula of the new national research centers on the arts, literature, and elementary subjects) with a view to making recommendations on arts curricula and on school programs to implement them.

d. The Endowment should work with the U.S. Department of Education to develop a plan for the inclusion of each of the arts in the National Assessment of Educational Progress. The plan should include analysis of whether arts education might best be assessed by (i) separate assessments for each of the individual arts, (ii) a general arts assessment, (iii) integrating arts assessments with other subject area assessments, or (iv) a combination of these.

e. The Endowment should provide limited funding to assist state-level development of model assessment plans, programs, and procedures, both with respect to programs and student testing.

f. The Endowment should encourage (i) state education agencies and arts education associations to recruit highly qualified arts teachers; (ii) state certifying agencies to raise standards for teacher certification and teacher preparation programs accreditation; and (iii) school boards to hire qualified arts teachers. The Endowment should encourage the arts sector to lend support to these efforts.

g. The Endowment should continue to identify areas in which there is a need for systematic and regular collection of baseline survey data on arts education, and it should disseminate the results of its studies and data to the arts education communities and the public. The Endowment should also provide limited funding to assist efforts to translate research into classroom practice.

h. The Endowment should appoint an ongoing Advisory Board (with representatives of the governance, education, arts, and business-producer sectors) whose purpose would be to institute a national dialogue on: (i) what students, at a minimum, should know of and about the arts when they graduate from high school, (ii) how required course units might be structured to include teaching of these minimum requirements, and (iii) what evaluation mechanisms might be appropriate and effective to assess whether students have actually mastered such materials and skills.

The Advisory Board should specifically advise the Endowment on: (i) activities and efforts which it could undertake to ensure that the recommendations in this report are addressed by the appropriate parties, (ii) development (with appropriate agencies and associations) of proposals for a master plan for arts assessment as part of the National Assessment of Education Progress, (iii) development of a plan by which exemplary school and district arts programs might be identified, recognized, and rewarded (e.g., exemplary schools, programs, and teachers); and (iv) the report to the president and Congress suggested for the Endowment's mid-1990s reauthorization.

i. The Endowment should provide a national model for the kind of collaboration necessary to make progress in arts education. The model should in particular include the U.S. Department of Education, the National Endowment for the Humanities, and the national associations that can influence arts education. The Endowment should assist states, localities, and the arts education community generally to develop a clearer vision of what arts education in the United States can and should be.

Appendix A: National Endowment for the Humanities

The National Endowment for the Humanities (NEH) spends a considerably larger portion of its budget on programs to improve elementary and secondary humanities education than the Arts Endowment does with respect to arts education. In Fiscal Year 1988 NEH expects to spend a total of about $17.9 million (or 12.8 percent of its total budget) in support of humanities education in the schools. This support comes from three of NEH's funding divisions: the Division of Education Programs, the Division of Fellowships and Seminars, and the Division of State Programs.

In Fiscal Year 1988, the Division of Education Programs estimates obligations of $8.5 million to elementary and secondary education—$8 million for grants to support summer institutes, academic-year masterworks study, conferences, workshops, and related activities, and an additional $500,000 for a national history center to conduct research on effective approaches to the teaching of history in the schools. In the Division of Fellowships and Seminars, a total of $3.9 million has been allocated—$3.7 million for summer seminars for school teachers, and approximately $200,000 in grant support for high school students to conduct research and writing projects in the humanities. In the Division of State Programs, which provides support to state humanities councils in the fifty states and Puerto Rico and the Virgin Islands, NEH estimates that about $5.1 million will be devoted to seminars and institutes for teachers and school administrators and to other educational programs at the elementary and secondary levels.

Many of NEH's other programs also have an impact on humanities education at the precollegiate level. The Division of Research Programs, for example, funds basic research in the humanities disciplines, much of which will ultimately benefit teachers and students in elementary and secondary schools. And the Division of General Programs provides support to museums, libraries, and television and radio stations for interpretive humanities programming for audiences of all ages.

Appendix B: National Science Foundation

The National Science Foundation (NSF) also spends more of its budget on science education than the Arts Endowment does on arts education. This conforms with NSF's enabling legislation of 1950 which authorizes and directs the Foundation "to initiate and support . . . science education programs at all levels in the mathematical, physical, medical, biological, social, and other sciences . . . and engineering education programs at all levels in the various fields of engineering."

NSF began research and education programming in Fiscal Year 1952 with $1.54 million of a total budget of $3.47 million. None of these funds, however, were dedicated to elementary or high school education. In Fiscal Year 1957, nonetheless, the appropriation for precollege education jumped to $10.2 million from $850,000, accounting for over a quarter of the agency's budget. NSF's Fiscal Year 1988 budget provides $89.6 million (or 5.2 percent) for precollege science education, including $45.2 million for precollege teacher preparation and enhancement; $37.5 million for material development, research, and informal science education; $3.7 million for the "young scholars" program; and $3.2 million for studies and program assessment.

The Foundation's programs cover every educational level from kindergarten through postdoctoral studies. NSF's support of programs for students is usually indirect. Fellowship and research grants, however, go directly to graduate students. Programs for teachers and faculty members are both direct and indirect. The Foundation has not supported education facilities but has supported and does support research facilities.

Direct teacher programs supported by NSF include summer or academic-year institutes (designed to upgrade disciplinary knowledge and improve instructional effectiveness), fellowships or scholarships to support individual advanced study, projects to create new curricula for the preparation of school science and mathematics teachers, and support for the establishment and initial operation of teacher networks.

Indirect support to improve science and math instruction has included projects to improve elementary school, middle school, high school, and college science and mathematics curricula; projects to create new high school and college science and mathematics courses; programs to develop new instructional methods, materials, and apparatus; support of science museums, radio and television programming, and other methods for accomplishing informal science and mathematics education; support for research on the processes of teaching and learning; and projects to gather longitudinal information on a variety of education-related topics including demographics and student achievement.

NSF targets specific student populations in undertaking these programs: those who are likely to enter one of the fields of mathematics, engineering, or science, those who are likely to enter other technical areas (such as the health sciences) where they will make significant but limited use of math, engineering, or science; and those who will associate with science as citizens, not vocationally or professionally. The Foundation tries to give appropriate attention to all these students, but historically its support for future scientists, mathematicians, and engineers has been the most consistent.

Appendix C: U.S. Department of Education

Because the entire budget of the Department of Education is devoted to education activities, it is difficult to draw precise conclusions by contrasting Department of Education funds spent on education-related activities with Endowment funds spent for arts education.

It is useful to note, however, that the department has directed a considerable portion of its resources to the support of education at the elementary and secondary levels, the same K–12 years that are the focus of the Arts Endowment's activities in arts education, and that the department has provided high levels of support to improve teaching, increase literacy, and improve education in specific areas such as science and education. It also has provided significant support for the collection of data on the condition of education in the United States. These areas—the improvement of kindergarten through twelfth-grade education, the strengthening of teaching, the enhancement of curricula in special subjects, and the support of research—are as important in arts education as they are in education as a whole.

In Fiscal Year 1987, the department devoted 43 percent of its $19.3 billion budget to programs that support elementary and secondary education. The largest portion of this is the approximately $6.8 billion provided through programs which serve students with special needs. These children include the economically disadvantaged, children of limited English proficiency, Indian children, children who live in families that migrate, handicapped children, and neglected and delinquent children.

The department allocates approximately $741 million of its budget to support several programs geared toward improving excellence in education. These include the Chapter 2 Block Grants to states, teacher training, improvement, and fellowship programs, literacy training, and funding to improve science and mathematics education.

The Department of Education recognizes the importance of arts education through a discretionary program within the Chapter 2 Block Grant for arts in education. In Fiscal Year 1987, $3.3 million was devoted to support two activities for Arts in Education Programs: (1) the Kennedy Center's education programs, which support a national network of state arts organizations and provide support for Kennedy Center Programs for Children and Youth and the American College Theatre Festival, both of which promote the expansion of opportunities for children and youth to participate in the arts; and (2) Very Special Arts, which develops programs that integrate the arts into the general education of disabled children and the lives of disabled adults.

In Fiscal Year 1987, $63.6 million was allocated to the Office of Educational Research and Improvement to collect data, conduct research, and disseminate information on the condition of education in the United States. While these funds are not exclusively used for elementary and secondary education, they play an important role because support for research and information is one of the principal ways the department assists in improving educational performance.

15

The NEA: Looking Back and Looking Ahead

Samuel Lipman

As we look forward to the 1990s and to the prospect of a new administration in Washington, the time seems ripe to attempt some consideration of just where matters stand in the public world of the American arts and some consideration as well of the role the National Endowment for the Arts has played—or has failed to play—in the complex filiation that always obtains between our recent past and our present.

Let me begin with some thoughts on how things looked some years ago, although not *in toto,* for to sketch the entire picture of the arts in America at any given time would require a very large book rather than a mere article. Two issues in particular seem worth focusing on: our working description of arts activity and the arts, and our working description of arts education.

The best place to start is with arts activity and the arts. By the early 1980s, the arts in America had reached a pinnacle of expansion and development unprecedented in our history. There is no need to cite statistics. It is enough to say that the operative word was *more*—more museums, more ballet companies, more modern-dance companies, more theater companies, more creative writing, more poetry, more symphony orchestras, more opera companies, more chamber music ensembles, more avant-garde groups, more exhibitions, more performances, more artists, more audiences, more patrons, more administrators, more press, more arts-conscious politicians. Everywhere—more, more, more.

With more, of course, went bigger. Bigger groups, bigger companies, bigger institutions, bigger staffs, bigger earned income, bigger budgets, bigger subsidies, bigger commitments, and, of course, bigger deficits. Perhaps the crowning confirmation of all this bigness was the happy news from the Census Bureau that in 1980 our artists, taken together as a class, amounted to at least one million souls, all struggling to create what at least some people some of the time might be open-minded enough to call art.

Much of this emphasis on more and bigger came from factors powerful in our history for many years and in some cases going back to the founding of the Republic. We Americans have always been a people with continental ambitions, and our goals in the arts have been little different in form from our goals in agriculture and industry. To feed a continent, to industrialize a continent, and, lest we forget, to school a continent—all this has required monumental labors to guarantee the production of monumental results. The American urge to provide culture was already evident in the nineteenth century in the very different successes of Ralph Waldo Emerson and Walt Whitman, of Jenny Lind and the Metropolitan Opera, of the Metropolitan Museum and the *Little Blue Books* of the Kansan E. Haldeman Julius. We have often seemed to have a hard time separating quality from quantity; indeed, when faced with a choice between the two, it has been our national bent, and often our national virtue, to choose quantity.

Clearly, quantity in itself is not the whole story of our artistic development. In literature, for example, we have had a powerful national art since the days of Washington Irving. In the visual arts of the past century we have nothing to be ashamed of and much of which to be proud; modern American painting is admired the world over and, *mirabile dictu,* even here at home. Our twentieth-century dance, helped along in the early years by the likes of Ruth St. Denis, Martha Graham, and Agnes de Mille—and, of course, by the immigrant George Balanchine—is properly our joy.

In the field of music, the situation has been a good bit more complicated, for here we have had to contend at one and the same time with the great achievement of the eighteenth and nineteenth centuries in Europe and with the contemporary European failure to inspire us by extending its own triumphant creations into the present. Our own disappointment in musical composition is perhaps no more than the local manifestation of a condition to be found throughout the Western world; even in this case, however, we happily possess many composers of the past fifty years and more who have written beautiful and enduring music. Of our orchestras, there is little that needs to be said: for the whole of this century, they have been universally accepted as the standard of the world; our choruses, too, like our singers and instrumentalists, have won worldwide recognition.

All in all, the great expansion in American artistic life that took place from the Great Depression to the end of the 1950s, aided by the great post–World War II expansion of college education, strikes me as a remarkable democratic achievement. By the 1960s, however, much had begun to change. Commercial television, so beguiling and full of hope when it transmitted shows like *Omnibus* in the fifties, quickly showed that sit-com characters and late-night talk-show hosts were to be the new cultural celebrities of our time; by the 1970s, educational television, once thought of as a university of the air, had become what it is today, an upscale vendor of semicultivated pabulum for the prosperous. Such general publications of intellectual quality as still existed began increasingly to devote themselves to discussions of politics and "life-styles"; the new trend in periodical journalism toward single-subject magazines guaranteed that the reader's prior educational achievement would become an ever less important requirement for his comprehension. In the media as a whole, the inflation of publicity and glamour had begun to make the arts in America into another branch of Broadway and Hollywood. Led by the sexual revolution of the 1960s, the cry of pleasure was everywhere in the air, and the forces of seriousness and reflection were in full flight. The consequence of these societywide developments was a gathering tendency to see the arts as entertainment and artists as entertainers, lavishly paid to sing for their suppers.

As the 1980s succeeded the 1970s, and in particular as the quasi-populist administration of Jimmy Carter came to its end, these developments in art and culture seemed to impinge with particular force on the National Endowment for the Arts, charged as it was with dissolving all our long-accumulated guilt about being the only country in the civilized world without a tradition of direct governmental support for culture. By the end of the seventies, this agency had been so successful at accomplishing its mission that it seemed to many as if all of America's artistic excellence could be laid at its door. All the activity and all the art, all the employment for artists and all the enjoyment for audiences, all the momentum of artistic civilization in this country—everything seemed to depend for its existence and continuation on the work of a federal agency delivering rather less than $150 million each year in subsidies doled out to thousands and thousands of grant applicants.

Such was not the case then and is not the case now; the NEA makes up only a small part of the funding for the arts in this country. It seems to me that the credit for the propagation of this myth of the NEA's necessary centrality belongs not to artists but to politicians who have manipulated the electronic media and the press.

It is now history that the Reagan administration walked into this situation with scarcely a thought in its collective head. At David Stockman's Office of Management and Budget the determining word in arts and humanities matters was *cut:* cut not to improve, cut not to alter in any thought-out way the endowments' policies, cut not simply to save money, but cut to destroy. This is not the place to go through the long and tedious arguments for and against government support of the arts and the humanities. My confidence in the intellectual probity of all the participants in the debate would be greater if the pro–government-support arguments came more often from those who wish to give their own money to the arts, and if the anti–government-support arguments came more often from those who believe that the arts and humanities require support—of any kind whatsoever.

In the end, of course, the president, aided by a blue-ribbon task force that gave federal art subsidies a clean bill of health, was able to reach agreement with a Congress strongly sympathetic to such support. The NEA budget was cut by only a small amount, and Frank Hodsoll, a career government official well placed in the administration and sympathetic to the idea of arts subsidies, was appointed the agency's chairman.

What was so unfortunate about all the ruckus over abolishing the endowments was that it tended to obscure the very real problems in the fields they served. We must never forget that in our society, government reflects what is going on in the country at large. At the NEA our systemic, debased idea of the marketability of art as entertainment affected the discussion of public policy in a thousand ways, large and small, gross and subtle.

Perhaps a personal recollection will be of some use here in describing just how far this putatively artistic gospel of consumer satisfaction had gone by the early 1980s. In one of the first meetings of the National Council I attended, I interrupted the usual discussion about the poverty-stricken state of American orchestras to ask why some of our great ensembles were paying (with NEA support) second-rank celebrity conductors hundreds of thousands of dollars for rather less than a half-year's work. In answer, I was told by an NEA staff member that the employment of such stars was the only way audiences could be inveigled into coming to hear the music.

As it was in music, so it was in the other arts. Institutions were measured by their turnstile count; museum exhibitions were evaluated in terms of drawing power (with the word *drawing* referring not to draughtsmanship but to box office); even the various avant-gardes, once thought to be hermetic, were praised as the coming inheritors of the salable mainstream. Administrators were praised, and large challenge grants awarded, on the basis of a continuing record of budget increases. Agency grants were continually described to the Council by staff members in terms of the "impact" they would have on the artistic field in question or even on the cause of the arts as a whole; it was proudly proclaimed that the major purpose of bringing interns from all over the country to Washington to work at the agency was to spread knowledge of the Endowment and enlarge its reputation. A major concern of the agency two years before the celebration of its twentieth anniversary in 1985 was how to arrange a prime-time television spectacular using the entertainment services of stars from the world of commercial culture to salute the Endowment. Everywhere the goal was to expand and enhance the arts' image as a bringer of pleasure. Everywhere the enemy was the dull image of the status quo. An artistic task well and repeatedly done was invariably seen as evidence that the responsible institution was in a rut—and whatever might be said in favor of old ruts, they certainly weren't as sexy as new waves.

It is not too difficult to see that turning art into amusement is an integral part of what the English poet and critic C. H. Sisson has called "the conversion of religion as well as political events, the 'arts,' and all particular knowledge to the purposes of a power-ridden entertainment world." But beyond the redefinition of the idea of art, this trivialization-through-expansion had a devastating effect on what had once been seen as a civilized glory: I refer here to the calamitous drop in the level of general arts education in America during the 1960s and the 1970s. Under the influence of the doctrine that to feel good is to be good, a two-tier system of the arts was established: professional glamour merchandised to the adult millions on the one hand, and the encouragement of the most aimless self-gratification by children on the other. The monument to the triumph of artistic glamour is, of course, public television, with its incongruous mating of movie stars serving as hosts to the hackneyed tragedies of the operatic stage.

The monument to the destruction of the idea of serious general arts education was *Coming to Our Senses,* the 1977 Arts, Education and Americans Panel Report which summed up where general arts education stood after the triumph of progressive education.[1] For *Coming to Our Senses,* the arts—or rather the cultivation of the senses—were seen as a necessary counterweight to reason, or the life of the mind. This whole approach was well put in a quotation from *Synaesthetic Education,* a 1971 book by Michael F. Andrews which *Coming to Our Senses* placed in a position reserved for approved insights:

> To most persons majoring in Art Education, the term is interpreted to mean a preparation for becoming a teacher who is to train individuals from the observation of nature and the ability to record accurately the socially agreed upon symbolic conventions and facts by a process of drawing and painting.... The term Art Education in this sense then, merely confuses the issue, which is not to teach teachers to teach the making of artists; but to free the individual so that he may discover his inner-self and nurture his individual ability to search for, find and apply truths in relation to himself.

Of course, there was nothing in *Coming to Our Senses* about general arts education having as its goal the training of young people in the skills and content of great civilization. The definition of art this 1977 report recommended was, at bottom, to be student-determined: "Existing standardized materials [should] be reevaluated constantly in order to meet the needs of particular student populations. Materials should be changed or amplified if they do not illuminate the students' life experiences or if they condition students to a narrow definition of acceptable forms of art." At the Endowment, this new approach to arts education was expressed by a policy of supporting not *art* in education but *artists* in education. There were plausible reasons for this policy: school performances given by artists rather than school classes given by teachers nicely avoided conflict with school bureaucracies for control of funds and curriculum, and the provision of performances in schools seemed a massive and welcome employment opportunity for unemployed artists.

Unfortunately, by the time I came to the Endowment in the early 1980s, the deleterious consequences of this policy, which in so many cases resulted in entertainment rather than teaching, were clear. Little arts education of any substantive kind was going on; teachers were sullen and hostile toward what was perceived as an unwanted invasion by artists; and the very idea of arts education, just because it was seen to depend upon the casual and irregular appearances of outsiders, increasingly seemed irrelevant, frivolous, and totally dispensable.

The time was ripe for a change in educational policy. Under Frank Hodsoll's energetic and patient leadership, several changes were made. The name of the program itself, which had been "Artists in Education," was changed to "Arts in Education." On the level of the allocation of funds, an attempt was made to change what was essentially an artist residency program into one which also allowed for the support of basic education. Furthermore, a strong attempt was made to bring arts teachers, and their representatives, back into Endowment planning, from which they had previously (and with good reason) felt excluded.

Public evidence of what had taken place at the Endowment has now been provided by yet another report, but this time (at least in my opinion) an excellent one. I have in mind *Toward Civilization*, which was prepared by the NEA over a period of about two years and submitted to Congress last May [1988]. This report documented the unhappy state of arts education in this country and made substantive suggestions for its amelioration. What seems to me special about this report—so well conveyed by its title—is that it takes a position on just what basic arts education is. Here are the report's opening words:

> Basic arts education aims to provide *all* students, not only the gifted and talented, with knowledge of, and skills in, the arts. Basic arts education must give students the essence of our civilization, the civilizations which have contributed to ours, and the more distant civilizations which enrich world civilization as a whole. It must also

> give students tools for creating, for communicating, and understanding others' communications, and for making informed and critical choices.

And, a bit later, the report goes on:

> The first purpose of arts education is to give our young people a sense of civilization. American civilization includes many cultures—from Europe, Africa, the Far East, and our own hemisphere. The great works of art of these parent civilizations, and of our own, provide the guideposts to cultural literacy. Knowing them, our young people will be better able to understand, and therefore build on, the achievements of the past; they will also be better able to understand themselves. Great works of art illuminate the constancy of the human condition. . . . Without knowledge of such supreme achievements, we are "culturally illiterate."

If this is to be the wave of the future, then this is one wave we can look forward to. The reader will have noticed that, in devoting myself to developments in NEA arts-education policy, I have not as yet had anything to say about the problem I raised earlier: the conversion of art into entertainment. If in arts education I am proud of what has been accomplished at the NEA and moderately optimistic about the effect of its new policy, in the rather more difficult area of our fidelity to the very idea of the arts we serve I am unhappy with the role the Endowment has played in recent years, and I am in no way sanguine about the future.

To illustrate the present situation, allow me to cite a letter I recently received from a person deeply committed to the field of choral music. Here is my paraphrase of what he wrote: For many among us, choral performance is especially valuable because, combining as it does significant literature with affecting music, it speaks directly to an audience. It is often an irrational concern of ours that we are unable to secure a public for chorus of an equivalent size to that for operas, ballets, and orchestras. Curiously enough, this sentiment is not restricted to artistic fields which have traditionally enjoyed only small audiences: it is widespread throughout the arts today. Yet there is no reason to think that the primary blame for the current direction of the arts in America rests with the people who share these sentiments. As I pointed out earlier, we have always thought of collective activities in terms of quantity and size, and in this country perhaps more than abroad, government has a remarkable record of reflecting the wishes of its citizenry. The problems of the arts are not at heart problems for government to solve; even so, the government does have a role: to inform and educate and to provide a desired leadership.

In recent years as well as over its entire history, the National Endowment for the Arts has not adequately served to make clear the present overexpanded and overhyped state of the arts in America. The Endowment has not sufficiently encouraged—and explained the reasons for encouraging—either public or private arts funding based on artistic commitment, taste, and knowledge. Too often the Endowment has accepted the mere existence of funding, both public and private, as a good in itself, without asking the reasons behind this funding and its effect on the education of the public. Too often the Endowment has treated the arts as a matter of the financial and social prestige of its backers rather than as a common inheritance of all. Too often the Endowment has failed to press the general case that the arts are a vital part of the civilization which binds our people to each other in the present and binds our past to our future. Above all, too often the Endowment has treated success in numbers as the criterion not just for funding but for the pride it takes in accomplishing its mission. The effect of all this has been to shake the confidence of artists, patrons, and the public alike, whose faith in art is vital to everything we do.

The most interesting presentations I have heard at the National Council on the Arts have centered on how marvelously successful organizations have grown and how others might follow in their footsteps. By contrast, the artistic presentations which have been made to the Council have usually been of a very drab and second-rate, show-and-tell nature. The discussions of the Council, a group of intelligent people reasonably representative of artists, arts institutions, and state arts agencies, have all too often focused on success by numbers, as if all that can be talked about in the arts is marketing strategy. State arts agencies are routinely complimented by Council members not for the quality of their grants—or even for the high quality of the activity going on in their jurisdictions—but rather for the year-to-year increases in their budgets; the same criterion of size is used when the discussion turns to local arts agencies. It is significant that when the Council focuses on the one Endowment program in which numbers are very difficult to adduce—the Literature Program, which supports individual writers and poets and small presses—the amount of discussion and interest seems to dwindle to the vanishing point.

There has recently been an important controversy which suggests that this habit of judging art by numbers has now come close to becoming a codified part of the way grants are to be awarded. I have in mind here the policy, proposed by Frank Hodsoll more than a year ago, of determining grant amounts by directly relating an institution's artistic ranking to its budget size. The announced goal of this new policy was to correct various inconsistencies resulting from the present system, whereby institutions of lower artistic ranking and lower budgets from time to time received a greater percentage of their budgets supported by the Endowment than institutions of higher artistic ranking and higher budgets.

The new policy would involve a major change in the functioning of the Endowment's peer panels, the groups of artists and administrators charged with making the primary decisions about grants. Hitherto, panels had based their judgments first upon artistic ranking and then adjusted the resulting grant amounts—on an ad hoc basis—so that questions of scale might be taken into account. According to the new policy, panels were to use the scale of applicants' activities, along with their artistic ranking, as a necessary factor in determining grant amounts. The change in the outcome of this new panel process would be great: if budgets were to be a required factor in determining amounts, larger-budget applicants, in a time of flat Endowment appropriations, would receive increased funding, while smaller-budget applicants would receive less. The signal sent to the world of art would be clear: henceforth, artistic achievement would properly be judged by money, not art.

The battle over the chairman's proposed new policy has raged for many months. The possibility of obtaining a more consistent set of grants seemed, at first, reason enough for many, including me, to support the new process. But as an attempt was made to put the new policy into practice, it became clear that the effect would be to make scale of activity the determining factor and a factor furthermore that would unduly reward large applicants. From various artistic fields came an almost unanimous defense of the present ad hoc process; the chairman, in turn, made a spirited defense of his position that fairness requires the explicit factoring of budget size into grant decisions.

I am happy to say that the National Council on the Arts was drawn into the controversy, and for the first time in my memory there were sustained discussions at the Council which explicitly recognized that big budgets and high levels of activity do not necessarily bring with them art of permanent value. These discussions took an often militant "art first, budgets second" position. At the National Council meeting in St. Louis in May [1988], a compromise between the chairman, intent on changing panel procedure, and the Council, united in opposition to the idea of grant-making by budget size, was arranged. According to this compromise, information about an applicant's budget size would be made available to panels, which they might use to provide consistency in their grant-making; in the absence of such consistency, the panels would have to provide explanations for any anomalies that may thus result.

It is difficult to say where we stand now. The primary importance of the artistic judgments made by peer panels, the very heart of the Endowment's traditional way of making grants, has come under attack. The chairman has been widely accused of wishing to impose some kind of formulaic funding. Furthermore, there have been indications that the Congress, under severe pressure in an election year from the artistic fields, might go so far as to use the upcoming Endowment appropriation bill to prohibit any change in the status quo. Should the Congress ever take this matter into its own hands, a questionable precedent would be established whereby the legislature would determine Endowment guidelines.

Unwisely, the defenders of the present system have seen fit to oppose *any* use of budget data in panel deliberations. Moreover, there has been much extravagant talk, from people who are highly capable of rational decision making, about the need to make grants on the basis of intuitiveness and subjectivity. Equally unwisely, the chairman pushed ahead too fast at the beginning with the imposition of his initiative, without waiting for a consensus to be reached outside Washington. What is more, he did not make clear the implications of his new policy—who would get more money and who would get less.

My own position in this matter is that panels should employ all available data in reaching their decisions; an applicant's budget size should always be taken into consideration, so that the amount of money granted might be in reasonable relation to the quality, activity, and need of the applicant. But just as important, there is no *necessary* correlation between budget size and the artistic needs and aspirations of an artist or of an institution. In awarding grants, it is always vital to be sure that artistic ranking is based on talent and aspiration, not on the advantages money can buy.

So important is all this for the future of the relations between the applicants and the Endowment, and indeed for the future status and working of the Endowment itself, that it behooves us to stand back and look dispassionately at the core of the controversy. This core is our old national problem of the supposed virtue of size. Size of audience, it goes without saying, is closely related to size of budget; within any given artistic field, institutions with larger audiences almost always have larger budgets. More expensive productions draw larger audiences; larger audiences cost more to satisfy (I almost wrote *to entertain*). Artistic ranking itself, properly the primary concern of panels, is often closely related to budget size; bigger budgets, after all, mean more money for artists, more money for productions and exhibitions, more money for administrators to arrange better presentations, more money for development personnel to raise more money for better presentations—and for bigger budgets.

None of this is necessarily wrong. It is all just a fact of life: the race is often to the large as well as to the swift. But to put matters this way is once again to load the discussion in favor of big budgets, big audiences, and the performance of entertainments that allow audiences to grow. Alas, it is no secret that today it is not the biggest and the busiest arts organizations that are under the strongest economic pressure; it is rather the medium-sized institutions, deeply rooted in medium-sized communities, that are beginning to feel the threat of financial failure. A quick glance at our marvelous symphony orchestras of intermediate budget size will show an increasing and unacceptable attrition rate over the recent past; the salvation of these institutions does not lie in the expansion of budgets, even if such expansion might bring larger government grants; it lies in the stabilization of their costs and, at the same time, the artistic education of their audiences and private contributors.

Above all, there is no way in which the concentration on largeness of budget per se as a criterion for support can do anything but further degrade the image of the arts and the civilization which we all wish to further. It is high time that we recognize the primary artistic contribution made by serious institutions and artists who cultivate neither the celebrity glamour of big budgets nor the artificially controversial hype of the so-called avant-garde cutting edge.

This position can be summed up in a credo: The greatest art, just as the greatest civilization, is the heritage of all. Therefore, education in art is the noblest function of the artist, just as education in the humanities is the noblest function of the humanist. To accomplish this function, the idea of art must be kept as something shining, golden—and serious. To cherish this elevated idea of art cannot be the task of artists alone; it also must be the task of all, politicians, patrons, and public alike, who cherish the future of civilization in a democratic and capitalist society.

Note

1. The American Council on the Arts issued a revised edition of *Coming to Our Senses* in July 1988.

16

The Museum in the City

Mark Lilla

Never has the American art museum been so popular; never has it been so confused. The signs of its popularity are everywhere to be found. The Department of Education's Institute of Museum Services has learned that visits to art museums rose from 42 million in 1975 to nearly 50 million in 1979, nearly a 20 percent increase in just four years. Whether these are repeat visits by a new, committed museum audience or simply one-time visits by those curious about cleverly packaged "blockbuster" shows, it is a significant development nonetheless that the museum is now considered among our major urban tourist attractions. Funding reductions at the national level hardly signify less interest in the museum, for the fact is that federal grants have never covered more than a fraction of American museum expenditures. And, as if to underline the museum's growing popularity, state and local governments, along with corporations and private donors, have increased their efforts to replace the lost revenues. So confident do many museums seem of their financial prospects that several cities have embarked on ambitious museum-building plans in the last decade, and a number of older institutions have added wings to hold the ever-expanding collections and crowds. Every one of these building projects has been considered a major commission by the architectural profession. Its most eminent members compete for the jobs, a telling sign of the broader cultural significance placed on the museum today.

Yet to all but the most inattentive museumgoers the signs of confusion are nearly as apparent as those of popularity. These are "growing pains," it is said, temporary problems induced by the extraordinary attention museums have only recently come to receive. Perhaps in response to the new museum audience, perhaps to encourage it, the museum building itself has recently become "user friendly." Permanent displays have been reduced to open up additional space for the packaged traveling show. These shows in turn draw larger crowds that feel more comfortable attending a publicized event with the aid of didactic printed guides, copious writing on the walls next to the works, tape recordings of show tours, one-way directions through the gallery (to see every work "in sequence"), a comfortable cafe or cafeteria, and the familiarity of the cardshop/bookstore at tour's end. Even more than the much maligned blockbuster shows of the 1970s, these structural concessions to the comfort of the new audience have been questioned by the traditional audience accustomed to roaming galleries without the restrictions of shows and programs. They are made especially uncomfortable by museum huckstering that lately seems to have acquired a life of its own. Museum shops now sell T-shirts, tote bags, prints and posters, stationery, cards, books, children's toys and games, jewelry, cutlery, and glassware. The Metropolitan Museum in New York has even established a bridal registry for the convenience of its affianced visitors.

Harmless, perhaps, but still one wonders. These programmatic and institutional activities were originally justified on the grounds that they would entice new visitors who, once comfortable in the museum, would return for the more serious shows and the permanent collection. A more plausible case has been made that blockbusters, bookstores, and cafés can generate much needed revenue for the museum's main tasks, but, again, there has been surprisingly little effort to learn just what the financial gains have been. (Museum directors have even begun to think that the costs of blockbusters—including transportation, insurance, and security—may, if anything, outweigh the income.)

Following these developments, the interested museum observer cannot help but feel that the objective of growth, and growth alone, has come to animate the work of all too many museum professionals today. Growth in the number of visitors is taken to be an unmixed good, it seems, no matter what works those visitors are shown or under what conditions they must see them. Growth in the collection is to be sought, no matter what the cost, what the effect on the private art market, or how infrequently the works may be seen by the public. The Association of Art Museum Directors may not be able to agree on what constitutes a high standard of quality in a collection, but it has little trouble agreeing on a code of ethics condemning "deaccessioning"—the practice of selling works from the collection to private collectors in order to raise money for other works, for construction, or for maintenance. Once a work is in museum hands, it must never be "lost" to private interests again—a rather bizarre notion when applied to collections of contemporary works, an increasing proportion of which move directly from loft to museum without ever touching the private hands from which they are being rescued.

But, in fact, unmitigated growth is neither the cause nor the sole consequence of the museum's current confusions. It seems instead to reflect a deeper absence of ideas, an insecurity about the fundamental principles of the museum as a social institution. Growth in audience and collection cannot mask the directionless drift of the American museum as it is buffeted by the moods and fashions of the moment, in art, politics, and entertainment. The museum today neither leads nor stands firm; it "responds." And those who demand this response continue to grow in number. Over the past twenty-five years, the museum has been told by ideologists that, as a progressive institution, its galleries must be open to ethnic, folk, and political art. It has been told by public officials to display popular works, in every part of the country (even on buses and trains, if necessary), if it wishes to retain public funds as a representative, democratic institution. And it has been told by the private art market that it must buy representative contemporary work if its collection is to remain an accurate barometer of aesthetic fashion. The museum has been told that art is not just art; art can also provide therapy, have a role in crime control and welfare programs, stimulate economic development, help effect income redistribution, serve as an educational tool, and be part of the entertainment industry. And, in almost every instance, the museum has "responded."

"Respond and thrive" is sound market strategy in private business. But in a major social institution like the museum it is a prescription for incoherence and, eventually, irrelevance. A museum that owns everything and shows everything, with no discernible purpose or standard, not only fails to serve art, it begins to bore the public. A public led to expect a museum "responsive to its needs" will soon tire of a place that can neither suggest something to which to aspire nor provide the truly responsive fun of television or the movies. One need only examine a museum's annual report, or that of the National Endowment for the Arts, to see that the American museum is at sea without the anchor of clearly articulated principles. To be sure, there *are* ideas, but they are contradictory and undigested ones that pander to every special interest without speaking confidently to the deeper purposes of this institution. Rising attendance has so far allowed museum professionals and public officials to avoid thinking through the questions of aims and purposes. But when the growth finally stops as someday it must—only the incoherence will remain.

II

It is, perhaps, a most telling sign of the museum's current problems that it has acquired a new set of highly articulate critics. What distinguishes the new critics is that they do not so much question particular acquisitions or shows as raise more fundamental questions about the political, economic, and aesthetic presuppositions of contemporary museum administration.

A number of important professional art critics must be counted among this group. These critics—perhaps the most prominent being Hilton Kramer, editor of *The New Criterion* and former chief art critic of the *New York Times*—cannot be dismissed lightly. They are not the enemies of high art nor, in most cases, of public funding of the arts. What they do object to is what they consider the distinct decline in aesthetic standards as museums have slavishly attempted to satisfy popular and political tastes. Entire shows, from the Museum of Modern Art's controversial *Harlem on My Mind* to the recent display of lesbian Judy Chicago's *Dinner Party,* are taken as evidence that museums have allowed themselves to be used by political propagandists. Potentially useful government programs meant to support art institutions, critics, or artists are criticized for substituting ideological criteria for aesthetic ones or for falling victim to a political process that distributes funds geographically without reference to artistic merit. The museum is also charged with a cowardly abandonment of traditional acquisition standards, reflecting instead the "camp" aesthetic of certain contemporary critics. And, while these new museum critics are not necessarily opposed to popular shows, they have expressed reservations about architectural concessions to the new visitors (such as those made at the Centre George Pompidou) as well as the questionable value of some of the more popular shows (such as the recent display of haute couture at the Metropolitan).

One is tempted to label these art critics "conservatives" or "neoconservatives," since most of their charges have been directed at the political Left. But it is quite obvious that their animus is not primarily political; it is aesthetic. They have clearly and consistently held that politics must play no role in the making of aesthetic discrimination and that this separation must be rigorously maintained, both in the private realm of criticism and in the public realm of the museum. The museum's task is to acquire and display the very best work available to it; that is all. It is an art institution and nothing more. And if there are to be government art programs they must do nothing to distort the public's unmediated appreciation of the best work available. Nonaesthetic criteria—historical, political, religious—are taken to be alien to the appreciation of art and to the proper management of the museum.

A genuinely political criticism of the museum has recently been offered by Edward Banfield in his controversial new book *The Democratic Muse.* To make this aesthetic/political distinction clear, it is worth noting that Banfield's conservatism has been attacked not only by critics on the Left but also by Kramer, who objects to the book's defense of political criteria in consideration of government art policies and internal museum policy. Banfield's is an important book primarily because it examines this political dimension from a principled, philosophical point of view. He recognizes that government funding of artists and institutions raises fundamental questions about the purposes and limitations of government; his book is, as most of his critics have failed to recognize, about American government and is only secondarily a book about the arts.

Banfield's main target is federal art programs, and about them he is quite clear: the federal government has no constitutional right to tax its citizens for the support of museums or artists or for the purchase and display of public works of art. "The American regime exists for purposes that are not served by art," he writes, "and the support of art is not among the powers that were given to the federal government." Banfield admits that "the public interest requires that there be a courthouse," but, in the most frequently quoted sentence of the book, wonders whether "it also requires that there be a statue in front of the courthouse." His case does not depend on the abuse of federal art programs (though he provides compelling evidence of such abuse), only on the impropriety of government distribution of what he calls "the art experience."

It is his definition of "the art experience" that underlies his other criticisms of the museum's distortion of art, as well as his bold proposal for the display of art reproductions in schools and even museums. If the viewing of art is reduced to a private, ahistorical, noncontextual "raw feel," then Banfield may be right that the museum can impede such an experience, that high-quality reproductions can evoke it at much lower cost, and that government distribution of it is probably unjustified. But we must be very clear that such arguments do depend heavily on just such an interpretation of what happens to us when we look at works in the museum (or on the courthouse lawn). Though Banfield's book is deeply political, his conception of art is profoundly asocial. What cannot be explained with reference to individuals leaves him highly skeptical. As if to underline this, he denies that great art institutions bring a country prestige, asking skeptically, "What exactly is national prestige? How is it measured?" How, one might add, is it consumed?

Art as consumption is a theme that has been explored exhaustively of late by a third group of museum critics, the arts economists. Ever since "arts policy" had become a governmental concern in the 1960s, it has seemed inevitable that the museum and its practices would come to the attention of the analytical economics profession. Some of the profession's most prestigious members—such as William Baumol and Dick Netzer—have written books on the subject, and "cultural economics" has been recognized as a legitimate, independent field of inquiry.

Generally, the arts economists look favorably on museums as public institutions, and few have political reservations about federal support for the arts. Indeed, some museums have even hired economists as in-house policy consultants. Yet they are critics of the museum, mainly because they see this institution in terms radically different from those of the average museum administrator. They believe that art exists only in the consumption of art and that the job of the economist is to ask whether that consumption has been "maximized," whether the distribution of payment matches the distribution of benefits, whether those payments and benefits are "progressively" distributed, and whether government intervention into the art marketplace may be justified on economic grounds. (Unlike Banfield, the economist ignores constitutional justification and speaks only of justification on the basis of efficiency or social-economic welfare.) Considered from the economic point of view, the museum comes to measure art consumption by the number of visits or visitors entering through the turnstiles each year, and the gifts and bequests a museum receives are simply lumped with taxes and gate receipts in the analysis of museum revenues. Once supply and demand, costs and benefits have been measured, it is possible to recommend changes in museum and government policy, again on purely economic grounds. For example, a group of economists has recently suggested that all the indirect government support museums receive— deductibility of gifts and bequests, property tax abatements, and so on—be ended so that the "real" level of government art support may be debated rationally and publicly.

If public monies are to be spent on the museum, the economist's voice probably should be heard in debates over taxing and spending. But it should not need restating that the science of economics is quantitative, not qualitative. Economists are quite gifted at devising schemes for increasing revenues or enticing visitors or using space efficiently; they cannot begin to discuss why a city would want a museum or any particular work or show. To economists, the museum problem is a "public finance" problem akin to financing roadways and setting subway fares, and they set themselves the task of analyzing growth, efficiency, and distribution. It is not an aesthetic problem, nor is it a political problem.

III

Each of these lines of criticism—the aesthetic, the political, the economic—reflects a perfectly consistent way of thinking about the museum in society. But it is an expensive consistency, one that sacrifices a realistic appraisal of the social functions museums have always served. Though ordinarily unsympathetic to the spirit of artistic achievement, the political and economic critics do have a point: the museum exists outside the boundaries of the private art world. It is a nonprivate institution with extra-aesthetic meanings and purposes. What are those meanings and purposes? The contemporary museum clearly has no idea, nor do the new critics, despite the justice of certain charges against the museum today.

If the American museum is to find a secure sense of its proper role in American society, it will have to recover it through an act of historical self-examination. How were most American museums founded? Who paid for them, and why? What did the founders hope to achieve in building them?

If we cannot speak confidently of the museum's "mission" today, we are fortunate enough to have evidence of what its original mission *was*. The history of the American museum is, so to speak, an open book. It began as an idea, the "museum idea." And, as Nathaniel Burt has written in his *Palaces for the People,* this is what distinguishes the American museum from the European.

> The American museum was and is an idea. The European museum was a fact. Almost without exception the European museum was first a collection. With few exceptions most American museums were first an ideal. Many of them were created, and sometimes even their buildings built, before they owned anything at all. Furthermore, almost without exception the larger American museums began with a deliberate appeal to the public. Most of the earlier European museums remained semi-exclusive cabinets and curiosities visible only to a few. The American museum began, and has remained, wide open.

The American museum idea was born after the Civil War and quickly spread to every part of the country, propelled by the tremendous economic growth of the new industrial age. Economic growth produced major social transformations, which, in turn, produced the museum. To put it bluntly, since then the history of the American museum has been the history of the American bourgeois class. Before 1870, the American merchant class was a relatively small part of our agriculturally based economy, and the few museums that served this class were mainly private galleries and teaching institutions in the Northeast. By 1930—only sixty years later—most major American critics had at least one public museum, and scores were scattered in improbable small towns across the country. The reason is simple: economic growth created a new middle class in virtually every part of the country.

But the museum was not the only institution built by the new American haute bourgeoisie. Countless libraries, colleges and universities, concert halls and opera houses, hospitals and charities were built with private funds during this same period. The "Age of Industry," the "Gilded Age" —whatever else we may think of it, this era can also lay claim to being the great age of American civic philanthropy. It is over, but in a sense it is still with us. We cannot walk through our older American cities without feeling we live among the ruins of that age, whose spirit speaks to us through its architecture and the grandeur of its public spaces.

The commercial republic, then, was simultaneously a republic of civic philanthropy as Adam Smith, for one, predicted would be the case. And the museum was one of its central concerns. For the most wealthy, the philanthropic impulse was expressed in monumental gifts to the city or, in the case of Andrew Mellon's National Gallery, to the entire nation. But American museums were not by and large the work of individuals. While they may have been pioneering individualists in corporate life, when it came to museum building the American philanthropists' first impulse was to form a civic association with the expressed purpose of bringing high culture to their fair cities. In New York, it was the "Committee of Fifty" that built the Metropolitan Museum of Art; in Boston, it was the members of the Atheneum that formed the Museum of Fine Arts; and in Detroit, it was the forty original members of the Founders Society that created what we now know as the Institute of Arts. In city after city these associations were formed. By and large, the members possessed only modest fortunes, and if one looks at their names today, one finds few that represent America's "first families." When the museum idea first took hold in the 1870s, museums went up in New York, Philadelphia, and Boston; in the following decades, businessmen in nearly every other American city followed suit in the hope of making their cities at least as respectable, as "advanced," as those back east.

It is unlikely that many museum founders knew very much about art; unless one went to Europe, one would have had little opportunity to see much respectable art on this side of the Atlantic. They were simply, self-made people for the most part, and their devotion to art was probably outweighed by their strong desire to improve their cities; if that meant museums, so be it. The museum builders were boosters first, art lovers second. And, like all acts of civic boosterism, their museum activities were a mix of respect for art, pride in their cities, desire for recognition, pure altruism, and raw arrogance. But every one of them believed in social improvement through culture and education.

American museums began as philanthropic enterprises, and so they remain today. College museums aside, private contributions remain the single largest source of museum income. Nor would it be surprising to learn that most of these private donations come from citizens of the city in which the museum is located. Museum trustees strengthen the ties between city and museum. They are usually private individuals drawn from the local business class, and, as trustees, they act in a special civic capacity somewhere between that of private individual and public official. The relation between a city and its museum is an intimate one, and the notion of donating art to a museum, or serving on the board of trustees, is one of the few distinctly civic acts open to private citizens. The focus of these acts is on *this* museum, *this* audience, *this* city. People simply devoted to art, or even to the "art world," can have no stake in seeing particular works in this museum rather than another; the city does. Even an international city like New York, which at times can seem like the whole art world, shows civic pride in its museums when it raises funds to keep Calder's *Circus* in the city or grieves the loss of Picasso's *Guernica* to Spain. Since its inception just over one hundred years ago, the building of the American museum has been a central part of the building of American cities.

IV

The word *civic* has been carefully chosen. For it is precisely its civic nature that has been lost, or forgotten, in recent discussions of the museum. By *civic* I refer not only to cities but to that sphere of human activity that rests uncomfortably between private and public life. That the civic is not the private is clear, but that the civic sphere is not identical with the public sphere must be explained.

Private life is intimate; public life opens up the possibility of anonymity. And if we are to believe its critics, modern bourgeois public life is unbearably anonymous. The marketplace and mall are public areas, but we enter them to attain personal satisfaction and while in them remain private individuals. Most public places today are meant to serve our shared, but still private, needs; we have come to speak of public parks and public squares just the way we would speak of public beaches or public lavatories. (And we often treat them the same way.) Perhaps "shared consumption" is the most precise definition we can give to our most common government programs, which have become forms of social cooperation, a sort of private (but compulsory) quid pro quo among people who live together. Nothing more is required for participation than an agreement to contribute in order to draw benefits. It is a compact unanchored to place or history, since it only exists now for those who agree to maintain it.

In the civic sphere men and women are not private or public consumers, they are citizens. They share places and purposes. They cannot dissolve their civic "compact" any more than they can jump out of their skin, nor can they take it elsewhere or deny its history. A city hall and a courthouse are civic buildings that represent, or should represent, more than a private office building ever can. The same is true of a civic monument: when we look at it, we should be reminded of some common event or leader we share by virtue of our citizenship. Monuments remind us that civic life is rooted in history, that civic events are not reversible, that civic goods are not exchangeable. When we step into a voting booth or put on a military uniform, we leave behind the private realm of home and hearth, but we also leave behind the anonymous public realm where we pay our taxes and cash our social security checks.

It is a fuzzy line we have drawn, one that perhaps can be seen best in urban places. When we step into the Washington Mall, we are meant to feel different from the way we do when we enter Central Park; we are meant to act differently as well. This distinction is a healthy one and in no way denies the virtues of Central Park. Frederick Law Olmsted designed Central Park in such a way that most areas allow private enjoyment of his carefully constructed "natural" wonder. Yet it is a private enjoyment we share publicly and one that Olmsted hoped would make all New Yorkers more "sociable." But in the Mall we are expected—joggers excluded—to act "civilly," to feel overwhelmed by the unbroken vistas of grand government buildings. We are equal members of society in Central Park; we are equal citizens in the Mall.

It is an interesting complication of modern political life that all projects undertaken with government funds are not civic in nature and that some privately funded ventures can rise to the level of civic acts. The welfare state, to take the most obvious example, has become a program of anonymous public consumption, whatever the civic aspirations of its founders. A privately initiated project becomes civic when it satisfies at least two conditions: it speaks to the shared purposes and experiences of its citizens by what it does or commemorates, and it is open to all citizens. In programs of shared public consumption, openness is not enough: there must be some attempt to ensure that the costs and benefits of such programs are equally shared. But beyond being open to all, the civic sphere is silent on questions of distributive equality. In part this is because the civic sphere is so often made up of the unique, the nonreproducible. While it makes sense for nearly every city neighborhood to have its own public playground, there is no reason for it to have its own city hall or civic square—or Mall, for that matter. The special power of civic monuments in particular is preserved by their singularity. We flock to our civic places—to the Mall, to Arlington Cemetery, to our state capitols—we do not expect them to come to us.

The museum is not at the center of American civic life, as are our most important government buildings or our commemorative statues and places. Nor is it central to the very operation of the city, as are the courts and city halls. But like our major public libraries (many of which were also founded through private philanthropic efforts), museums were built with the understanding that they were to stand for something we have, or should aspire to, in common. Not devoted to private or shared public consumption, the museum was to be a *symbol* of the importance a city's citizens placed on art. And, perhaps more important, it was to serve as a symbol of the importance of having the highest achievements in Western high culture be available to all. The library was meant to represent the same civic commitment to learning, at a time when few could expect to own books.

We cannot claim for the museum or library the civic status of our most precious institutions. When we vote or serve on juries, we define ourselves as citizens by these very acts. Looking at pictures cannot be construed as an act of citizenship. But when we are in our cities' museums, we are there by virtue of being citizens, looking at shows and collections organized for us in that capacity. Private galleries are open to the public, buying or not, yet there is no pretense of having served the public by showing works. Galleries belong to the art world, and properly so. Just as a library is meant to represent something more than a bookshop, so the museum was created to offer more than a gallery ever could.

The history of the American museum shows it to be a civic institution of a very special kind. Bypassing local governments in most cases, private citizens gathered together to make an offering to their fellows, and by so doing became more than private people. One can see the motives for these acts in the rhetoric of nineteenth- and early twentieth-century philanthropy. Museums, the philanthropists believed, would provide the moral uplift needed to raise the common man (read: urban worker and immigrant) to a level of culture at which he could be expected to act like a citizen. The museum, like the library, was to be a preparation for civility. Citizens of the nineteenth century had tremendous faith in the transformative powers of civic institutions generally, a faith we can see reflected, if only faintly now, in that century's ambitious architecture. Their faith in museums in particular rested on two simple beliefs. First, they shared the classical belief that art shapes the soul and that great art shapes a great people. Second, they hoped that making the highest achievements of Western (and later, non-Western) art available to all would attract the loyalty of the common man to the civilization of which he was a part. Even if we read a little self-interested fear of the new urban "masses" into the philanthropists' actions, it is hard to fault the result. In just sixty years, most American cities had made available, to all classes, works of art previously in private hands.

It is in the civic world that the educational function of the museum is rooted. Most museum charters state that these institutions are devoted to education, and this is normally taken by museum officials as a mandate to arrange their shows and collections to enhance their "art-education value." Many even run special art education programs for children and adults. But we must read these charters as expressing more than a guide for operations. They were also meant to be statements of purpose: the founders thought the educational function of the museum was principally served by its *being there.* By being there as a symbol of civic intent and by leaving its door open to all, the museum does most of what it can do to educate the public. If the museum goes beyond that, if it offers classes or distributes books or produces guides, it may do a better job. But what is distinctive about that job is that it takes place in a civic setting.

Perhaps the most tired charge against the museum is that it is elitist or antidemocratic. Not every city has a museum; only certain works are shown, and these works may be difficult to appreciate or may represent class biases in taste, and so on. If the museum had been founded with public funds to facilitate the shared, private consumption of art, these criticisms would carry some weight. If the museum was just another public institution, we would have to be concerned that those who benefit also pay and that their tastes are represented. Distributing good reproductions might be more democratic in this case.

But the museum is a profoundly democratic institution when considered from the civic, as opposed to the simply public, point of view. To use contemporary political jargon, the museum is an "empowering" institution meant to incorporate all who would become a part of our shared cultural experience. All citizens have the opportunity to walk into a museum and appreciate the highest achievements of their culture. If they spend some time there, they might learn something; if they spend enough time, they may be transformed. This is precisely what the museum founders had in mind when they brought great collections to their own cities. They understood what we, perhaps, have forgotten: that museum education is above all civic education.

V

These are, of course, abstractions. And the problems our museums face are unrelentingly concrete. Should we open a new wing? If so, who should build it? Should we display more works from the permanent collection or bid for more traveling shows? How can we ensure that our shows are historically sound yet accessible to the public? How much "marketing" can the gift shop engage in without becoming vulgarly commercial? How much of this museum's budget should be devoted to expanding the contemporary collection?

But unless our museums directors and public officials recover a historical sense of the museum's social role in America, they will never be able to make sense of their new environment. When the growth finally stops, they will find themselves piloting rudderless ships, prey to every crisis and challenge. But once the civic nature of the museum is reasserted, these museum challenges look a little less threatening. Museum architecture can once again become a part of civic architecture, with the same monumental aims and public constraints. Museum education can be shaped as a form of civic education that enfranchises citizens into a significant mode of Western cultural expression. And in civic education the task of shaping the collection can acquire an appropriate extra-aesthetic standard.

This is not a prescription for museum reform. It is, if you like, a plea for sober self-examination and self-defense. In the face of its new, articulate critics, the museum should be able to defend itself confidently as an exemplar of that shrinking realm of American life: the City.

17

Art, Culture, and Identity

John Wilson

All three words of my title are baffling. They offer rather good illustrations of terms which are not (a) just jargon and dispensable, (b) technical terms with clear meanings (such as we find in the natural sciences), but also not (c) ordinary, everyday terms of which the meaning is entirely clear. Like *role, neurotic,* and many others, they have crept into our everyday language and therefore may be presumed to be doing (or at least to have a chance of doing) some real and important work, but it is not at all obvious just what they mean and what work they are supposed to do. I am tempted to (and will) add that this makes it all the stranger that sociologists, educationalists, and others who ought to know better use the terms quite blithely and uncritically, as if we already knew well enough what they meant and could happily go on to employ them for theoretical and practical purposes. But we do not.

I too want to say something about the things, and not just about the words, so what I say about the words will be far too brief and sloppy; I look to other philosophers to improve upon it. But I hope at least to make the sense in which I shall be using them clear enough to do business with them.

I

1. *Art.* I shall use this to cover anything that can be viewed aesthetically. Exactly what it is to view something aesthetically, or whether there is such an independent view, is much disputed by philosophers (Strawson[1] is the best introduction), but it seems reasonably clear that we talk about things ("art objects") in a way which is radically unlike talk about their weight, size, economic value, moral or political merits, or religious virtues. It is one thing to ask if a picture is heavy, or a good financial investment, or corrupting the morals of the young; it is another to ask if it is a good (beautiful, elegant, charming, etc.) picture. So too with music, literature, and indeed anything that normally falls within the ambience of aesthetics.

What makes aesthetics so important for the educator is that it appears to be an indispensable form of thought or experience for human beings; I mean that it is not, and could not be, optional (*pace* Hirst:[2] see Wilson).[3] It is inconceivable—ultimately, I think, for conceptual reasons to do with the human mind, particularly the unconscious mind—that there should be people who never used terms like *nice-looking, tidy, elegant, ugly,* and so forth. Certainly "art" in the sophisticated, as it were Bloomsbury, sense of "high art" (*les beaux arts*), "high culture," is an option in fact taken up only by a minority, and certainly there may be a more or less sharp divorce between art and (say) religion, or politics, or morality, or (a very difficult divorce to make at all) nature. But if we take "the aesthetic viewpoint" in a sufficiently wide and sufficiently pedestrian sense, then that viewpoint is something we are landed with. All people (we might say) order their lives and surroundings, sometimes, for nonutilitarian purposes and purposes that are not directly connected with enterprises like religion or politics.

2. *Culture.* The importance of these points emerges when we consider the ground marked by "culture," because any culture (if I may speak for a moment as if we already knew what we are talking about) must, on this account of art, contain aesthetic elements. A culture, we might say as a sighting shot, consists of the practices and forms of life which distinguish a social group from a group of animals: the styles, rules, values, and other elements distinguishable in various patterns of human life. This is still very vague (and perhaps ought to remain so at this stage), but it will include, for instance, such things as cooking, dancing, certain language uses that are not purely utilitarian, dress, social rituals, and so forth.

In primitive cultures (if one dare use a word like *primitive* in these egalitarian days) the aesthetic element is, in fact, a good deal more visible than in modern technological, utilitarian cultures: there is, perhaps, less science, less instrumental adopting of pragmatic means to pragmatic goals, more ritual, more expressiveness. But at the same time there is also less differentiation of different features: anthropologists are often at a loss to say whether a particular practice is aesthetic, or religious, or moral, or a piece of incompetent science—partly because these distinctions (in themselves pretty difficult to draw) are not clear in the minds of individuals in that culture. The forms of thought are, as it were, less externalized, not seen so sharply as existing in some transcendental way, with their own standards to which individual practice has to conform, but seen more as an intimate and personal expression of individual or social feeling. It is perhaps for this reason that "culture" seems more sensible as a piece of terminology when we talk of primitive cultures: the question, for instance, of whether science and mathematics are part of "our culture" in advanced societies is a bit baffling—we feel that we want to say yes, because of course science and mathematics go on in our society, but we hesitate because they are not (always) interwoven in the personal lives of all individuals in it. (Jet airplanes and atomic bombs exist in various countries, but it sounds odd to say that they are part of our culture in a way that it is less odd to say that—perhaps—hamburgers and automobiles are.)

3. *Identity.* Here again I have tried to concentrate on the points about "culture" which affect the still more baffling notion of "identity." For if "identity" has something to do with what, as it were, permeates and somehow constitutes one's life and if "culture" refers not to options in which an individual might or might not be interested (as a man might or might not be interested in, say, Beethoven or quadratic equations), then culture is going to have some importance for one's identity. In particular, perhaps, one might think of childhood experiences of food, drink, the rituals of personal relationships, dress, and many other things which might be seen as basic from a developmental or psychological point of view—even though, ultimately, one might want to say that they are less valuable, or fine, or noble than the Beethoven symphonies or quadratic equations that the child only came to appreciate much later in life.

I shall take "identity," for the purposes of this essay, to be closely connected to or perhaps the same as "psychological security." Questions like "Who am I, really?" or "Where does my real self lie?" are usually asked by people who, at this or that time, feel insecure, uncertain of themselves (and of their place in the world), unsure of what it is about themselves that they can or want to rely on. And clearly one of the things that might contribute to a sense of psychological security, or that might shatter it if absent, is the network of cultural experiences which an individual is used to enjoying—or, better, which he is used to wearing as a garment that both comforts him and gives him some sort of dignity. The "art" or "aesthetic" elements of this network will hence be important.

II

All that is, as I have said, too brief and sloppy, but at least we can see how unsurprising it is that we make so much fuss nowadays about the preservation of various "cultures," about "multicultural education," and so forth. On the whole, educators and others proceed uncritically here. It is simply taken for granted that a person's identity, or security, either must or ought to reside in his culture (which therefore ought to be preserved at all costs), and this is reinforced by a kind of relativism which denies the whole idea of criticizing that person's culture, either wholly or in part, on the grounds that no such criticism can be sustained—one is as good as another. These are the ideas I want to explore.

1. The first and most obvious point is that there are of course many *other* and many *different* features on which people may put their money, beside putting it on their culture. One may rely on being white (black, yellow, etc.), British, a woman (man), a Christian (Buddhist, etc.); also, on being physically strong, or rich, or clever, or morally virtuous, or politically powerful. None of these are, as they stand, *cultural* features—and there is, naturally, a lot of dithering about whether what we want to preserve is to be identified in terms of race, or religion, or nationhood, or what. Briefly, it is an entirely open question (i) what people *do* in fact rely on (which may not be the same as what they *think* they rely on) and (ii) what they *ought* to rely on. The answer to (i) must involve a good deal of empirical research, in which what the relevant individuals say would not always be taken at face value (one may easily think one's identity or security rests on this or that feature, but when the chips are down, it may easily turn out that one was deceived).

2. In such research (though of course I am not primarily concerned with it here) we should have to start by establishing a proper set of *categories*—that is, different types of candidates for what people may rely on. Here I want only to point out that—for reasons that would themselves repay study—there is a strong temptation to overemphasize what one might call *socially visible* features. We think at once of a person's social group, or race, or culture, or his standing in relation to other people in terms of money or political power. (When feminists, for example, talk of "power," they are not thinking of the enormous power a mother has over her infants at home, but of social or political power.) In trying to set up categories, one main label ("social") would have to take its place alongside another, which might be called "psychological"; for even sociologists will (if pressed) admit that security may be found in the love one might have for another person, or one's hobby, or one's pets, or plenty of other things that could not (unless the word were extended to vanishing point) sensibly be called "social." It is in fact an open and important question how far identity/security actually is, or ought to be, social at all. (Does anyone really believe that people who are socially much esteemed—film and TV stars, for instance—are actually any more secure in themselves than other people?) Most psychologists, after all, would reasonably claim that features like a secure childhood, having parents who exercise discipline with love, being able to enjoy and appreciate friendship and affection, and other such things counted far more—partly because they affect us much earlier—than what happens to us in "society." That is not, of course, to say that what happens to us socially is unimportant: we may be enslaved, tortured, deprived of all sorts of things. But it is to say that these things may be overemphasized just because they are more easily visible.

3. If we now approach what for educators must be the crucial question of what people ought to put their money on—a question I find them curiously reluctant even to raise—it seems still more strange to opt for social features. For one thing, as religious people have constantly stressed, such features are fragile: we may lose our money, our social status, our power; our race or culture may be persecuted and disappear; changing circumstances, even without human intolerance, may necessitate dramatic social changes that—if we have been foolish enough to rely on social features—leave us psychologically bereft and in a vacuum. Secondly—and this is where the crunch comes—features in our own culture and society may not be, in themselves, good enough to rely on. They may not be worthy. This may be true in at least three ways:

a. First, some things which are apt to spring to our minds first may be positively wrong or pernicious. One might be (people are) attached culturally to practices like female circumcision, not caring for old people, crippling the feet of children, persecuting Jews, and many other things.

b. They may be unworthy because they are trivial in comparison to other things. (I was at school with a boy whose ancestors, he claimed, came to Britain with the Norman Conquest; being the sort of boy he was, he paid attention to history only if one of his ancestors was personally involved. The history teacher said to him something like, "For goodness' sake, forget about your wretched ancestors and concentrate on something of greater historical importance." Quite right. But now compare that with the liberal passion for helping everyone find out about and celebrate their "roots." My own roots are shallow: two generations back my ancestors were foundlings, dumped on the doorstep. End of inquiry into the Wilson genealogy, but fortunately my security, such as it is, does not lie there.)

c. A little less obviously, they may be antieducational. Many cultures have practices which prevent, for instance, the rational discussion of important issues or which even prevent the adoption of rational modes of thought (science as against witchcraft). Although these features may be more difficult to identify than features which are positively wicked or boringly trivial, they must be, to educators, of very great importance. It is bad if a culture practices a wrong moral code; a nuisance if they practice a code which includes a lot of unnecessary conventions (when they should be concentrating on important matters); but, in a way, worst of all if they do not allow proper consideration and discussion of morality in general. (So, too, with art.)

III

This is perhaps enough to show, at least, that we cannot simply take cultures for granted. The point may be put this way: there is nothing, *in point of reason,* that makes some practice or feature good just because it is mine. The fact that they are my ancestors, that this is the sort of music my family plays, that these religious or moral beliefs are *my* beliefs shared by my social group, goes no way at all to show that these things are true, or worthwhile, or valuable. Of course it is understandable that I am attached to them, but that is a different matter. It is one thing to like a tune because "It's our tune, darling," another thing to like it because it is a *good* tune.

This is something which (like many things in education and indeed life) we know perfectly well when we keep our heads. Any even moderately sane Englishman knows that the English are, by and large, not good at cooking, art, or running the economy, and the sensible thing would be to get some Frenchmen to do the cooking, Italians to do the art, and Germans or Japanese to run the economy. This is not a flippant point; it simply raises, in a sharp form, the question, When we consider any product of activity, are we going to value it (a) because it is English (French, black, feminine, etc.) or (b) because it is good? We give all our allegiance *either* to some kind of irrelevant criterion (such as nationalism) *or* to the standards which are above any culture or social group, the standards which are appropriate to the art, or the business, or whatever it is. In practice, of course, people often prefer to do the former, because their dignity (identity, need for security) will not allow them to do the latter—although the latter is in itself clearly more sensible.

Some Britishers (I regret to say) refused to play German music during World War II; some Israelis still refuse. Well, that is (as I said above) understandable. But to that extent they have simply turned their backs on music and indulged their own autistic feelings—just as much as the Nazis did when they rejected products on the irrelevant grounds that they were Jewish products. Either we are going to go in for this sort of gang warfare, in terms of nations or cultures or creeds or ideologies or color or sex or whatever other boring and ultimately trivial distinctions we can find, or we are going to set our faces in the opposite direction, the direction which makes us look away from ourselves and seek our identity in truth, in things that are worthwhile in themselves (not because they are *ours*), in values that are really valuable and not just cultural products.

I am saying, then, that anyone seriously interested in *education* (rather than promoting some political movement) must encourage students (and himself) to seek their identity (security) *not* in terms of their own culture per se, that is, just because it is theirs, but in culture-free terms, that is, by reference to what is really valuable and worthwhile. For it is this latter, plainly, that ought to constitute our identity (as a religious person might say, "Put your trust in God, not in princes or cultures or the changing world"). The whole of education consists (because that is part of what "educate" means) of playing down the individual self and directing it to something true or beautiful or valuable outside, rather as described by Iris Murdoch.[4] That does not destroy or (ultimately) threaten the self so much as transform it: we become liberated from our own petty concerns and caught up in the beauty of a really good piece of music or literature, the truths and methods of science, the dialectic of philosophy, or whatever it may be.

That is, of course, in itself not enough to lay down any kind of educational blueprint or recipe. It would be wrong, and anyway useless, to take some student, shake him till his teeth rattled, and say words to the effect of "Look, forget all about *your* culture, background, etc., and concentrate on what's really good"; people are naturally attached to their cultures and have to be weaned from them, so far as that is desirable in the interests of education, gradually and with care. But they do have to be weaned—even if their cultures (as will be unlikely) happen to represent what is best in art, science, philosophy, and so on. Even fifth-century Athenians should have realized that the Parthenon, Sophocles, and all the other glories of Athens were to be admired because they were good, not because they were Athenian. I have heard it argued that identity with one's own roots, or culture, or social group is a necessary "developmental stage" (an argument used by some tolerably sophisticated people to justify "black studies," "women's studies," and other such symptoms that show how easy it is to abandon educational criteria in favor of political or sociological ones). Well, that is not obviously an absurd argument, and it is (I suppose) for empirical researchers to tell how we may most swiftly and efficiently turn out students who pursue the real goods rather than the false ones. But we need to be suspicious here, because the whole weight of prejudice, fashion, and other kinds of autism is on the side of politics, "culture," "society," and the various pressure groups that make themselves felt.

Art is in one way in a strong position here, in another way in a weak one. It is, or seems to be, weak because there are no very obvious proofs that some art is better than others—that, to put it sharply, students in many cultures would be well advised to drop their boring folk music and start to try to appreciate classical music, because classical music is better (more enjoyable, more rewarding, less ephemeral, deeper, a possession—when one has it—that one would not willingly lose, as one might willingly forget the latest pop tune; one might say many things here). Of course, in a way this is wrong; there are proofs, but not in the sense of "proof" that mathematicians, or scientists, or historians use. It can (if a person will open his eyes and ears) be shown, and shown reasonably (i.e., without illegitimate forms of persuasion), that Leonardo's drawings are more interesting than the doodles I make during tedious committee meetings, that, briefly, good or great or classical art is better than the other stuff. But it cannot be shown quickly (as you can show a geometrical proof quickly), so it is particularly important here for educators to keep their nerve and maintain the student's concentration upon what is in fact really good, even (and particularly) when it is not immediately perceived as such.

But art is also in a strong position, because (as Plato first said) beauty is the most immediately attractive and appealing value. Truth is, at least sometimes, grimmer and harder. It is, or ought to be, easier to show students *something* good in Shakespeare (or whomever) fairly quickly than to show them something good about quadratic equations or the life cycle of the newt. (I must declare prejudice here: I think equations and newts are ultimately more boring and of less importance to all men than Shakespeare is. Maybe lots of students warm to newts and atomic weights with an immediate fiery glow, in the way I warm to Wagner or Raphael.) If not, we must be doing aesthetic education all wrong, for it is an essential component of such education that the student *enjoys* and feels passionate about, deeply moved by, the art object—it is not enough that he knows a lot about its origins or history or surrounding social conditions. Indeed, one of the most interesting questions about art is why it has to be beautiful in order to work: one has the intuition that it is not so much that art does a certain job and just uses beauty as an overlay to make the job attractive, but that the beauty is an essential part of the job (not as in a didactic poem, which could just as well be put into prose).

To conclude (and crisply—there is a good deal too much of the eirenic and the latitudinarian in most such discussion), I want to say that any educator, indeed any serious person, ought on reflection to realize that identity or security ought *not* to be sought in one's culture, that all of us have to be weaned and helped away from our cultures toward what is truly valuable in a transcendental, culture-free way, and that it is at best patronizing and trivial, at worst crippling and cruel, to encourage particular cultures to adore themselves in mirrors. Instead of feeling narcissistic (or guilty) about one's culture, one should have something better to do. Art—when freed from wholly improper connections with culture—is one of these better things.

Notes

1. P. F. Strawson, "Aesthetic Appraisal and Works of Art," in *Freedom and Resentment and Other Essays* (London: Methuen, 1974).
2. P. H. Hirst, *Knowledge and the Curriculum* (London: Routledge and Kegan Paul, 1974).
3. John Wilson, *Preface to the Philosophy of Education* (London: Routledge and Kegan Paul, 1979).
4. Iris Murdoch, *The Sovereignty of Good* (London: Routledge and Kegan Paul, 1970).

18

The Artists-in-Schools Program of the National Endowment for the Arts: Analysis and Criticism

Ralph A. Smith

The purpose of this essay is to submit the Artists-in-Schools Program of the National Endowment for the Arts to systematic analysis and criticism. The reaction to AIS programs suggests a need for such scrutiny. AIS programs are both praised and criticized, though often without benefit of relevant critical criteria. Such criteria derive from an understanding of the nature of policy and the demands and obligations policy imposes on thoughtful and responsible policymakers. The approach of this paper consists of asking several questions which can be asked of any policy,[1] including the Endowment's specific policy of employing artists in the schools. A familiarity with the Endowment's AIS policy is presumed, that is, a policy whereby funds are allocated to state arts councils and a few other organizations which in turn administer grants to schools for the purpose of employing artists for varying periods of residence. Now to the questions.

1. Is the AIS policy actually a policy; that is, is it clear about what should be done and toward what end?

This question presupposes a notion of policy as something conceived and adopted only after careful consideration. It assumes that policy deliberations issue not only in decisions of what to do, which is to say policy is always addressed to actions, but that policies are designed to determine, organize, regulate, or systematize activities in order to bring about that state of affairs which marks a policy's purpose. We may ask, then, what is the state of affairs which marks the purpose of the AIS policy and to what extent does the AIS policy contain provisions for regulating and systematizing pertinent activities? Or, simply, is the AIS policy clear about what should be done, how it should be done, and toward what end?

On the matter of purposes and aims the literature of AIS programs is far from clear. A reading of official publications, guidelines, and articles by

Endowment representatives reveals confused and contradictory statements of purpose. Indeed the Endowment's 1976 guidelines are so equivocal that one is justified in asking whether the Endowment really knows what it is doing. For example, the guidelines, issued under the imprint of the Endowment's Education Program, contain several statements which describe benefits ostensibly educational in nature. But then in suggesting questions that may assist persons in the preparation of evaluation procedures, the guidelines state (parenthetically) that "Artists-in-Schools is an artist-oriented program, so evaluation efforts should be tailored to the special nature of the program. *Strictly educational criteria may not always accommodate to the uniqueness of the Arts-in-Schools program*" (emphasis added). Repeat: "may not"! There is much that could be said about these parenthetical remarks, but let it suffice to say that in stating that the schools should tailor their programs to the AIS policy, the Endowment has got things backward. Not only that, the Endowment cannot have it both ways. Either AIS programs are educational programs, as advertised, in which case educational criteria are relevant in evaluating them, or AIS programs are not educationally pertinent and must be justified on other grounds. Now a policy that equivocates on basic and fundamental purposes fails to satisfy a minimal condition for something's being designated a policy in any significant sense of the term.

2. Does the AIS policy have an adequate conception of implementation and enforcement?

The aspect of policy being picked out here involves institutional considerations, the assumption being that without some kind of institutional network within which policies can be enacted and enforced there can be little or no basis for determining the effectiveness of a policy. A well-articulated system of state art councils and cultural organizations provides the institutional support for the AIS policy and guarantees a certain measure of systematic regulation. In this respect the AIS policy satisfies one of the more obvious conditions of an educational policy. By permitting great latitude in the implementation and assessment of AIS programs, however, the starch is taken out of enforcement, which tends to leave questions of effectiveness hanging,[2] with one notable instance to be mentioned later, namely the Western States Arts Foundation study of AIS programs. What is more, regulative and evaluative efforts are rendered more problematical when artists are deployed in both the school *and* the community, this latter being a more recent aspect of the AIS policy. It may be concluded then that a system of arts councils and cultural organizations provides the minimal institutional network necessary for the allocation of funds and assignment of artists to schools and communities but that no firm control is exercised over this network.

3. Is the AIS policy a truly educational policy, or does it subserve noneducational ends?

Once more the 1976 guidelines suggest that on the one hand AIS programs are educational programs and that on the other they are not, this latter because of the statement that AIS programs are artist-oriented and thus educational criteria may not be relevant in evaluating their effectiveness. Consider this last point.

On the face of it the AIS policy is a contemporary instance of federally subsidized employment of artists, the precedent for which was set by the WPA projects of the thirties. And there would be no reason to believe that the real purpose of the AIS policy is any different except for the equivocating about purpose in the literature. Now if the employment of artists is the real purpose of the AIS policy, then one wishes that the Endowment would say so and desist from its pedagogical doubletalk. This would not, as we shall see, necessarily justify the AIS policy, but it would at least lend the statements of AIS officials an air of sincerity. After all, it would not be the first time in recent history that the government has tried to use the schools to solve essentially economic, social, or even political problems. Idle and unappreciated artists are a potential source of tension and unrest, and it might well be in a society's interest to keep them busy. This is the implication of Saul Bellow's recent remarks comparing the situation of writers and literature today and in the thirties. "The difference," he says, "is that in the thirties crackpots were not subsidized by their families. They had to go it alone for several years. Or at least until the New Deal . . . recognized that a great government could *buy* the solution of any problem and opened WPA projects in many parts of the country. . . . Hopkins and Roosevelt, seeing how much trouble unhappy intellectuals had made in Russia, Germany, and Italy between 1905 and 1935, thought it a bargain to pay people twenty-three dollars a week for painting post-office murals and editing guidebooks. This plan succeeded admirably."[3]

One can appreciate the point being made by Bellow without endorsing everything the government does to help artists. It is naive to assume, as the Endowment's guidelines do, that practicing artists in schools will not only provide artists with opportunities to communicate with a larger audience but will also contribute to their creative development and enhance their position in society.

This hardly seems the way to nurture artistic development. If the government wants to help artists, and there is no quarrel with this idea here, there are many things it can do that would be more effective and more appreciated by artists than by making them temporary schoolmasters. Asking artists to educate school and community merely complicates their lives and interferes with their work.

And so an answer to the question of whether AIS programs subserve noneducational aims must be ambivalent. This ambivalence is probably what animated Elliot Eisner to ask the Endowment what had been done to secure information about the effectiveness of AIS programs.[4] He discovered that no one had bothered to find out. Not only that, there seemed to be some impatience that the question should even be asked. But more on the subserving of noneducational ends and the effectiveness criterion below.

4. Did the AIS policy originate from a legitimate source?

Government has the obligation to promote the general welfare of its citizens, one aspect of which is the aesthetic welfare or the aesthetic good. There is thus no question of legitimacy as far as its decision to employ artists in the schools is concerned, for a prima facie argument could be made that doing so has the potential to contribute to aesthetic well-being. Whether it is the most sensible way to promote such well-being is another question.

So far as the wisdom of the AIS policy is concerned, a few words are necessary on the way cultural and educational policy gets made in the government. Much has been written about the diffusion of cultural and educational policymaking throughout the several branches of government. Practically every major division has its own special assistants on educational and cultural affairs, not only the Endowments, HEW, and the State Department, but also Interior, Commerce, and several others, including the Pentagon. Observers agree there is a need for at least some centralization and coordination. Charles Frankel, for example, was dismayed upon entering the State Department as assistant secretary of state for cultural and educational affairs to find that Office of Education officials were so seldom consulted when the State Department framed its educational policies and programs.[5]

This lack of coordination and communication probably contributes to the confusion of function and mission. For example, Endowment officials speak both of "not being in the education business" and of "getting out of the education business." What is more, the education program of the Endowment has a larger budget than anything in HEW's arts and humanities branch. But there is more. A power struggle of sorts exists between the Endowment and the educationists, a number of whom have quite understandably become critical of the Endowment's doubletalk. The Endowment's failure to acknowledge criticism of its policies has not helped things. The situation of the Endowment vis-à-vis the educationists is part of a larger development which over the last two decades has seen a dramatic growth in the cultural services field. While there are numerous instances of cooperation between members of the new cultural establishment and the educational establishment, a situation is developing which is generating second thoughts about some of the possible unanticipated consequences of a burgeoning cultural bureaucracy in which government increasingly calls the tune. Some of this second thinking turns on a realization that the cultural establishment has now become a competitor for educational funds, one effect of which has been an increase in the size of their educational budgets and staffs. Educational grants to cultural organizations must of course be at the expense of other organizations, namely the schools. Nor, as the new cultural establishment becomes impressed with its achievements, should it come as a surprise if it begins to say it can do a better job of aesthetic education than the schools, just as paraprofessional teachers have been known to demand equal status with certified professionals because they say they do as good if not a better job than the teachers they assist. Some educationists are also beginning to think about the precedent being set, which is becoming an unquestioned practice, of permitting uncertified artists to teach in the schools at a time when school populations and budgets are shrinking. The schools do not really need the artists, but a case could be made that the cultural establishment does, that is, all those directing, coordinating, and implementing AIS programs. Again funds are flowing into cultural organizations that could be going to the schools where ultimately the long-range task of aesthetic education must be accomplished.

The emergence of a cultural services field may thus have unexpected consequences which school people would do well to ponder. One cannot imagine the legal, medical, and engineering professions permitting unlicensed lawyers, doctors, and engineers to practice part-time in their respective areas. To do so would violate an important principle of professionalism, the principle of quality control. In this respect it might be noted that educators have sometimes been observed to betray a peculiar death wish: they do not always act in the interests of their own survival.

That AIS programs are popular with school, community, and a segment of the educational profession is, of course, comprehensible. It has to do not only with the rise in the general popularity of the arts but also with the image teachers of art have of themselves. In embracing the AIS policy teachers of art are only doing what seems natural—according entré to members of their primary reference group, the group to which they look for inspiration and identification. To deny sympathy to this "secret sharer" of one's very own self would indeed be odd. But the image of the artist-teacher is not ordained, and other images of teaching and profession now compete with it or at least claim the right to supplement it. This is to say that the creative dimension of aesthetic education is but one dimension and that there are others, such as the historical, the social, the critical, and the cultural.

In response then to the question of whether or not the AIS policy originates from a legitimate source, it has been seen that an answer requires taking into account the policymaking apparatus of government, its links with the cultural services field, and some possible consequences for the schools of this new situation in culture and education.

5. Is the AIS policy justified, that is, can its purpose or objectives be shown to be (a) specific to the domain or subject area in question and (b) consistent with an acceptable general educational objective or philosophy.

This is the most important question that can be asked of any policy as it goes to the heart of the matter. And in this respect there can be no equivocating about the justifiability of the AIS policy: *In light of what a policy is and does and the criteria which are relevant to evaluating its effectiveness, the AIS policy of the National Endowment for the Arts cannot be justified.* It is difficult, for example, to justify a policy aimed at the schools which isn't clear whether or not it is intended to achieve educational outcomes. It is even more difficult to justify a policy that is loosely or casually enforced. But without clear objectives and systematic enforcement, estimates of effectiveness will be hard to come by. In this respect the Endowment's impatience with Eisner's question is understandable. If the Endowment doesn't know what its policy objectives are, it is difficult to know what counts as policy effectiveness.

It is important to note, however, that effectiveness is an ambiguous notion. There are effective arguments as well as effective practices, and since all practice cannot possibly be evaluated—it would be prohibitively expensive to attempt to do so[6]—effectiveness often implies likely or probable effectiveness which is established by cogent or reasonable argument set forth in behalf of practice. And even effectiveness of practice involves consideration of types of effectiveness. The question must always be, Effective with respect to what? What is more, effectiveness is only a necessary, not a sufficient, condition for the justifiability of a policy. Even if a policy is successful in bringing about that state of affairs which marks a policy's purpose, this does not mean the policy is thereby justified, for it is precisely that purpose or state of affairs which stands in need of justification in order for the policy as a whole to be acceptable. Policymakers must be prepared to defend the worthwhileness of their policies and not only their effectiveness. And if the policy is an educational policy, then the justification must be on strictly educational grounds. Neither the popularity of a policy nor its widespread endorsement necessarily satisfies the justification criterion. Preference for a policy can be ascertained through polls. But this cannot prove that the purpose of the policy is such that any thoughtful person ought to approve of it since the fact of a thing's being desired does not count as evidence for that thing's desirability. Questions concerning desirability or what ought to be preferred are dealt with on an entirely different level of thinking and of discourse.[7]

With this point in mind we may look once again at the purposes of the AIS policy with respect to effectiveness and justifiability. If AIS programs are primarily for artists and not for the schools' clientele, then an analysis of the policy's educational philosophy is beside the point. But then, it could be said, so are AIS programs, and the schools should have no part of them. The 1976 guidelines' parenthetical qualifications notwithstanding, however, there is enough in AIS publications to suggest that there are after all educational objectives. Some AIS writings do not equivocate about purpose. Some writers see artists and AIS programs as harbingers of significant educational reform. At this point a few asides are in order.

First, we should not expect cogent statements of educational aims from writers who have little or no background in education. The absence of such background, however, does help explain the extraordinary naïveté of AIS publications. This is not intended to offend the sensibilities of those who write them. People find their way into government jobs from a variety of places and tend to do what is expected of them. They write and think as others before them have or as those around them do, and uppermost in their minds is what people who count will think of what is written. Having said all this, however, AIS literature taken generally must be recognized for what it is: pure cliché. Mindlessness, it seems, is not the exclusive property of educationists. Some examples of this mindlessness have already been discussed, and it would be tedious to set out further instances. The task may thus center on considerations which any educational policy must take into account in order to be justified.

In any policy deliberation some reflection is required on the role of education and the function of schooling in a society such as ours. This usually involves setting forth notions of essential human nature, ethical and social ideals, and images of the good life. At this level of generality, statements of educational purpose may be somewhat vague, as they tend to refer to matters of a more or less ultimate nature. AIS publications characteristically favor this level of educational discourse. We read, for example, that the purposes of AIS programs are "to enrich creativity" and "to enhance children's powers of perception and their ability to express themselves and communicate creatively."

A defensible educational policy must go beyond such generalities to describe subject-specific purposes, to outline the factual knowledge, concepts, and methods and procedures the young must master. Intermediate or domain-specific purposes must be so articulated that the relationships to higher-level objectives are made clear.[8] In the case of arts education this involves the use of art and aesthetic theory which elucidates the conceptual baggage of the arts. This is also to say that the principal objectives of instruction in the arts should be primarily *aesthetic* and not extra-aesthetic.

It follows that the attainment of aesthetic objectives entails rather extensive work in learning how to create, confront, and criticize works of art. This may seem obvious, but not when one considers the extra-aesthetic outcomes stipulated for AIS programs. In addition to domain-specific instruction, although in some cases it is not clear that this is very important, AIS programs are said to have the potential for humanizing schooling generally, in which case artists are seen as "catalysts" of educational change; that is, AIS programs can ease problems of racial integration, cultivate the disposition to learn generally, aid the handicapped, develop interpersonal relations, engender a general creativeness, and build ethnic identity—to cite just a few AIS objectives.[9] The prospect of artists marching into schools also generates euphoria and evangelical zeal. In recent testimony in behalf of AIS programs, the arts were proposed "as an ideal context, a context for a euphoric kind of synthesis, in which better, richer, more profoundly humanizing education can take place."[10] It would take an essay in cultural history to explain how such miraculous powers have come to be ascribed to art,[11] but as a sample of AIS rhetoric it is standard.

This extra-aesthetic power ascribed to art requires comment. True, art is power and energy and has its peculiar potencies, but the power potential of art is for both good and evil. Art may be beneficent or maleficent with respect to its effects on persons and societies. And it is noteworthy that it is the potential of art for the latter that serious critics have recently been stressing. But AIS writers do not breathe the air of serious cultural criticism. To AIS writers art is not only benign, it is a stimulant and a curative, the best possible prescription for schooling. As Nancy Hanks has said, let artists pop into schools and doubtless all sorts of wonderful things will begin to happen.[12] If the potential of art for good and evil were properly understood, if the literature from Plato to Tolstoy to Steiner were known, much of the nonsense would not get written. And it should be pointed out that if one of the capacities of art is to induce action, another and perhaps more important function is to induce inward states of reflection and contemplation. There is a significant body of aesthetic opinion which holds that art is essentially nonutilitarian, its essence consisting in its efficacy for bringing about aesthetic experience in beholders, a kind of experience that is intrinsically gratifying and which leads nowhere in particular. As Dewey said, aesthetic experience contains no signposts; it is an experience having characteristics distinct from scientific and other types of mental activity. At this moment in culture this view of art's function would seem to have much to recommend it, at a time, that is, when—to refer to Saul Bellow once again—the world is so much with us as spectacle and crisis.[13] But now we are talking of aesthetic and art theory, which AIS publications choose to ignore. Rather, AIS writers prefer what elsewhere has been called a Trojan

Horse approach to schooling: gain entry for art and artists under any pretext or subterfuge and then let art and artists do what only art and artists can.

But enough. The central consideration to remember in responding to the justification question turns on the kinds of reasons given in support of a policy. The justification question demands that the right kinds of reason be given. Popularity and effectiveness of practice may figure in such reasons, but they are never sufficient. This is why the Western States Arts Foundation study of AIS programs, while it reports positive attitudes toward AIS programs, cannot be taken as a justification of the AIS policy. A few words are in order about this study.

The Western States Arts Foundation study[14]—termed "the first comprehensive study of AIS"—will, of course, be used to promote more AIS programs. One can already read the proposals and testimony—"according to," etc. But the study is superficial and exhibits the public relations aspect of the new cultural services field that is its shame. First the latter. At the time of this writing a media blitz is under way consisting of the dissemination of study highlights, a study summary, and short films all purporting to show the merits of AIS programs, *before,* that is, the technical report of the study containing accounts of research design, methodologies, and modes of analysis has been made available. (One is curious about the films. Were they made for the purpose of collecting data, in which case they should be part of the technical report, or were they made after the fact for the purpose of promoting AIS programs? If so, what does it say of a study that builds into its budget funds for promoting its conclusions? Would a public relations campaign have been launched to disseminate negative results?)

But criticism need not await the technical report, for it is apparent from the study's summary statements that the study is highly biased. For example, references to "increased creativity" are assumed to be instances of positive response and evidence of the successfulness of AIS programs. Of course, the expression "increased creativity" is meaningless until creativity is operationally defined and distinctions are drawn between quantitative and qualitative dimensions and many others. But the point is that creativeness is not a universally shared goal of arts instruction in the profession of teaching art. A respectable body of opinion holds that as an objective it is too vague and ambitious and not distinctive of arts education. And neither are attitudinal or affective values, which are emphasized in the WSAF study, held in uniformly high esteem throughout the profession. The cognitive aspects of arts instruction are increasingly being stressed, that is, a mastery of the concepts by which experience in the aesthetic domain can be structured. If the study of AIS programs assumed cognitive objectives to be important, its study summary might well have an entirely different character.

As for the attitudes of artists, administrators, and students solicited by the study, they can for the most part be discounted. Artists cannot be expected to bite the hand that feeds them; administrators have everything to gain and nothing to lose by endorsing AIS programs; that is, AIS programs cost them practically nothing and they receive free publicity in return; and students, though their opinions are worth noting, cannot always be expected to know what they need most. This is not to say that the opinions of these groups are completely beside the point; it is that in themselves they are insufficient to ground the worthwhileness of AIS programs. Certainly artists would express a willingness to return the following year. Of course, administrators, teachers, and students would like to have them back. But these are not the only choices. Given a choice, would artists prefer to work on their own at government expense or in an AIS program? Are administrators willing to strengthen requirements in the arts for the purpose of developing aesthetic learning? Or are AIS programs merely a way of having the arts without paying the freight that would be required if the arts were to become a major item in the budget?

It is not to be doubted that a cameo appearance by an artist or group of movement specialists can stir up things for a while, that is, get up people's "energy levels."[15] But what of long-term effects and the matter of alternatives? What would a new art department or more teachers and more equipment do for a school? Only the attitudes of the art teachers (and not other teachers) reported in the WSAF study deserve comment, for admittedly they are an important court of appeal. But I have suggested that teachers do not always act in their best professional interests. If confronted with criticism of AIS programs and the possibility of selecting alternative kinds of assistance, their responses might exhibit a greater range. And, of course, even teacher preferences, as this paper has indicated, are not the only consideration in satisfying the justification criterion. The kinds of reasons given by teachers for their preferences must be educationally defensible.

6. *To what portion of the school population does the AIS policy apply?*

It is estimated that AIS programs reach only 2 to 3 percent of the total school population. This fact in itself makes laughable the exaggerated claims set forth for AIS programs as far as their potential for educational reform is concerned. Neither can one envision the significant increase in the number of students reached that would be necessary if the arts were to have the kinds of consequences reformers talk about.

7. *Can the AIS policy be justified in terms of cost?*

This question is best discussed along with the next, and last, one.

8. *Have alternatives to the AIS policy been duly considered?*

We are forced once again to recall the confusion of purpose that marks AIS writings. If AIS programs are not intended primarily to further the learning of pupils, then AIS policies cannot be justified and the cost question is irrelevant. If, on the other hand, AIS programs are intended to have educational consequences, then the question of costs and alternatives is pertinent. The principal alternative, of course, is the strengthening of existing school programs. This could involve the hiring of additional staff, the purchase of supplies and equipment, and the support of faculty members' travel and further study. It could also involve support of local research efforts. School programs could also be strengthened by improving teacher preparation programs, perhaps by upgrading their laboratory, clinical, and internship functions. In short there is much that federal assistance could do to strengthen the profession of the teaching of art, which needs all the support it can receive. The increase in cultural activities in the society has not resulted in a commensurate increase in aesthetic studies in the schools. Strengthening the profession is the most effective way to contribute to the reform of aesthetic instruction. A small art staff in a high school might thus want to ask whether it is in their best interests to have, say, $40,000 spent on artists-in-residence (e.g., painters, poets, sculptors, movement specialists, dancers, etc.) or on needed supplies and equipment which will be around long after the artists have departed. I realize that teachers do not usually have this choice—it is usually a case of accepting the gift horse or nothing. But simply taking thought might encourage teachers to establish their own priorities rather than having them decided by others.

Conclusion

The questions asked of the AIS policy in this paper suggest that the policy is in need of reassessment by the Endowment and by teachers. But I am not optimistic that this will happen, and for this reason. The AIS policy is politically popular, which means that questions of validity and justifiability are secondary considerations. And who in his or her right mind criticizes anything done for artists in our time? For those who teach the arts to do so borders on professional suicide. Having said this, however, it should be emphasized that the point of this paper has not been to undermine federal assistance for artists; rather, it has been to question the policy of tempting artists into schools. Let artists do what they do best where they do it best and give them, at least some of them, money to do it. As for the cultural establishment that arranges things between artists and schools, the plea here is for more sense and less nonsense, for more rationale and less mystique, in short for more professionalism and less public relations. Above all, if the AIS policy is to continue, which is likely, then there is an obligation on the part of the cultural establishment to take account of serious and responsible criticism. It contributes nothing to cultural and educational diplomacy to act as if the AIS policy, or any other, has divine sanction in the light of which all criticism is deemed heretical and in bad faith.

Notes

1. These questions are discussed at greater length in R. A. and C. M. Smith, "Justifying Policy for Arts Education," an unpublished manuscript that draws significantly on Donna H. Kerr's *Educational Policy: Analysis, Structure, and Justification* (New York: David McKay, 1976).

2. Remarks by those involved in administering and advising AIS programs bear this out.

3. Saul Bellow, "Writers and Literature in American Society," in *Culture and Its Creators,* ed. J. Ben-David and T. N. Clark (Chicago: University of Chicago Press, 1977), p. 173.

4. Elliot W. Eisner, "Is the Artist in the School Program Effective?" *Art Education* 27, no. 2 (February 1974). Questions about AIS programs have also been raised by Vincent Lanier in two articles in *Arts and Activities:* "Instructional Media: The Artist-Teacher Re-Visited," 69, no. 3 (April 1971); and "Instructional Media," 69, no. 4 (May 1971).

5. For a revealing and often entertaining account of how the government works, see Charles Frankel, *High on Foggy Bottom* (New York: Harper and Row, 1969).

6. In this respect I agree with Robert Stake in "To Evaluate an Arts Program," *Journal of Aesthetic Education* 10, nos. 3–4 (July–October 1976).

7. R. A. and C. M. Smith, "Justifying Policy for Arts Education."

8. For one effort to relate high-level to intermediate objectives in aesthetic education, see R. A. and C. M. Smith, "The Artworld and Aesthetic Skills: A Context for Research and Development," in *Arts and Aesthetics: An Agenda for the Future,* ed. S. Madeja (St. Louis: CEMREL, 1977).

9. For a sampling of the range of outcomes stipulated for AIS programs see the following: B. Schiff, *Artists in Schools* (Washington, D.C.: GPO, 1973); S. Madeja et al., *The Artists in the School: A Report on the Artist-in-Residence Project* (St. Louis: CEMREL, 1970); B. Morrison, "The Artist as Teacher," *Saturday Review* 53, no. 51 (December 19, 1970); R. Tyrell et al., "Artists-in-Schools: Why Bother?" *Art Education* 27, no. 9 (November 1974); J. Kerr, "Arts Projects as a Vehicle for Educational Change," *Art Education* 25, no. 9 (December 1972) and "Artists in Educational Settings: A Report from the National Endowment for the Arts," *The National Elementary Principal* 55, no. 3 (January–February 1976); M. Merrill, "The Federal Government and Arts in the School: Easing Integration through Special Arts Projects," *Music Educators Journal* 62, no. 6 (February 1976).

10. From testimony given before a House Committee on Select Education in the fall of 1975.

11. The story is partially told in Jacques Barzun's *The Use and Abuse of Art* (Princeton: Princeton University Press, 1974).

12. Nancy Hanks, "Education through Art: A Gateway," *Art Education* 24, no. 7 (October 1971).

13. As Bellow puts it: "The power of a true work of art is such that it induces a temporary suspension of activities. It leads to contemplative states, to wonderful and, to my mind, sacred states of the soul." In this statement Bellow is one with a tradition of aesthetic theory dating from the eighteenth century.

14. "Study Summary" (Denver: Western States Art Foundation, 1976). The study was supported with a grant from the National Endowment for the Arts.

15. The expression is from S. R. Shapiro et al., *Artists in the Classroom* (Hartford, Conn.: Connecticut Commission on the Arts, 1973). This is not an Endowment publication, but it shares the Endowment's outlook. In fact, AIS publications tend to look alike: artists and young children pictured in predominantly action poses with much dancing, making of faces, and joyful sprawling about. The photograph on the cover of this particular publication doubtless conveys the authors' notion of what an AIS program should look like: an adult artist sits cross-legged and barefoot on the floor, making a face at a child who returns the expression. Cf. the conclusion to Ross Norris's "SAIR: The Student Artist-in-Residence," *Art Education* 30, no. 2 (February 1977), p. 26.

19

The Arts in Alternative Schools: Some Observations

Barbara Leondar

The state of the arts in the public schools is even more deplorable than the state of everything else. Friends of the arts, then, have reason to welcome the educational disestablishmentarianism currently astir on the North American continent. Suddenly, from Canada to Mexico, "alternative schools" are ubiquitous. Humanistic in conception, Utopian in outlook, these schools would seem to provide a natural home for the arts. That, at least, was the assumption which led me to visit dozens of such institutions and to study the manifestos of hundreds more. What follows is an informal account of a year's observations.

"Alternative schools" has become a generic designation encompassing a broad range of experimental institutions, public, private, and denominational. Virtually every major metropolitan school system now supports at least one unconventional school; almost every state and province, even those as educationally recalcitrant as Alabama and Virginia, now claim at least one free school. Thickets of such experiments flourish on both coasts; clusters surround the great university centers of Canada and the American Midwest. But significant numbers, following the lead of earlier Utopians, have retreated from the cities to the open land, to farms, ranches, and wilderness country. Rural or urban, they include Summerhill and Leicestershire variants, community and parent cooperatives, drop-out centers and live-in communes, peripatetic academies and ecological survival institutes. Although such endeavors tend to be aggressively independent, they have nonetheless already spawned a national and several regional information exchanges, a weekly newsletter, a handful of employment centers, and a growing number of producers of avant-garde educational materials.

Because such schools often exist on a shoestring and sometimes vanish as abruptly as they materialized, it is impossible to estimate how many lives they touch—how many children, how many teachers, how many parents. In any case, their interest rests not on numbers alone but rather on the influence which they may exert—indeed, *intend* to exert—upon conventional patterns of schooling. Although a few are truly counterschools, viewing themselves less as alternatives than as rebukes to existing institutions, most regard themselves as harbingers of future mass education. For this reason, although some receive visitors in such numbers as to strain their resources, they continue to entertain with the cordiality of missionaries. Characteristically, then, alternative schools are serious, self-conscious, and principled. They are prepared to resist charges of amateurism or enthusiasm with a set of rational and internally consistent premises from which their practice derives.

These premises are of special concern to art educators. They fall into two classes: assumptions about human growth and learning, on the one hand, and on the other, a set of values which those assumptions are presumed to decree. The accord between these two may be less than complete. "Every individual learns best through his own personal experience," notes one school. "We believe in the right of every individual to be free to experience the world around him in his own way." One may wonder whether the opening clause provides sufficient warrant for the concluding imperative, or whether, in fact, that "right" conceals a nest of unexpressed and prior convictions. In any case, the real interest of the statement resides in its implied values. Freedom, individuality, and the diversity which must result from many individualities—these are the Utopian trinity, the fundamentals which, however variously interpreted and realized, command universal allegiance.

Freedom in the alternative school often means not merely avoidance of coercion but absence of all restraints except those required for health and safety and for preservation of the rights of others. The free school student can, for the most part, do exactly as he chooses (and that includes choosing to do nothing) provided he does not endanger himself or unduly exasperate his fellows. Even compulsory attendance laws, which apply to experimental schools operating within public school systems, are likely to be loosely observed.

The emphasis on individuality and diversity dictates that students be able to select according to taste and interest from a rich mix of activities. Even more important, it requires that those activities all be judged equally worthy. This Benthamite proposition engenders marked uneasiness among conventional schoolmen and probably contributes generously to the disorientation which afflicts the first-time free school visitor. After all, not only is push-pin as good as Pushkin, but making jelly or making out is on a par with making music, a course in astrology is equal to one in astrophysics, and an hour's T-group is neither better nor worse than an hour's tedium. The brochure of a California school makes the point merely by its choice of rhetorical style; the relentless series of parallel units insists on the equality of each of its members: "Students are involved in such areas as mountaineering, creative sewing and design, organic gardening, computer building, word sensitivity, minority studies, existential philosophy, yoga, meditation, sex education, pottery, weaving, geometry, diving, and gourmet cooking." The list is not uncharacteristic.

One further value, widely held among alternative schools, deserves to be noted. Since Dewey, American educators have proclaimed their interest in "the whole child" while in reality attending only to a narrow range of behavior. The new Utopians, attempting to redress the imbalance, place human encounter and emotional growth at the center of their concerns. They seek to foster intuition and insight, gusto and passion, self-actualization and self-expression. As one experimentalist writes: " . . . love and freedom are integral parts of education, as they are of life. Allowing children to be happy emotionally and psychologically and to develop their full potential as human beings are more important to us than forcing them to learn to read or write and do arithmetic and homework. Happy children will become happy adults, and happy adults do not make war, commit anti-social acts, or destroy other living things."

Not every alternative school goes quite so far. Many—especially those within public school systems, but by no means only those—retain some authority, impose some structure, or insist on some academic preparation. Often an all-elective school will establish distribution requirements. Or an elementary school may impose formal reading instruction upon nonreaders approaching middle-school age.[1] And secondary schools commonly offer appropriate instruction for those seeking college admission; in such cases, college requirements may impose stringent limits upon a student's choices. The descriptions which follow, therefore, should be distrusted; for every generalization, a dozen counterinstances could be cited. At best, these examples represent frequent, but by no means universal, practice. Alternative schools are as idiosyncratic as the children they cherish.

Individuality, diversity, intuition, expressiveness—in such schools, surely the arts must flower. Where none need tolerate laborious "appreciation" classes, where no one is ordered to practice (or else), and where each is encouraged to celebrate his own idiom, there surely shall the Muses dwell. Yet, every value implies a rejection of its opposite. Where freedom and expressiveness reign, other qualities retreat. In too many alternative schools freedom has been purchased at the cost of discipline and commitment. Some students flit restlessly from one to another transitory attraction, sampling a smorgasbord of interests and activities. Others sink phlegmatically into apathy and ennui. Few muster the doggedness and purpose to pursue a problem, aesthetic or intellectual, as far as it may lead. Younger children, oddly enough, seem less vulnerable to this infection than their adolescent siblings. (Utopians count this as evidence of the damage inflicted on adolescents by prior conventional schooling.) In elementary schools founded on the British integrated-day model—in schools, that is, which bulge with a heterogeneity of tools, books, paints, games, scraps, records, and other materials freely available to children—pupils often produce paintings, crafts, sculpture, and poetry of astonishing quality. Even here, however, music languishes, as does dance, the latter perhaps because it requires a disciplined *group* (rather than an interested individual); the former certainly because mastery of an instrument and a notation necessitates direct instruction of a kind such schools eschew. And of course it still remains to be seen whether free school youngsters entering adolescence will continue to avoid the temptations of frivolity and self-indulgence.

If freedom has its price, so too does social growth, which is often purchased at the cost of privacy and silence. Free schools are noisy. Even their designated quiet zones—libraries, meditation spaces, listening rooms—rustle more than most such places with the sounds of aggregate human living. Many secondary schools have student lounges, or smoking rooms, or retreats where, invariably, the sound system operates at such a volume as to preclude conversation and to screen out other noises. Although there students can withdraw from the unremitting social pressures and intrusive demands of others, their retreat is at best partial: they must still conceal their interior life, avoid eye-to-eye contact, maintain an inscrutable mask. The student who writes or sketches commits a social indiscretion; he draws attention to himself and thus disrupts the tacit pretense at isolation. Some wealthy schools, wired up for electronic learning, provide a few soundproof listening booths and a number of less claustrophobic audio stations where students can plug into temporary privacy. That listening booths, where available, are in constant use and must be reserved well in advance is scarcely surprising. But experimental schools are poor for the most part and count themselves lucky to possess a single quiet area. In most elementary schools even this minimal amenity is lacking. Of the "silence, exile, and cunning" which Joyce took to be the condition of art, the first two are reserved for the onset of puberty.

Nor does the faculty fare better. Indeed, teaching in a free school demands far more than the normal allotment of dedication and constancy. Since the job requires the teacher to be ceaselessly, patiently, cheerfully accessible to kids, his day is likely to disintegrate into an incoherent mix of harassment, crisis, and distraction. Whatever its personal rewards—and some, it should be emphasized, find these immeasurably rich—adult life in alternative school lacks aesthetic and intellectual focus. The restless motion and relentless sociability which characterize the students' style impose themselves willy-nilly upon the staff. The result, of course, is to deny students those models of sustained and disciplined purpose which might invite emulation. In alternative schools, sometimes by accident but more often by design, the psychological tempo of the student prevails.

Insofar, then, as the arts demand of their practitioners stern concentration, periodic isolation and withdrawal, even on occasion blind resistance to social proprieties, to that extent they have suffered in alternative schools. Paradoxically, they may have suffered most in those schools which are most free—free, that is, of adult authority and externally imposed structure. In such schools new tyrannies, subtler than their predecessors, may breed. Indecision, indolence, and indifference can paralyze aspiration; disorder and distraction can compel and prohibit as effectively as rules, schedules, and penalties. Especially as reinforced by other affirmatives—for example, by the constant promotion of interpersonal responsiveness and community participation—the freedom of alternative schools can prove to be merely an alternative coercion. This is not to deny that such schools honor achievement in the arts. On the contrary, they celebrate its appearance more fervently than do conventional institutions. But their celebration is at the same time an acknowledgment of the obstacles to creation in such an environment.

By contrast, what flourishes in alternative schools are the crafts: leather and metal work, pottery, textiles. That this should be so seems altogether predictable. In part, it responds to economic need. Free schools are poor and craftwork is salable. In part it responds to an antitechnological bias as well as to an impulse for self-sufficiency and simplicity not unlike that which characterized American Utopias of the nineteenth century. But its fundamental impetus is social. Handicrafts require neither the isolation nor the concentration demanded by the fine arts. In fact, nothing is more companionable than an evening gathering of craftsmen around a country hearth, and this scene is as regularly reenacted in residential free schools as is evening study hall in traditional institutions. That the products of such communion are of uneven quality matters little; what counts is the process, not the product.

Yet a genuinely aesthetic motive is sometimes apparent as well. In those instances, emphasis shifts to the artifact, and the esteem accorded the craftsman represents a tribute to precision, inventiveness, and artisanship. Where these values prevail, the boundary between art and craft may blur. At a Quaker farm school high in the New Hampshire hills, my query about fine arts facilities produced a tour of the meeting room where one of two pianos was housed, a visit to the pottery shed and adjacent outdoor kiln, and an exploration of the subterranean studio where seven imposing looms all but overpowered a lone easel, a small sculpture table, and a tired photographic display. The designs emerging on the looms, however, were visually striking and technically adept. Here the free school style, modified by traditional Quaker concerns, had yielded a unique amalgam of the useful and the aesthetic. Still, that combination, although found now and then, is as rare in free schools as elsewhere.

Nonetheless, the prospect for the fine arts is not uniformly bleak. Experimental schools sometimes offer real alternatives in aesthetic learning. Although few have attempted to educate students as potential audiences, some have evolved thoughtful, even imaginative, means for encouraging and refining the practice of the arts.[2] And where schools persist in neglecting this task, after-school alternatives—compensatory education for the aesthetically deprived—are emerging. These share the characteristic goals and style of the free school. Whether in school or out, four approaches predominate.

The Open Studio

The open studio is exactly what its name implies—a workroom equipped with the tools and materials of one or more of the arts. Some schools will station an instructor or other adult in the studio, but most eschew supervision on the grounds that an adult presence curtails exploration and encourages dependency. If a teacher is on hand, he is likely to remain inconspicuous, intervening only if summoned or if equipment is egregiously abused. Supervised or not, the open studio remains open to all students throughout the school day and often beyond it. No registrations, authorizations, passes, signatures, or other clerical impediments bar the way; the student is free to attend his Muse whenever she beckons.

The open studio has flourished in progressive nursery schools for years and, under the influence of British practice, has become increasingly common in elementary education. Among secondary schools, although still a rarity, it has at least won acceptance as sound practice. And in alert suburbs the open studio has by now become a mandatory feature of new public school construction. Generally it is one element of a more comprehensive system which includes open laboratories and industrial shops; sometimes, unfortunately, it remains the poor relation in that family. Timberlane Regional High School is perhaps not untypical. Built five years ago to serve the five hundred children of four tiny rural communities, none of which had ever boasted a secondary school, Timberlane includes two spacious and well-outfitted open shops for wood and metal work, three superbly equipped open laboratories for biology, chemistry, and physics, and a single crowded art studio. The latter, though nominally open, is scheduled for classes during much of the day, so its accessibility is substantially reduced. By contrast, the Sanborn Middle School in affluent Concord reserves the entire basement of its two-story plant for the arts. Here, in an architectural setting as elegant as any on the continent, alcoves are equipped for easel painting, for wood, metal, and clay sculpture, and for pottery, leaving available for elective use a large central space with movable work tables. In a studio of these proportions, two or three classes (limited, as a rule, to ten children) can meet simultaneously without disruption of privacy and without curtailing spontaneous use of the facility by individuals.

Obviously the open studio is best suited to the visual arts. Nowhere is dance popular enough to merit its own space, while music requires rather different arrangements. Creative writing, however, remains a puzzle. Two Newton teachers claim considerable success with a modified version of the open writing lab. Although institutional rules require that students register for and attend the lab, once enrolled they are under no compulsion to write nor will they receive formal instruction in technique. On an ordinary day, perhaps a quarter of the class, gathered in corners or on the fringes of the room, will be otherwise occupied. The rest, sprawled over tables, hunched above typewriters, or strung out on window seats according to their bent, will be in the throes of composition. What they compose is under their own control, as is the amount and kind of assistance they receive. Some students will submit work in progress to a friend or teacher; some will display only finished artifacts. Some seem to want the merest nod of approbation, some a detailed critique, some the applause of the entire group. Although flexible enough to accommodate such diverse preferences, the laboratory setting nonetheless puts the writer on public view, a circumstance which would seem to multiply the psychic discomforts of composition. For the graphic artist, on the other hand, such a milieu seems nourishing. The young observer in the studio can incorporate in the most casual and offhand fashion a rich knowledge of media and technique. His fellows are, as a rule, happy to discuss or to demonstrate. If several students confront related problems, they can constitute themselves an informal class and request appropriate instruction. But perhaps most desirable of all is the opportunity afforded by the open studio to explore at leisure, to pose one's own problems, to fail, if need be, and try again or try another way, always without penalty to the ego or damage to the academic record.

The Artist as Schoolteacher

The open studio system abandons formal instruction or at least minimizes it. This, of course, is consistent with the more general goal of reducing constraints and expanding choices. But at the same time it reinforces—or in any case does not ameliorate—the aimlessness and dilettantism which may afflict the free school student. Least of all does it offer him a model on which to pattern his own behavior, or provide him with a sense of the practicing artist as an embodied human being. Adding to these considerations the further one that the practitioner is likely to prove the most ardent advocate of his calling, many schools have sought to attract working artists to their faculties. Estimating the success of such recruiting efforts is precarious, since the distinction between artists who teach and teachers who paint or act or dance is necessarily a fine one, ultimately decidable only by the practitioner. Still, certain patterns emerge.

The most common is one borrowed from university practice—that of the artist-in-residence. In return for work space, and perhaps board and housing, the professional makes himself available to students. He will offer tutelage if requested, but, from the school's point of view, his most important function is merely to be visible and, within reason, amiable while doing his own thing. Obviously such an arrangement once again favors the visual and certain of the performing arts, since what the composer or poet does is not readily accessible to observation. Obviously, too, such activity as *is* observable will vary in quality from school to school and, within the school, from month to month, artists being individuals of disparate talents and uncertain inspiration. Thus, although the Sudbury Valley School numbers among a staff of twelve a musicologist, a painter, a sculptor, and a photographer, a random visit may find the part studio bare, devoid even of signs of recent occupation, while the only music emanates from the stereo set in the smoking room. Even when the artist's activity is prominent, his apparent effect on students may remain negligible. In fact, so perverse are the ways of adolescents that the continuing presence of a practicing artist—his very ordinariness in the school setting—may discourage rather than excite students' interest. Nonetheless, the salutary influence of a devoted professional upon a youthful community can scarcely be discounted. If he never answered a question nor offered an explanation (though it is hard to imagine that happening), his example as a man who takes himself and his work seriously ought to guarantee his welcome.

By contrast, the visiting artist imported into the school for a single performance appears as an exotic and can exert a lively impact. Unfortunately, the impression often conveyed by such visitors is a compound of glamour and mystification, designed to dazzle rather than enlighten. The very conditions of the visit may thrust the artist into the role of entertainer rather than of teacher. Even if he resists the temptation to preserve a professional distance between himself and his audience, his interchange with the numbers of children who will have something to say must necessarily be abbreviated and fragmentary. Still, enlightenment need not be dull, nor communication superficial, provided the artist is himself clear in his intentions. The Arena Stage of Washington represents perhaps the happiest conquest of the hazards of an isolated visit. Veterans of nightly improvisational performances for general audiences, the Arena troupe spends its days in schools and its weekends in teachers' workshops. Experience has taught the troupe to reject engagements shorter than half a day or audiences larger than two hundred. Given this number, each member of the troupe will engage a group of ten children for approximately two hours in the creation of improvised roles and situations around themes suggested by the children themselves. For a final hour the entire group will reconvene so that adults and children together can perform for their peers. Because the Arena company sees its purpose as teaching children to make dramatic art of their own experience, its members avoid censoring the children's themes. In racially tense Washington where most teachers are white and most students black, theirs could be a disastrous course. Instead, they have learned to coax from the incipient explosion itself the conception of art as a paring and shaping of life, an imposition of coherence on chaos. That they do so without preaching, almost without language itself, is a tribute both to their skill and to their art. Unhappily, the momentary transformation wrought by Arena Stage is rarely sustained by the schools it visits. Though the company may suggest what school can aspire to, its brief performances cannot, after all, affect children deeply and permanently.

Like Arena Stage, the Teachers and Writers Collaborative of New York sends its members into conventional public schools to offer children an unconventional experience. But unlike the theater company, the Collaborative's teacher returns to his class once a week. He thus maintains continuity while escaping the invisibility which may cloak the resident artist; his arrivals become celebrations interrupting the weekly routine. In fact, he occupies much the same position as the art or music specialist supplied by the school system, with the important difference that he is not a part of the system nor is he a certified teacher. Instead he is likely to be a young poet with a published volume or two to his credit, a growing reputation, and a serious commitment to his craft.

The Collaborative's teachers come into the classroom to help children write poetry. That they succeed, often beyond anyone's predictions, is substantiated anew by each issue of their monthly newsletter, which regularly displays samples of student work. Although suspicious of mechanically applied methods and skeptical, as poets will be, of generalizations, they have nonetheless evolved a loose technique which, in one variation or another, dominates the Collaborative's practice. Its elements will be familiar to readers of Herbert Kohl, a founder of the Collaborative, and to fans of the *New York Review,* where Kenneth Koch recently described his classroom adventures:

> Rhyme is wonderful, but children generally aren't able to use it skillfully enough to make good poetry. It gets in their way. The effort of finding rhymes stops the free flow of their feelings and associations, and poetry gives way to sing-song. There are formal devices which are more natural to children, more inspiring, easier to use. The one I suggested most frequently was some kind of repetition: the same word or words ("I wish") or the same kind of thing (a comparison) in every line. . . .
>
> A poetry idea should be easy to understand, it should be immediately interesting, and it should bring something new into the children's poems. This could be new subject matter, new sense awareness, new experience of language or poetic form. I looked for other techniques or themes that were, like wishes, a natural and customary part of poetry. I thought of comparisons and then of sounds, and I had the children write a poem about each. As in the Wish Poems, I suggested a repetitive form to help give their poems unity: putting a comparison or a sound in every line.
>
> Some things about teaching children to write poetry I knew in advance, instinctively or from having taught adults, and others I found out in the classroom. Most important, I believe, is taking children seriously as poets. . . . Treating them like poets was not a case of humorous but effective diplomacy, as I had first thought; it was the right way to treat them because it corresponded to the truth. A little humor, of course, I left in. Poetry was serious, but we joked and laughed a good deal; it was serious because it was such a pleasure to write. Treating them as poets enabled me to encourage them and egg them on in a nonteacherish way—as an admirer and fellow worker rather than as a boss.[3]

One clue to the Collaborative's success, manifest in Koch's remarks, is its desanctification of poetry. Koch relieves verse-making of the burden of holiness too often imposed on it by teachers whose reading ceased with Tennyson; he returns the poem to the world of discourse and to the arena of children's immediate concerns. At the same time his attitude is thoroughly practical; he sets forth without preconceptions to find a technique that works, and he tinkers about until he has found it. How much his search is aided by professional intuitions can scarcely be guessed, though they would seem to be crucial. While that fact magnifies the value of his insights for teachers who are not poets, it also underscores an important gap in the Collaborative's procedures. Explanation has been systematically ignored; no attempt has been made to understand, in logical or psychological terms, why one approach works and another fails, or even to examine what it means for a technique to "work." Doubtless it is unjust to accuse the Collaborative of slighting a task it never chose to undertake. Yet the neglect of so unique a fund of experience is surely regrettable. What that experience, diligently combed, might reveal about the sources of children's aesthetic capacities, their nature, development, and variation, needs to be known. As long as the Collaborative continues to tinker without conceptualizing, its success must remain local and isolated, unexplained and unexplainable.

The Student as Apprentice

Both the open lab system and the introduction of professional artists into the classroom imply an acceptance of the school as a world unto itself. An opposing view, however, regards the school as an artificial, sometimes noxious, enclave which, by isolating young people from the real business of life, unduly prolongs helplessness and dependency. Some argue further that teachers who merely teach, those whose sole occupation is school-mastering, will never be taken seriously by adolescents since they lack the authority conferred by genuine achievement. John Holt is among those who have lately arrived at this view:

> What is most truly and deeply nutty about schools and schooling is not the idea that someone decides what and how and when someone else should learn something, or even the idea that all this should be done in a building shut off from the rest of the world, but the idea that learning should or can take place in an institution *that doesn't produce anything but learning*. . . . Any game, or puzzle, or activity, that is not worth the time and attention of the adults will soon be seen by the children as not being worth their time either. No one can get children truly interested in reading, or writing, or whatever it may be, who does not himself do these things regularly, and in their presence, and not for their good and pleasure but for his own.[4]

These two beliefs, taken together, underlie the "school without walls" exemplified by Philadelphia's widely imitated Parkway Program. Parkway has no classrooms of its own. Instead, its students learn science in research labs, mathematics in engineering or insurance offices, and languages in foreign consulates. And of course they study art history in museums, music in recording studios, writing in newspaper offices and television stations. Other smaller schools sometimes apprentice individual students to local master craftsmen. Although particular arrangements vary, there exists a common underlying intention: to evict the arts from schools, where they are alien and embarrassed, and to send children forth to encounter the artist on his own turf.

Where schools have failed to provide such opportunities, after-school alternatives are emerging. Their appearance is perhaps the newest wrinkle in aesthetic education. Saturday piano lessons are not, of course, strikingly novel; out-of-school instruction has long prevailed as the dominant pattern of training in the arts. But except for a gifted elite, those children lucky enough to discover the arts out of school generally did so under tutors whose accomplishments were pedagogical (or commercial) rather than creative. What is novel, then, is the inauguration of out-of-school centers where serious, committed artists stand ready to initiate children into their crafts. All of these, however, are still too new to permit evaluation. The Cherry Street Studio, for instance, came into existence earlier this spring and for the present remains only a building housing sixty painters, sculptors, and printmakers whose studios are always open to young people. The Touchstone Center, an even more ambitious experiment in authorship now getting under way, expects to reproduce a journal of international children's writing. These endeavors all emanate from New York City, but rumors suggest that their counterparts on the West Coast and elsewhere are already being planned.

Again, it is perhaps unjust to require of a new and precarious enterprise that it add to its other vexations that of systematic analysis and research. Yet fundamental questions need answering, and the day-by-day accumulation of events which might supply those answers may be difficult to recapture in later retrospective study. While the practical goals of these experiments merit applause, they need not preclude, as they now do, the equally worthy purposes of research and evaluation.

The Student as Teacher

Big kids have probably always taught little ones. In primitive societies they may be the primary tutors; in our own popular folklore the role of big brother, though invested with lofty condescension, will also require as its price some tutelary responsibility. Lately a convergence of events has sparked a new interest in the effectiveness of juvenile teachers. Among those events was Dolores Durkin's study of children who learned to read before entering school, a study which found that preschoolers had been instructed by siblings as often as by parents.[5] This discovery had already shaped the practice of some British infant schools where instruction in reading—and in almost everything else—proceeded very informally, relying less on teachers than on the willingness of peers to share their skills. Again, Ivan Illich has recounted the success of Spanish-speaking Harlem teenagers in teaching their native language quickly and efficiently to adult volunteers.[6] And experiments in cross-age tutoring in American public schools have suggested that tutors learn at least as much as their pupils from such an experience.

Much of this needs to be said only in order to be dismissed. Peer teaching in alternative schools—and there is much of it—proceeds from entirely different motives. It is the product not of a concern with the efficacy of teaching and learning but rather of the expression of allegiance to a cause. In fact, its symbolic importance may outweigh its practical effects, for the student-as-teacher embodies an egalitarian principle high in the scale of free school values. "All may learn and all may teach," proclaims one school's brochure, announcing its elimination of distinctions based on academic rank or achievement. Clearly, unless students are empowered to teach—and moreover, to teach their teachers—that proclamation will be hollow.

Proclaiming away all such distinctions, however, does not erase them. Perhaps it is a tribute to innate human modesty that the student who chooses to teach is, as a rule, one who has already achieved substantial competence. Since, in academic subjects, such expertise will be rare, the young instructor is likely to be teaching a performance skill—typing, dressmaking, sports, auto repair, or one or another of the arts or crafts. At the Palfrey Street School in Watertown, an eighteen-year-old painter of great promise teaches a beginners' class of fellow-students. In an experimental school in Los Angeles, a sixteen-year-old guitarist joins with a literature teacher to offer a course in poetry and song. At the Murray Road School in Newton, a high school filmmaker receives academic credit for teaching animation techniques at a nearby junior high. In many schools, individual tutoring or casual instruction in an open lab has grown so routine as to attract little notice.

But if in alternative schools and in conventional ones the rationale for peer teaching differs, its practical effects do not. The most predictable of these is wretched teaching—wretched, that is, if teaching is valued for its clarity, logic, and coherence. The young teacher does not begin at the beginning, does not proceed in sequence, does not define his terms or explain his assumptions or offer reasons for his judgments. He does not, in short, lay bare the workings of a mature intellect; patently, he cannot. Countervailing strengths, however, may offset these shortcomings. Not the least of his assets is enthusiasm. Scarcely a substitute for coherence when the instructor is an adult, enthusiasm may nonetheless count importantly in the young teacher. His obvious pleasure in his activity, his eagerness to pursue it despite recurrent and inevitable frustration, his patience and shrewdness, intensity and persistence, all provide that model of discipline and purpose so rare in free schools. Moreover, the young teacher's bumbling may lend his example extra weight: he is not so far ahead of his students that the gap appears forbidding. They rightly see him as one of themselves, distinguished from them by will and perseverance. Some surely must recognize, at least subliminally, the latent presence of those qualities in themselves and the consequent possibility of a corresponding achievement.

The greater benefits, however, may accrue to the tutor. The worn observation that one learns his subject best by teaching it still nurtures a kernel of truth. Under the questioning of students, the teaching artist must seek words to describe habits, assumptions, and intuitions which lie on the fringes of awareness. He must, however incoherently at first, explain and justify what he is about. In the process of finding language for this peripheral knowledge, he brings it into conscious focus, gains insight into his own procedures, and can alter or refine them voluntarily. He must also begin to formulate his own aesthetic, to demonstrate why *this* is better than *that,* and to support his judgment with reasons sufficient to withstand his pupils' challenges. Assuming that critical self-consciousness is to be desired in the artist, this early training would seem invaluable.

Peer teaching in the arts is an innovation of a different order from those described above. Less amenable to planning and more dependent on a spontaneous confluence of circumstances, it cannot be programmed into a curriculum. It need not, however, exclude other modes of instruction; in fact, it probably serves best as a supplement to a more nourishing diet. How rich a supplement it is remains to be discovered. Once again, its consequences need to be better understood, if only because it is a style likely to prevail for some time.

A final distinction—between alternative schools on the one hand and, on the other, out-of-school alternative arts programs—perhaps needs to be emphasized. For the most part the arts are withering in alternative schools, decisively in secondary though less irrevocably in elementary schools. Many alternative schools have traded the formalism of conventional institutions for an equally forlorn disorder. Theirs is an extreme response to desperate circumstances. But pessimism would be premature. Lively minds populate both camps; where they have attained influence, reform follows—in the public schools, reform inspired by the experiments, and in alternative schools, reform stimulated by students' incapacity to bear the burdens of self-determination. But reform is slow, and if despair is unjustified, impatience is not.

Alternative programs in the arts, however, are another matter. Whether operating, like the Teachers and Writers Collaborative, within schools ossified by habit and custom, or like the Cherry Street Studios, entirely outside the system, these approaches bring a new and welcome vitality to the teaching of the arts. Especially heartening is the readiness of practicing artists to bare their mysteries to children. If such programs flourish and multiply, they may yet undo the mischief of generations of schoolmasters.

Notes

Consistent with common usage in 1971, when this article was first published, the term "he" is used in the generic sense.

1. But see Neil Postman's argument for abolishing reading instruction entirely in "The Politics of Reading," *Harvard Educational Review* 40 (May 1970): 244–52.
2. Implicit in this approach (and explicit, too, in the emphasis on learning by doing) is the assumption that potential audiences should be educated by doing what the artist does. Whether this practice also implies, as Dewey argued, that reader and listener are in some sense author and composer *manqué,* re-creating the work in the act of responding to it, is a question schools prefer to ignore. And they are equally indifferent to the difficulties of reconciling Dewey's notions about art with the Benthamite egalitarianism that informs the free school curriculum. Although Dewey is enjoying a new vogue among free schools, one suspects that he suffers the same fate there as elsewhere; he is still, alas, more quoted than read.
3. Kenneth Koch, "Wishes, Lies, and Dreams: Teaching Children to Write Poetry," *New York Review* 14, no. 7 (9 April 1970): 18–22.
4. John Holt, *New Schools Exchange Newsletter,* no. 36 (no date), p. 2.
5. Dolores Durkin, *Children Who Read Early* (New York: Teachers College Press, 1966).
6. Ivan Illich, "Why We Must Abolish Schooling," *New York Review* 15, no. 1 (2 July 1970): 12–13.

20

Is Art Above the Laws of Decency?

Hilton Kramer

The fierce controversy now raging over the decision of the Corcoran Gallery of Art in Washington to cancel an exhibition of photographs by the late Robert Mapplethorpe was an event waiting to happen. If it hadn't happened at this time and at this institution, sooner or later it would surely have erupted elsewhere. The wonder is that it didn't occur earlier, for it involves an issue that has haunted our arts institutions, their supporters, and their public for as long as government money—taxpayers' money—has come to play the major role it now does in financing the arts.

The issue may be briefly and in the most general terms stated as follows: Should public standards of decency and civility be observed in determining which works of art or art events are to be selected for the government's support? Or, to state the issue another way, is everything and anything to be permitted in the name of art? Or, to state the issue in still another way, is art now to be considered such an absolute value that no other standard—no standard of taste, no social or moral standard—is to be allowed to play any role in determining what sort of art it is appropriate for the government to support?

The Corcoran Gallery's decision was prompted by the special character of Mapplethorpe's sexual imagery and a quite reasonable fear on the part of the museum's leadership that a showing of such pictures in Washington right now—especially in an exhibition partly financed by the National Endowment for the Arts—would result in grave damage both to the Corcoran itself and to the whole program of government support for the arts.

Yet it may help to put this controversy in perspective to be reminded that it isn't only in relation to the exhibition of provocative sexual images that this issue has lately arisen. In the storm caused by Richard Serra's now legendary sculpture, *Tilted Arc,* which came into existence as a United States government commission, the question of sexual imagery played no part. *Tilted Arc* consisted of an immense and completely abstract steel wall and thus belonged to the genre of overscale Minimalist sculpture in which representational imagery of any kind is entirely absent.

What proved to be so bitterly offensive to the community that *Tilted Arc* was commissioned to serve was its total lack of amenity—indeed, its stated goal of provoking the most negative and disruptive response to the site the sculpture dominated with an arrogant disregard for the mental well-being and physical convenience of the people who were obliged to come into contact with the work in the course of their daily employment.

When the General Services Administration, the federal agency that had commissioned *Tilted Arc* through its Art-in-Architecture program, conducted a public hearing over the fate of this work, a number of art world eminences claimed, predictably, that the removal of the offending sculpture from its site on the plaza of the Javits Federal Building in lower Manhattan would constitute an act of cultural barbarism no different in spirit from the campaigns waged against artistic freedom in Hitler's Germany and Stalin's Russia. My own view of the matter, if I may paraphrase a famous observation by George Orwell, is that you would have to be an art world intellectual to believe a thing like that. At the very least, such a belief betrays a woeful lack of understanding of the categorical differences—political and moral differences—that distinguish acts of violently enforced totalitarian repression from the inevitable disagreements of taste and value that are a legitimate and indispensable feature of democratic societies.

In the case of Richard Serra, moreover, it was certainly possible to admire him as a sculptor while thoroughly approving the decision to remove *Tilted Arc* from its site. This was, in fact, my own position. As a member of the prize jury for the 1985 Carnegie International Exhibition in Pittsburgh, I did not hesitate to award the top prize that year to the sculpture that Mr. Serra created for the plaza of the Carnegie Museum of Art. While I found *Tilted Arc* to be repulsive in every respect, I found the Carnegie's sculpture to be a very beautiful work of art. Which proves what? Only that we are not obliged to accept, either as critics or as citizens, every judgment rendered by the art world establishment as inviolable or irreversible writ, especially where the public has an urgent and legitimate claim to a grievance. To suggest that such grievances and the need to address them are in any way comparable to acts of totalitarian repression contributes nothing but an element of demagoguery and intimidation to what ought to be a serious debate about what standards are to be observed in spending the taxpayers' money on public financing of the arts.

Getting the Issue Exactly Wrong

In the case of the Mapplethorpe exhibition, which the Corcoran Gallery found it prudent on June 13, 1989, to cancel prior to its opening, even in the face of what everyone knew would be the inevitable uproar, we are once again being asked to accept the judgment of the art world establishment as absolute and incontestable. (The fact that the Washington Project for the Arts immediately appropriated the right to show the exhibition in Washington only serves to underscore this point.) We are being told, in other words, that no one outside the professional art establishment has a right to question or oppose the exhibition of Mapplethorpe's work even when it is being shown at the government's expense. In this instance, to be sure, the government did not cause the photographs in question to be created. Mercifully, they were not commissioned by a government agency. But such an agency did contribute funds to support their public exhibition, and by so doing it gave the public and its elected representatives the right to have a voice in assessing the probable consequence of such an exhibition—a task that the art establishment has lately shown itself to be utterly incapable of performing in any disinterested way.

Here again, to suggest that the public's legitimate interest in this matter amounts to political repression is to get the whole issue exactly wrong. The public's right to have an interest in the fate of this exhibition began on the day that tax dollars were allocated for its public display. There was no public outcry, after all, though there was a certain amount of private outrage, when Mapplethorpe's pictures were exhibited in commercial galleries. Some of the people who went to the galleries to see the photographs, unaware of what it was they would be seeing, had plenty of reason to be shocked at what they saw depicted in the work. This was especially the case, as I myself witnessed on one occasion, with parents who are in the habit of making the rounds of the art galleries in the company of their young children.

Public Money for Pornography?

What is it, then, about some of these photographs—the ones that are the cause of the trouble—that makes them so offensive? It isn't simply that they depict male nudity. There are male nudes in the Minor White retrospective now on view at the Museum of Modern Art that no one, as far as I know, has made any fuss about. In today's cultural climate, in which it has become commonplace for schoolchildren to be instructed in the use of condoms, it takes a lot more than a museum exhibition of pictures showing the male genitals to cause an uproar.

What one finds in many Mapplethorpe photographs is something else—so absolute and extreme a concentration on male sexual endowments that every other attribute of the human subject is reduced to insignificance. In these photographs, men are rendered as nothing but sexual—which is to say, homosexual—objects. Or, as the poet Richard Howard wrote in a tribute to Mapplethorpe, "The male genitals are often presented . . . as surrogates for the face."

Even so, these homoerotic idealizations of male sexuality are not the most extreme of Mapplethorpe's pictures. That dubious honor belongs to the pictures that celebrate in graphic and grisly detail what Richard Marshall, the curator who organized a Mapplethorpe retrospective at the Whitney Museum last summer (not the same exhibition as the one in dispute at the Corcoran, by the way), identified as the "sadomasochistic theme." In this case, it is a theme enacted by male homosexual partners whom we may presume to be consenting adults—consenting not only to the sexual practices depicted but to Mapplethorpe's role in photographing them.

The Issue Is Not Esthetics

I cannot bring myself to describe these pictures in all their gruesome particularities, and it is doubtful that this newspaper would agree to publish such a description even if I could bring myself to write one. (There can be no question either, of course, of illustrating such pictures on this page, which raises an interesting and not irrelevant question: Should public funds be used to exhibit pictures which the press even in our liberated era still finds too explicit or repulsive to publish?) Suffice it to say that Mr. Marshall, who presumably knows what he is talking about in this matter, assured us in the Whitney catalog that Mapplethorpe made these pictures "not as a voyeur but as an advocate" and "sympathetic participant."

Even in a social environment as emancipated from conventional sexual attitudes as ours is today, to exhibit photographic images of this sort, which are designed to aggrandize and abet erotic rituals involving coercion, degradation, bloodshed, and the infliction of pain, cannot be regarded as anything but a violation of public decency. Such pictures have long circulated in private, of course. They belonged, and were seen to belong, to the realm of specialized erotica. In that realm, it was clearly understood that the primary function of such images was to promote sexual practices commonly regarded as unruly and perverse or to aid in fantasizing about such practices. The appeal of such images for those who were drawn to them lay precisely in the fact that they were forbidden. They belonged, in other words, to the world of pornography.

It may be asked whether the disputed Mapplethorpe pictures really differ from earlier works of art that, owing to their violation of conventional taste, caused the public to denounce them, only to embrace them later as treasured classics. The example that comes to mind is Manet, whose two most famous paintings, *Dejeuner sur l'Herbe* and *Olympia* (both 1863), were attacked as indecent when they were first exhibited in Paris.

For a true counterpart to Mapplethorpe in nineteenth-century art, however, it isn't in a master like Manet but in graphic artists who specialized in pornographic images that we will find an appropriate parallel, and we still don't see much of that art on public exhibition in our museums even today.

What has turned these Mapplethorpe photographs into a public controversy is not that they exist. We may not approve of their existence, and we may certainly regard both the creation and the consumption of them as a form of social pathology. But so long as they remained a private taste, they could not, I believe, be seen to be a threat to public decency. What has made them a public issue is the demand that is now being made to accord these hitherto forbidden images the status of perfectly respectable works of art, to exhibit them without restriction in public institutions, and to require our government to provide funds for their public exhibition.

Ostensibly, these are demands that are being made in the name of art. That isn't the whole story, of course—it never is where art is made to serve extra-artistic purposes—but before looking into the extra-artistic aspects of this matter, a prior question must be addressed. Are these disputed pictures works of art? My own answer to this question, as far as the Mapplethorpe pictures are concerned, is: Alas, I suppose they are. But so, I believe, was Richard Serra's *Tilted Arc* a work of art. This is not to say that either *Tilted Arc* or the Mapplethorpe pictures belong to the highest levels of art—in my opinion, they do not—but I know of no way to exclude them from the realm of art itself. Failed art, even pernicious art, still remains art in some sense.

Writing some years ago about the Marquis de Sade, to cite a relevant example, Edmund Wilson observed that "the Marquis constitutes, unquestionably, one of the hardest cases to handle in the whole history of literature." Yet Wilson felt obliged, however reluctantly, to include Sade in the history of literature, and for similar reasons I believe we must accord Mapplethorpe a place—though not the exalted place being claimed for him—in the annals of art photography. It doesn't solve any of the problems raised by the Mapplethorpe pictures to say they aren't art. It is only a way of running away from the difficult issue, which doesn't lie in the realm of aesthetics.

What has to be acknowledged in this debate is a fact of cultural life that the art world establishment has never been willing to deal with—namely, that not all forms of art are socially benign in either their intentions or their effects. Everybody knows—certainly every intelligent parent knows—that certain forms of popular culture have a devastating effect on the moral sensibilities of the young. Well, it is not less true that certain forms of high culture are capable of having something other than a socially desirable impact on the sensibilities of young and old alike. How we, as adult citizens, wish to deal in our own lives with this antisocial element in the arts should not, I think, be a matter for the government to determine, for systematic programs of censorship are likely to have consequences that are detrimental to our liberties. (The question of protecting children is another matter entirely.) It is when our government intervenes in this process by supporting the kind of art that is seen to be antisocial that we as citizens have a right to be heard—not, I hasten to add, in order to deny the artist his freedom of expression, but to have a voice in determining what our representatives in the government are going to support and thus validate in our name.

A Dedication to Pernicious Ideas

Unfortunately, professional opinion in the art world can no longer be depended upon to make wise decisions in these matters. (If it could, there never would have been a *Tilted Arc* controversy or the current uproar over the Mapplethorpe pictures.) There is in the professional art world a sentimental attachment to the idea that art is at its best when it is most extreme and disruptive. This is the point of view that prompted an art student in Chicago to think he was creating a valid work of art by spreading out an American flag on the floor and inviting the public to walk on it, and then recording their responses to what was at the time a proscribed practice (now that the Supreme Court has ruled in its favor, I suspect that this particular idea will lose some of its appeal to "advanced" taste). It was this notion of equating artistic originality with sheer provocation that also led the Southeastern Center for Contemporary Art to give a grant of the government's money to Andres Serrano, now famous for the work that consists of a photograph of Christ on the Cross submerged in the artist's urine. This is the kind of thing people mean when they talk about the "cutting edge." Basically, it is a sentimentalization as well as a commercialization of the old idea of the avant-garde, which everyone knows no longer exists—except, possibly, in the realm of fashion design and advertising. The phenomenon of the avant-garde in art died a long time ago and now lies buried under the millions of dollars that have been spent on the art that bears its name.

In lieu of an authentic avant-garde in art, we now have something else—that famous "cutting edge" that looks more and more to an extra-artistic content for its fundamental raison d'être. In the case of *Tilted Arc*, the "cutting edge" element consisted of the sculptor's wish to deconstruct and otherwise render uninhabitable the public site the sculpture was designed to occupy. In the case of the disputed Mapplethorpe pictures, it consists of the attempt to force upon the public the acceptance of the values of a sexual subculture that the public at large finds loathsome—and here I do not mean homosexuality as such but the particular practices depicted in the most extreme of these pictures. In both cases, we are being asked to accept the unacceptable in the name of art, but this is sheer hypocrisy, and all the parties concerned know it is hypocrisy. What we are being asked to support and embrace in the name of art is an attitude toward life, which nowadays is where the real cutting edge (no quotation marks required) is to be found.

If our agencies of government are incapable of making this distinction between art and life, the public will have more and more reason to be concerned with the way tax dollars are being spent in the name of art. The problem won't go away, and it can't be argued away by cries of repression or censorship. Much of what the government spends on the arts still goes—and ought to go—to supporting the highest achievements of our civilization, and it would be a tragedy for our country and our culture if that support were to be lost because of a few obtuse decisions and a dedication in some quarters to outmoded and even pernicious ideas. But if the arts community is not prepared to correct the outrages committed in its name, there will be no shortage of other elements in our society ready and eager to impose drastic remedies. This is a problem that the art world has brought upon itself.

21

Artistic Freedom: An Art World Paradox

E. Louis Lankford

Two events have recently riveted the attention of arts watchers nationwide and embodied the tensions that exist between the art world and other segments of society. First, in the summer of 1989, a proposal was made by Senator Jesse Helms that an appropriations bill before Congress be amended to bar federal funds from being used by the National Endowment for the Arts and other federal agencies and institutions to support the creation, performance, or exhibition of materials which might be considered obscene. Second, in the spring of 1990, Cincinnati's Contemporary Arts Center and its director were indicted by a grand jury for pandering obscenity and "improper use of a minor in a photograph."[1] There are striking similarities between these events: each generated an enormous amount of controversy and public and private dialogue; each caused an outcry from the arts community, charging that Constitutional First Amendment rights had been abridged; each created a need to define obscenity and distinguish it from art; each was triggered at least in part by an exhibition of photographs by Robert Mapplethorpe; each has challenged those who create and interpret arts policies to come to grips with the threat of censorship; and each has occasioned reflection from within and without the world of art about the state of the arts in contemporary society and the nature of the art world in its relation to other social institutions. Unfortunately, in matters of controversy, impassioned rhetoric sometimes takes the place of informed, reflective opinion. The tasks undertaken here are to provide descriptive accounts of events and an analysis of key concepts, notably censorship, obscenity, and artistic freedom, and to assert that aesthetic education can provide an effective means for the resolution of issues.

The Helms Amendment

In the summer of 1989 Senator Jesse Helms introduced an amendment to an appropriations bill, whose beneficiaries included the National Endowment for the Arts (NEA), the National Endowment for the Humanities, the National Gallery of Art, and the Smithsonian Institution, which prohibited the use of federal funds to "promote, disseminate, or produce obscene or indecent materials, including but not limited to depictions of sadomasochism, homoeroticism, the exploitation of children, or individuals engaged in sex acts; also, material which denigrates the objects or beliefs of a particular religion or non-religion; or material which denigrates, debases, or reviles a person, group, or class of citizens on the basis of race, creed, sex, handicap, age, or national origin."[2] After some negotiations in Congress, a modified version of the amendment was adopted which retained a list of forbidden content but qualified it with the phrase "and which, when taken as a whole, do not have serious literary, artistic, political, or scientific value." Further, it became the NEA's responsibility to monitor and judge materials produced by its grant recipients to ensure compliance.[3] The bill was signed into law by President Bush in early autumn. Also among the rules newly established for the NEA: new grant recipients were to sign an agreement pledging not to use NEA money to produce art that is obscene.[4]

Jonathan Yardley of the *Washington Post* observed that it was "just the kind of legislation that politicians dread: a bill they can scarcely afford to vote against, yet one that makes them look foolish, and even philistine, for supporting it"; what politician would dare refuse to support a bill against obscenity, child exploitation, and bigotry?[5] And yet, what politician wishes to appear uncultured?

Reaction from the art world was vociferous. Editorial pages and conversations expressed diatribes against hypocritical, self-proclaimed guardians of decency, and voices rose against perceived infringements on freedom of expression.[6] In protest, many artists and arts organizations turned down NEA grants, refusing on principle to sign the oath.[7] Some viewed the bill in terms of its effect upon the NEA's mission, claiming that government funds are necessary to encourage new and diverse ideas in the art world and to "free artists from commercial and ideological restraints."[8] Art is "a vital forum for our culture's self-expression and self-examination," wrote the editors of *Artforum*. "In trying to limit what we see . . . the government is trying to limit what we think and are." The action by Congress toward the NEA was perceived as a move toward social conformity and the intolerance of difference.[9]

But even within the art world, a few observers were talking as though such action from Congress was inevitable, given the state of the arts in society. Hilton Kramer, writing in the *New York Times,* agreed that freedom of expression must be protected but that it's also not too much to expect that taxpayers demand accountability for the use of public funds. Kramer tried to encapsulate the issue in a question: "Should public standards of decency and civility be observed in determining which works of art or art events are to be selected for the Government's support? Or, to state the issue another way, is everything and anything to be permitted in the name of art?"[10]

In response to accusations that his proposal was tantamount to government censorship, Senator Helms wrote: "I do not propose that Congress censor artists. I do propose that Congress put an end to the use of federal funds to support outrageous art that is clearly designed to poison our culture. Those who insist on producing such garbage should be required to do it on their own time and with their own money. Taxpayers should not be required to pay for it."[11]

Many in the art world were unconvinced by Helms's argument, claiming correctly that artists and their patrons are also taxpayers. Artist Chuck Close considered it ironic that Congress approved the bill, which he viewed as repressive, amid celebrations of the bicentennial of the Bill of Rights and as the political climate of Eastern Europe warmed toward democracy. The bill, Close predicted, "will ultimately affect the kind of art that's made, because organizations will not invite artists to show whose work is problematic. But it could also have an opposite effect, that of making more artists go out and do controversial things."[12] The accuracy of his last forecast was almost immediately confirmed. *U.S. News and World Report* cited a nationwide rash of provocative exhibits, designed to blur the boundaries of art and obscenity and affront public tastes.[13] It is unlikely that such gratuitously offensive work has been of benefit to the arts; quite the contrary, even aside from childish motives and the impoverishment of aesthetic value, such art has served to erect still higher the walls separating the art world from the rest of society.

In October 1989 Congress created an independent commission, headed by John Brademas and Leonard Garment, to review the policies and procedures of the NEA. Among its recommendations, released in late summer 1990, was that matters of obscenity be left to the courts. Nevertheless, the commission declared that "the Endowment, in making grants, should act to strengthen, not to weaken, public confidence in its prudence and sensitivity as a steward of public funds. If the Endowment loses the trust and support of the American people, it will have failed."[14]

By late October, following months of bitter disputes, Congress approved an appropriations bill authorizing funding of the NEA for an additional three years. The legislation dropped the controversial list of forbidden subject matter. Instead, the bill requires the NEA chairman to ensure that grants are made "taking into consideration general standards of decency and respect for the diverse beliefs and values of the American public."[15]

The chairman of the NEA, John E. Frohnmayer, had in fact vowed in an earlier resolution adopted by the National Council on the Arts—a board of advisors to the NEA, to use "responsibility, accountability, and sensitivity to bring quality art to the American people."[16] But slogans can belie the difficulties and consequences of acting on them. As *Artforum* editors mused, "Quality is not some Platonic ideal but is and must be constantly debated and revaluated. Different artworks have different constituencies."[17]

The Contemporary Arts Center

Cincinnati is a city that "casts itself as a bulwark in the war against pornography."[18] It has virtually eliminated, via the efforts of community pressure groups and rigorous law enforcement, adult bookstores, X-rated theaters, nude dancing in bars, massage parlors, and magazines appealing to prurient interests. It was no surprise to some that the Contemporary Arts Center's (CAC) decision to exhibit "Robert Mapplethorpe: The Perfect Moment" stirred up a hornet's nest. The Mapplethorpe show had gained instant notoriety in June 1989, when the Corcoran Gallery in Washington, D.C., canceled it before it opened, purportedly out of fear of political reproach and economic consequences. Indeed, several of the photographs from the show were used as evidence by Senator Helms to underscore the supposed need for his legislation.

By early March 1990, several weeks before the scheduled opening of the exhibit in Cincinnati, citizens' groups and law enforcement officials had already mobilized their efforts to halt or censor display of the Mapplethorpe photographs. The CAC board chairman resigned, complaining that opponents of the show were putting pressure on his employer, a local financial institution. Failing to appease their opponents by promising to isolate especially controversial works and refusing to admit minors, attorneys for the CAC filed a suit requesting that the court decide on obscenity issues before the show opened. The court dismissed the suit, clearing the way for legal action by the city prosecutor, city police, and county sheriff. A grand jury indicted the CAC and its director, Dennis Barrie, shortly thereafter on misdemeanor obscenity charges punishable by fine and/or imprisonment. On April 7, amid a record opening day crowd, police cleared the gallery for one hour in order to videotape the exhibit as evidence. An impromptu demonstration ensued; protestors jeered at police, chanted "the whole world is watching, the whole world is laughing," and waved banners and signs, including one that read, "If you give artists freedom of expression, soon *every* American will want it!" Within days, federal judge Carl Rubin had issued a court order barring further police interference with the show, pending trial; officials were forbidden from closing the exhibit, confiscating any photographs, or interfering with public access to the show.[19]

Robert Russell, a professor in art and aesthetic education at the University of Cincinnati, wryly observed that the people who set out to shield the public from Mapplethorpe's work had accomplished just the opposite. Attendance at the CAC had reached unprecedented levels since the show opened, and membership at the Center had sharply increased. People who had never before heard of Mapplethorpe or the Contemporary Arts Center were flocking to view the "obscene" works of art.[20] Even so, events made many in the arts community nervous. Ruth Mayer, director of Cincinnati's Taft Museum, speculated that it put "in jeopardy all of the arts institutions of the city who try to present new and experimental work."[21] Alene Valkanas, executive director of the Illinois Arts Alliance, echoed the sentiments of many others when remarking that it wasn't just Barrie and the CAC on trial, "it was every museum in America and the arts as a whole."[22]

"Robert Mapplethorpe: The Perfect Moment"

Of the 175 pieces comprising the exhibit, seven were cited by the grand jury as being in violation of obscenity codes. Of these, five are part of what has been dubbed the "X-Portfolio," described in the *Cincinnati Post* as a "series of pictures, created in 1978 and representing a relatively early period in the artist's work, [which] focuses on masochistic behavior sometimes associated with, but not exclusive to, male homosexual sexual-behavior patterns."[23] The other two photographs cited depict children, one nude, the other seminude.

The foci of political and community pressures have been these seven art works and the art world that had made them available for public viewing. Media coverage, which was extensive, focused on the content, or subject matter, of the controversial works and broader issues about censorship and public funding. Relatively little has been said about the aesthetic quality of the photographs taken in the context of the whole show.

Images exhibited may be roughly divided into three categories: portraiture, still life, and figure studies. Mapplethorpe's portraits frequently feature major figures in the arts; included are Andy Warhol, Louise Nevelson, Leo Castelli, Laurie Anderson, and a number of self-portraits. Most are marked by an arresting combination of mystery and wit, rendered with meticulous detail and an eye for subtle gradations of value.

The still life images inspired the title of the show: fruits, vegetables, but most often flowers have been captured in film at "the perfect moment" to unveil their ripe colors, sensuous forms, and textures. These exquisite photographs, some printed on linen or silk, demonstrate that Mapplethorpe was a master of his medium. The singular verdure of the flora allows them to be transformed via Mapplethorpe's keen and creative eye into visual metaphors for virility and femininity. One visitor, a college student, was moved to remark that these photographs were more sensual than the figure studies.

As described in the show's brochure, the figure studies, "like classical Greek sculpture, seem primarily intended as tributes to the beauty of the human body," but also occasionally succeed in blurring distinctions of gender and race. Mapplethorpe's photographs of nude black and white men, often presented life-size, exhibit the same craftsmanship and eye for lighting and composition as the still lifes. A few echo Leonardo's famous drawing "Studio del Corpo Humano," depicting a male figure enclosed in a circle and square to emphasize proportion.

Two photographs cited by the grand jury depict children. One photograph of a nude boy shows him perched on an overstuffed chair, staring into the camera's lens. There is an impish brazenness about his pose and expression. A photograph of a young girl shows her sitting on a weathered stone bench, her knee up to reveal that she wears no underwear. Her expression is disarmingly innocent. The propriety of this photograph is questionable; as one woman commented after seeing it, "This little girl is too young to know what's going on. In a few years she might be horribly embarrassed to learn that this picture of her was displayed for all to see."

The "XYZ Portfolio," as it was called by the Contemporary Arts Center, is a suite of approximately twenty photographs, including many small still lifes and figure studies. Although the subject matter of a handful of them has proven to be most controversial, from an aesthetic standpoint these are among the weakest photographs in the show. Poorly lit, unimaginative compositions with a documentary quality about many of them, they might fit the category that Danto calls "the arts of disturbation." Danto explains that such work is frequently characterized by "improvisational and shabby execution" and is designed to confront viewers in a disturbing way, via obscenity or danger.[24] Despite the risk of sharing the outrage of Senator Helms and critics of the CAC, many people willingly submitted to the confrontational quality of these photos and waited in long lines to do so.

Crowds accompanied "The Perfect Moment" all along its tour route. The exhibit was organized in 1988 by the Institute of Contemporary Art at the University of Pennsylvania, with partial funding by the NEA. It was showing in Chicago at the time of Robert Mapplethorpe's death in 1989 at the age of forty-two. The show closed at the Institute of Contemporary Art in Boston in October 1990, the day before a jury of four men and four women in Cincinnati reached their verdict on the CAC.

Is It Obscene?

Obscenity laws are primarily adopted to prevent extreme social offensiveness and to suppress corrupt and morally subversive ideas and behaviors.[25] While obscenity and its suppression have existed in various forms throughout history and across cultures, in the United States its definition has been of paramount importance. There has been concern that the application of obscenity laws may infringe upon Constitutional First Amendment rights, which guarantee freedom of speech and have traditionally been interpreted as having broader applications in freedom of expression.

Current legal language commonly applied in obscenity cases has its roots in the Supreme Court's decision on the Roth case in 1957, which upheld the legality of the Comstock Law of 1873 and generally echoed a more contemporary opinion expressed by the American Law Institute.

The Comstock Law forbade all manner of products deemed "obscene, lewd, or lascivious" from being transported through the mail.[26] The law was named after Anthony Comstock, a lobbyist for the Society for the Suppression of Vice, who in his lifetime boasted the destruction of some four million obscene pictures, including daguerreotypes and photographs, engravings, paintings, and transparencies. "In the guise of art," he warned, "the foe to moral purity comes in its most insidious, fascinating, and seductive form."[27]

The American Law Institute (ALI) was a group of judges, scholars, and lawyers whose purpose was to synthesize and reduce principles of law to clear language. Their "Moral Penal Code" stated that "a thing is obscene if, considered as a whole, its predominant appeal is to prurient interest, i.e., a shameful or morbid interest in nudity, sex, or excretion, and if it goes substantially beyond customary limits of candor in description or representation of such matters."[28]

To the ALI's familiar "prurient interest" clause, Justice Brennen, who wrote the court's majority opinion on the Roth case, added that in order to condemn material as obscene it must be "offensive to the community's conscience" and "utterly without redeeming social importance."[29] The Supreme Court reinforced its ruling in 1973 (*Miller* v. *California*), insisting that materials, to be judged obscene, must meet three tests: the dominant theme appeals to prurient interest; the material is an affront to community standards, as judged by a reasonable person; and the material lacks serious artistic, literary, scientific, or political value.[30]

Some critics of the NEA bill containing the list of forbidden subjects claimed that it covertly circulated and legitimized conservative definitions of obscenity without real strength of law. By naming subject matter which *might* be considered obscene *if* it met the *Miller* test, the bill in effect created an unreasonable fear of that subject matter based upon imagined legal consequences.[31] In Cincinnati, the legal consequences were more real than imagined.

The Trial

There has been considerable discussion about the strength of the case against the CAC; scholars of law observed the progress of the trial with keen interest. While there is ample evidence that the Mapplethorpe exhibit had been an affront to some segments of the community, it is less clear whether the exhibit, taken as a whole, appealed to prurient interests. Even more contentious was the charge that it lacked artistic or political value, given that politics and the art world had been at the heart of the controversies and, especially, given the significant aesthetic merit of Mapplethorpe's work.

The trial drew throngs of people from across the country; media representatives packed the courtroom, and marchers (without permits) filled the streets outside. For four days the attorneys for the defense, First Amendment specialist H. Louis Serkin and co-counsel Marc Mezibov, faced off with prosecutor Frank H. Prouty, Jr., in the selection of the jury. Of the eight selected, none had ever been to the CAC and few had heard of Robert Mapplethorpe.[32]

Early in the proceedings, Hamilton County Municipal Judge David J. Albanese ruled that the CAC was an art gallery, in the eyes of the court, not a museum. The distinction is important, since under Ohio law a museum is allowed to exhibit even obscene artifacts if it is for educational purposes.[33]

But that was not the only blow suffered by defense attorneys. To their astonishment and dismay, Judge Albanese granted a prosecution request to isolate the contested photographs from the exhibition as a whole; jurors would see only the photos in question. Judge Albanese held that each photo could be considered individually because each was created individually.[34] According to the *Columbus Dispatch,* the judge pronounced: "The court believes the retrospective is a vehicle for displaying the five S & M photographs."[35]

Witnesses for the defense included John Walsh, director of the J. Paul Getty Museum and past president of the American Association of Museum Directors. In April, that association had passed a resolution endorsing "the validity of the Robert Mapplethorpe exhibition, 'The Perfect Moment,' in its totality" and praising the CAC and its director "for upholding the highest standards of the museum profession."[36] Walsh and other defense witnesses generally expressed those sentiments while on the stand.

Serkin and Mezibov also submitted depositions from parents of the children depicted in the two child-related photographs. The parents claimed that they had commissioned the photographs and that they had no objection to Mapplethorpe's portrayal of their children, now adults.[37]

On Friday, October 5, 1990, after a two-week trial, the jury deliberated for a little over two hours before reaching its verdict: Barrie and the CAC were acquitted of all charges. Jurors interviewed later admitted that they found the photos "lewd" and "distasteful," but determined that serious works of art do not have to be pretty.[38]

"This is a great day for this city, a great day for America," said Barrie to a crowd of supporters following the verdict. "A major battle was fought here, for the arts, for creativity. . . . Stay strong, be vigilant and don't let this ever happen again."[39]

Barrie's last admonition should be taken seriously by the art world, for these same words could well serve as the motto of special interest groups who consider themselves to be watchdogs of morality and who have taken a special interest in art.

The Question of Censorship

One of the most puzzling questions is whether or not events that have affected the NEA and the CAC constitute censorship. Many who marched outside the courthouse in favor of the CAC obviously thought it did, since banners carried messages like "Welcome to Censornati" and "The Perfect Moment to Stop Censorship." The Helms amendment has been variously described as "censorship of the arts" and as "proper management of public funds."

Harold Lasswell, in the *Encyclopedia of the Social Sciences,* defined censorship as "the policy of restricting the public expression of ideas, opinions, conceptions, and impulses which have or are believed to have the capacity to undermine the governing authority or the social and moral order which that authority considers itself bound to protect."[40] It's easy to understand how the same actions can be viewed as censorship by some and as protection of the public welfare by others.

Most often associated with freedom of the press, censorship as a response to obscenity has precedents in the visual arts. Yvonne Morse noted in her thought-provoking history, *Freedom of the Visual Arts:* "Censorship of the visual arts has included repressions based on economic, social, political, moral, or esthetic grounds by government and religious officials, as well as by groups of citizens, individuals, or society in general."[41] Describing measures more extreme than current NEA controls, Morse reported that federally sponsored exhibitions were carefully screened during the postwar McCarthy era and that "the federal government conducted a security check on artists before granting federal commissions for painting and sculpture to be placed in public buildings."[42] Back then, they were looking for Communists.

Supreme Court Justice Stewart once observed, "Censorship reflects a society's lack of confidence in itself."[43] Forces of society must seek to strike a balance between permissiveness and control and encourage the responsible exercise and protection of citizens' rights of choice and expression. Robert Stearns, director of the Wexner Center for the Arts, located at the Ohio State University, offered this reminder: "An important point shouldn't be forgotten when public support is administered in a democracy: that minority constituencies deserve the same benefits and protections, under the law, as the majority."[44]

It is difficult to claim with certainty whether either the Helms amendment or the actions against the CAC were instances of censorship. The Helms amendment did not forbid the creation or exhibition of any art form; rather, it placed restrictions on the allocation of federal funds to the arts. It should not be assumed that supporters of such legislation are philistines or enemies of the art world. Many an art lover, recognizing that "who pays the piper, calls the tune," has pondered the wisdom of any sort of direct government involvement in the arts. Arguing that the government's spending on the arts is pitifully low in comparison to other kinds of federal support, while true, will change few minds about the correctness of Helms's actions. Given a choice, most taxpayers wouldn't give a dime to a program they didn't believe in. This is a society that prides itself in sensitivity to the threat of censorship; if even voices in the press are uncertain about its application through the Helms amendment, that in itself provides reason for doubt.

The Contemporary Arts Center's case is slightly more problematic. The threat of confiscation lingered in the air. Nevertheless, it is impossible to ignore the involvement of citizens' groups in the urging of legal action for the protection of community standards. And, presumably, the grand jury consisted of reasonable persons making judgments of value.

Regardless of whether or not censorship has occurred, aggressive action directed toward artistic expression has. In his essay entitled "Censorship: But Deliver Us from Evil," aesthetician Eugene F. Kaelin stressed the inevitability of social control but also the wisdom of exercising flexibility, tolerance, and educated discrimination toward the furtherance of a democratic civilization: "All societies embody forms of social control: folkways, mores and laws determine what ought to be avoided for the good of that society. And yet, if that society is to continue to grow and to function in the life patterns of individuals living therein, folkways, mores and laws must be amenable to sensible change. . . . As long as this change is possible, society is healthy; when not, it is already dead."[45]

Art World Attitudes

A widely published editorial cartoon by Jules Feiffer depicts a goateed painter defiantly proclaiming to the general public, "I dedicate my life as an artist to the free expression of my contempt for what you are." He then adds, "Fund me."[46]

This parody effectively represents many attitudes about artists and art shared by those inside and outside the art world. Controversial art has often become a synonym for good art and even for art itself. One state's arts council director spoke for many in the arts in claiming that "art, most of the time, is going to be controversial. That's what art is supposed to be about—continual questioning, prodding, controversy."[47]

Kramer asserted that such attitudes are at the root of many of the problems currently facing the art world. Artists and their audiences must stop imagining themselves to be apart from or above the social and moral standards that attend the rest of society. "There is in the professional art world a sentimental attachment to the idea that art is at its best when it is most extreme and disruptive."[48] Others have used stronger language than Kramer's. An editorial in the *Wall Street Journal* condemned the contemporary art world as being "utterly contemptuous of the notion of educating the tastes and refining the aesthetic sensibilities of the citizenry. Its goal, instead, is deliberately to outrage those tastes," often while hiding behind the claim of making some mysterious "statement" only comprehensible by an art world elite.[49]

Cultural critic Jacques Barzun has speculated that the art world's tendency toward controversy is largely the result of a misplaced sense of purpose: "The arts should criticize life, and not merely denounce it." By replacing a desire to uplift, invigorate, and restore humanity, with a desire to confront, dumbfound, and humiliate, the art world has increasingly robbed culture of its self-confidence and succeeded in alienating itself from society. Continuing to raise the voltage on art as shock treatment can have dire results.[50] As Kramer warned, "If the arts community is not prepared to correct the outrages committed in its name, there will be no shortage of other elements in our society ready and eager to impose drastic remedies."[51]

An argument frequently heard in defense of controversial art is that history books are filled with examples of art that offended their original audience yet today are considered work of genius, for example, Impressionism. The implication that offensiveness is a barometer for future levels of adulation is so absurd that it hardly warrants discussion. No one has yet invented a reliable crystal ball. Responsible decisions must be made in the present. "We dont' want to do things at the Wexner Center for the sole function of offending people," said Robert Stearns. "And you always have to be careful in understanding the difference between bogus confrontation, as opposed to valuable insights which may offend someone."[52]

Artistic Freedom

Artistic freedom may be taken as the right of artists to choose without coercion the media, methods, form, and content of expression they prefer, provided that the artists or artworks do not infringe upon others' rights of choice and expression. This concept extends to the exhibition and performance of works of art and to attendance at exhibitions and performances.

John Dewey observed that it is a common misconception that the only prerequisite to freedom is the removal of obstructions, which theoretically would result in an indeterminate range of choices available to the whims of every individual. Individuals, however, exist within a physical and social context of interactions. Freedom, rather than being a natural condition, is an achievement which occurs when people in society are collectively aware of choices and the consequences of choosing and act so as to ensure the greatest range and benefit of choices.[53]

It is interesting to consider that the social institution of art has been in large measure responsible for its own ability to exercise freedom. As aesthetician David Novitz explains, the art world has its own means of perpetuating and regulating itself: "There are, for example, schools of fine art, art critics, gallery directors, philosophers of art, artists and their audiences, all of whom try, in one way or another, both to advance certain views of art while challenging and even proscribing others. They do this not just because they sincerely subscribe to certain artistic values, but also because, as officers of the art world, they have an interest in perpetuating some views of art and undermining others."[54]

In this light, and considering the prevalence of certain attitudes within the art world, it is not so apparent that the finger of blame for recent challenges to the arts point outside the world of art. If blame is appropriate at all, it resides in the dynamic and tense relationship between art and society, a relationship brimming with misunderstanding, arrogance, and suspicion. In order to protect its own ability to exercise artistic freedom, the art world should undertake a more active program to build trust in that relationship. As Kaelin noted, "The aesthetic institution may not without some peril to its own existence be isolated from the other institutions of societies."[55]

Aesthetic Education: Escaping the Paradox

Artistic freedom is a paradoxical aspect of the art world. In order to provide an environment that fosters maximum latitude and protection for artistic choices, the art world must sustain a positive, nurturing relationship with other segments of society. By creating opportunities for free expression, however, the art world opens itself to the possibility that what is expressed will go against the grain of predominant social norms and mores. By encouraging and defending such controversial work, it risks losing ground in its societal relationships; hence, it slips in its ability to guarantee freedom of expression.

One of the most potentially effective means of resolving this paradox is to engender a healthy environment for the arts through education. Dewey was a firm believer in education as a vaccination against censorship and other social ills. "I shall begin to believe that we care more for freedom than we do for imposing our own beliefs upon others in order to subject them to our will, when I see that the main purpose of our schools and other institutions is to develop powers of unremitting and discriminating observation and judgment."[56]

Aesthetic education, through rigorous programs of artistic and aesthetic inquiry, can play a central role in the development of an art world with a sense of responsibility toward itself and society, as well as development of a society committed to freedom of expression. Aesthetic educators must be aware of that role, plan for it, and seek the resources necessary to accomplish it. Stephen Mark Dobbs, pondering the often unspoken motivations of art educators, concluded: "We sincerely believe the informed, thoughtful, sensitive, and rational person to be indispensable to the democratic process. We teach because of strong convictions that our contributions are seminal to an orderly and progressive and humane society. . . . Our mission [is] to convey the purpose and meaning and utility and pleasure of art and its quintessential role in the lives of individuals and societies."[57]

It makes a sad commentary that, in a recent survey conducted by the U.S. Department of Education, only 7 percent of public secondary school teachers ranked citizenship as a "very important" goal for students.[58] Perhaps it has become unfashionable to think of schools as places where young people can develop aptitudes and attitudes directed toward responsible and constructive membership in a community. More plausibly, citizenship as a goal has been de-emphasized because educators have become increasingly preoccupied with trends designed to ensure that America can compete in the world marketplace. This leaves little energy to attend to loftier ideals.

Much as we would like to believe that it's an automatic, self-generating condition, freedom of expression is a lofty ideal, and its only chance for preservation and growth is through a thoughtful, critical, well-informed, well-educated populace. For artistic freedom to flourish, that means a citizenry well educated in the arts. Four propositions may help achieve that goal.

1. *Controversies, issues, and problems facing the arts should be addressed in classrooms.* Engaging in discourse about controversial topics might help students to better analyze and resolve such topics in the future. Obviously, some issues are more complex and sensitive than others, and educators must use judgment in the suitability of a topic for a particular audience.

People who are knowledgeable about art recognize that artworks can carry powerful ethical connotations. As Edmund B. Feldman put it, "You cannot touch art without touching values. . . . When we study the arts of many lands and peoples, we sensitize students to the fact that values shape all human efforts and that visual images can affect their personal value choices."[59]

In a 1989 student exhibit at the Chicago Art Institute, one artwork invited visitors to tread on an American flag spread on the floor and respond to the query, What is the proper way to display the American flag? This work further fanned the flames of the Helms amendment controversy. Students in class might be asked questions to help them think about this work and its social impact. What message do you think the artist is trying to convey? Is it an effective way to convey that message? Do you think this piece might offend anyone? Why? What effect might its exhibition have on the reputation of the artist? of the Art Institute? Does its message or its aesthetic significance outweigh the risks that it will offend people or damage a reputation? What do you think would constitute a proper response to this piece by the public? How did this piece come to be regarded as a work of art? Do you think that it's a work of art? If so, is it a good work of art? There are no pat answers to these questions, yet addressing them will engage the intellect and the emotions in the challenging world of values in art and society.

2. *Students should learn about the social dynamics of the art world.* Most students probably have little idea of the drama and work behind the scenes at art galleries, museums, studios, and performance halls. Who are the players in these dramas, and what are their roles? Artists, curators, art dealers, and a host of others together comprise the art world, and their combined ideas and efforts, in effect, allow art to exist. The art world meshes and sometimes collides with other social institutions, such as politics, religion, economics, education. Aesthetic educators should point

out these roles and relationships to students, who one day will play their own parts in the successes and failures of the art world. Criticism and evaluation of the art world should be an important element of aesthetic education. As R. A. Smith succinctly noted, "Art must occasionally be challenged as well as cherished."[60] And isn't it altogether preferable to provide constructive criticism from within than to bear the brunt of destructive criticism from without? As Jacques Barzun noted: "We do art no honor and no justice when we represent it as invariably humane, heroic and disinterested in its intentions, exclusively good in its effects, and thus not subject to reproach or accountability—sacred. Such compliments, whether sincerely meant or thoughtlessly repeated, deny art the very importance which they appear to claim for it . . . to acknowledge [art's] power entails the obligation to examine how that power is exercised."[61]

3. *Criticism should be an integral part of aesthetic education.* This is certainly not a new idea, and many are the voices, particularly in visual art education, advocating and directing its practice. It bears repeating here because so much depends upon the astute application of art criticism by all those within or affecting the art world. As Kaelin put it, "Enlightened criticism is the institutional control on the license of artistic freedom. And this is what no society has yet succeeded in achieving on a massive scale. It cannot be done, moreover, unless aesthetic judgment becomes a universal requirement for graduation from institutions of public instruction."[62]

4. *The concept of artistic freedom should be addressed as it pertains to the context of education.* This proposition applies to what students learn and to what educators teach. Responsible educational decisions are based on the perception of student maturity, aptitude, and background and must be made in a context of diverse community goals, strengths, needs, standards, and interests. A teacher's decision to not show Mapplethorpe's "X–Portfolio" to elementary school children is not an act of censorship. It is ludicrous to suppose that aesthetic educators have the same choices as artists and other members of the arts community. Educators must be highly selective in order to capitalize on limited opportunities to broaden and deepen students' aesthetic experience.

But this doesn't mean that educators mustn't consciously strive for maximum freedom of expression for themselves and their students within that context. Students, particularly those aspiring to membership in the art world, must realize that artistic freedom is a privilege which should not be abused. They should understand that artistic decisions can have far-reaching social consequences. This lesson should be taught so as to instill pride and respect, not fear and timidity.

In conclusion, it's worth noting that, if nothing else, the recent controversies about art have renewed convictions that the arts are powerful catalysts for social change and that artistic expression can shape thought and feeling. Recognition of this power is a mixed blessing, so long as there are those who fear and loathe that power and seek to suppress and control it. A comprehensive program of aesthetic education can be a vital force in turning a negative environment for the arts into a positive one, marked by understanding, cooperation, appreciation, and respect. The best guarantee of artistic freedom is the healthy relationship of a responsible art world and a well-educated, vigilant citizenry.

Notes

1. Jim Massie, "Police Raid Exhibition of Photos," *Columbus Dispatch,* 8 Apr. 1990, p. 1A.

2. Text of the Helms amendment as quoted by Jonathan Yardley, "Jesse Helms and the Art of Pragmatism," *Sunday News Journal,* Wilmington, Dela., 6 Aug. 1989, p. K1.

3. Rita Price, "Grants Pit Freedom vs. Funding," *Columbus Dispatch,* 14 Oct. 1990, p. 1B.

4. Beth Lindsmith, "Censorship and the Arts: Nightmare on Helms Street," *Ohio State Quest* 12, no. 2 (Spring 1990): 4–5.

5. Yardley, "Jesse Helms and the Art of Pragmatism," p. K1.

6. For a stirring example, see Gary Indiana, "Democracy, Inc.," *Art Forum* (September 1989): 11–12.

7. Christopher Phillips, "NEA Grants Spurned," *Art in America* (September 1990): 59.

8. Miriam Horn and Andy Plattner, "Should Congress Censor Art?" *U.S. News and World Report* (September 1989): 23.

9. Ida Panicelli and Anthony Korner, "Humani nil a me alienum puto (Nothing human is alien to me)," *Artforum* (September 1989): 1.

10. Hilton Kramer, "Is Art above the Laws of Decency?" *New York Times,* 2 July 1989, sec. 2, pp. 1, 7.

11. Jesse Helms, "It's Job of Congress to Define What's Art," *USA Today,* 8 Sept. 1989, p. 13A.

12. Chuck Close quoted by Grace Glueck, "Border Skirmish: Art and Politics," *New York Times,* 19 Nov. 1989, sec. 2, pp. 1, 25.

13. Horn and Plattner, "Should Congress Censor Art?"

14. Commission Report quoted by Hilton Kramer, "Misreported, N.E.A. Report Says Clean House of Special Interests," *New York Observer,* 1 Oct. 1990.

15. "Arts Endowment Gets Three More Years," *Columbus Dispatch,* 28 Oct. 1990), p. 4A.

16. Brian Wallis, "Controversy Dogs NEA Council," *Art in America* (September 1990): 59.

17. Panicelli and Korner, "Humani nil a me alienum puto."

18. Isabel Wilkerson, "Trouble Right Here in Cincinnati: Furor over Mapplethorpe Exhibit," *New York Times,* 29 March 1990, pp. A1, 9.

19. The events at Cincinnati's Contemporary Arts Center were widely covered by the media. Especially useful to this author was "The Mapplethorpe Exhibit: Special Report," *Cincinnati Post,* 9 Apr. 1990, pp. A1, 4–5.

20. Russell's observation, communicated to the author at the 1990 National Art Education Association convention, was confirmed with figures published in local newspapers.

21. "The Mapplethorpe Exhibit: Special Report," *Cincinnati Post.*

22. Quoted by Patricia Lopez Baden, "Verdict Seen As Vindication for the Arts," *Cincinnati Enquirer,* 6 Oct. 1990, pp. A1, A7.

23. "The Mapplethorpe Exhibit: Special Report," *Cincinnati Post.*

24. Arthur C. Danto, *The Philosophical Disenfranchisement of Art* (New York: Columbia University Press, 1986), pp. 117–34.

25. James C. N. Paul and Murray L. Schwartz, *Federal Censorship* (New York: Free Press of Glencoe, 1961).

26. Ibid., pp. 18–24.

27. Yvonne Linsert Morse, "Freedom of the Visual Arts: The Role of Governments," in *An Intellectual Freedom Primer,* ed. Charles H. Busha (Littleton, Colo.: Libraries Unlimited, 1977), pp. 114–15.

28. Paul and Schwartz, *Federal Censorship,* p. 142.

29. Ibid., pp. 144–46.

30. Debra Dennis, "Case Could Reach Supreme Court," *Cincinnati Post,* 9 Apr. 1990, p. A4.

31. Carole S. Vance, "Misunderstanding Obscenity," *Art in America* (May 1990): 49–55.

32. Mark Siebert and Lew Moores, "Lewd, But Art, Jurors Say," *Cincinnati Enquirer,* 7 Oct. 1990, pp. A1–A2.

33. "Art Photos Obscenity Trial Set," *Columbus Dispatch,* 7 Sept. 1990, p. 5B.

34. "Are Five Photographs a Fair Test?" *Newsweek,* (17 Sept. 1990), p. 36.

35. Jim Massie, "Cincinnati Art Director Gets Aid in Obscenity Case in Washington," *Columbus Dispatch,* 9 Sept. 1990, p. 2E.

36. "Going to Bat for Barrie," *Art in America* (June 1990): 47, 207.

37. Lew Moores, "Museum Experts Testify," *Cincinnati Enquirer,* 3 Oct. 1990, pp. E1–E2.

38. Siebert and Moores, "Lewd, But Art, Jurors Say."

39. Lew Moores, "Mapplethorpe 'Not Obscene,'" *Cincinnati Enquirer,* 6 Oct. 1990, p. A1.

40. Quoted in *An Intellectual Freedom Primer,* pp. 12–13.

41. Morse, "Freedom of the Visual Arts," p. 103.

42. Ibid., pp. 121–22.

43. Quoted in *Commentaries on Obscenity,* ed. Donald B. Sharp (Metuchen, N.J.: Scarecrow Press, 1970), p. 310.

44. Robert Stearns, "On Censorship," *Wexner Center for the Visual Arts Calendar* (February 1990): 2–3.

45. Eugene F. Kaelin, "Censorship: But Deliver Us from Evil," *Arts in Society* 4, no. 2 (1967): 217.

46. Released through Universal Press Syndicate, dated 27 Aug. 1989.

47. "Opinion on the Arts: Educate, Don't Gag," *Columbus Dispatch,* 24 Sept. 1989, pp. 1–2 G.

48. Kramer, "Is Art above the Laws of Decency?"

49. Irving Kristol, "It's Obscene But Is It Art?" *Wall Street Journal,* 7 Aug. 1990, p. A16.

50. Jacques Barzun, *The Use and Abuse of Art* (Princeton, N.J.: Princeton University Press, 1974), p. 135.

51. Kramer, "Is Art above the Laws of Decency?"

52. Stephanie Schleappi, "Obscene Art Questioned," *Ohio State Lantern,* 24 Aug. 1989, p. 7.

53. John Dewey, "Philosophies of Freedom," originally published in 1928, is included in Dewey's anthology of essays, *Philosophy and Civilization* (Gloucester, Mass.: Peter Smith, 1968).

54. David Novitz, "The Integrity of Aesthetics," *Journal of Aesthetics and Art Criticism* 48, no. 1 (Winter 1990): 18.

55. Eugene F. Kaelin, *An Existentialist Aesthetic* (Madison: University of Wisconsin Press, 1966), p. 354.

56. Dewey, "Philosophies of Freedom," p. 297.

57. Stephen Mark Dobbs, "Art in the Mainstream Is Our Lifestream," *Art Education* 35, no. 5 (September 1982): 4.

58. Cited in *NAEA News* (February 1989), p. 5.

59. Edmund B. Feldman, "Art in the Mainstream: A Statement of Value and Commitment," *Art Education* 35, no. 5 (September 1982): 6.

60. Ralph A. Smith, "Professor Feldman and the NAEA Take AIM: An Agenda for Further Discussion," *Art Education* 35, no. 5 (September 1982): 18.

61. Barzun, *The Use and Abuse of Art,* p. 22.

62. Eugene F. Kaelin, *An Aesthetics for Art Educators* (New York: Teachers College Press, 1989), p. 79.

22

An Overview of the Strategic Issues in American Arts Education

Samuel Hope

Let us begin by agreeing that we teachers of the various arts are important individuals in American society because we carry major responsibilities for the future of our civilization. If we do not see ourselves this way, there is not much use in proceeding either with this article, with prolonged discussion, or with our professional lives. If we are not convinced that our function is vitally important, we cannot expect to receive public understanding and support.

Let us also agree that the primary purpose of education is to develop the intellectual capabilities of individual minds, to make men and women truly free by enabling them to think for themselves about all areas of human experience, including the arts disciplines.

Let us also agree that art deserves serious study by everyone, that there is more to art than can be gained by experience alone.

Let us finally agree that we live in a society so complex by nature that educational and cultural policy development is becoming infinitely intricate and difficult at the same time as our professional involvement with it is becoming increasingly necessary.

If we agree about each of these points and believe them with all sincerity, we must face the fact that most public opinion on these issues is contrary to our own. When we use the old maxim that what is done speaks louder than what is said, we realize the following from what is being done:

1. Professionals in arts education have little status anywhere, not even in the arts community and, some would say, not even among themselves.

2. Education's purpose is widely regarded as being preparation for work at the individual level and maintenance of economic superiority at the national level. The life of the individual mind seems of little concern.

3. Art is rarely thought of as being much more than entertainment, at least by the general public and, increasingly, in the arts community as well.

4. Policy development for culture and education is increasingly conducted in the oversimplified terms typical of propaganda technique applied to economic and political power plays.

Given this state of affairs, what reason is there to believe that we can prevail with a program based on substance, rigor, and individual accomplishment? How can serious teachers of art expect to succeed now, given all the problems that exist? For one thing, times have changed and are continuing to change. Values inimical to the achievement of high educational and cultural aspirations are being challenged. For another, most of us have not changed. We remain committed to arts education and to its role as a progenitor of civilization.

Therefore, if we play our cards right, there is every chance that we can make significant gains. In order to play our cards right, however, we must become increasingly analytical. At the same time, we must become increasingly focused and direct. Our strategic and tactical skills must be improved, and our commitment to basic artistic and educational principles must become stronger.

Let us turn now to the issues: first, issues that confront us, and second, issues that we must confront. I ask you to share these two lists of issues with me by considering each element primarily in terms of the analytical, strategic, and tactical needs they project for advancing the cause of serious education in the various arts.

Issues Confronting the Arts Education Profession

The Cultural Formation Complex

Even though it may make us uncomfortable, we must recognize that there is a powerful system of cultural formation at work in the United States. The fact that this system is not controlled from a central governmental source does not mean that such a system is nonexistent. Our democracy simply provides everyone with opportunities to struggle constantly for position. The elements of our cultural formation system are engaged in such a struggle. Some players have more money and influence than others, and, for the most part, it is they who have the most control.

We all recognize that many elements of the cultural formation complex are not particularly friendly to the cause of arts education. The media, particularly television, are perhaps the greatest challenge we face. However, even the formal educational system is not always supportive. One has only to remember the tremendous battles waged every year to preserve curriculum-based K–12 arts education programs to realize that in the aggregate of its actions, our K–12 education system often winds up teaching the vast majority of students that art is unimportant.

If we look at the system of cultural formation and its ability to influence the development of individual minds, we must ask ourselves two questions: What real influence do we have, and what real influence should we have? I leave you to ponder the meaning of your own answers for the future of the field.

Values

Two obvious groups come to mind concerning matters of art and arts education: those who care about these matters and those who don't. Most of us probably would agree that those who don't care far outnumber those who do. We probably would agree also that those who do care are fragmented in their efforts to convince those who don't care that they should care.

Scholarly literature is full of analyses addressed to the origin, development, and condition of American values. We often characterize ourselves as a rather nonintellectual, pragmatic, and technique-oriented society. All three of these conditions frequently are cited as root causes for the low priority accorded to matters of art. There is also the terrible problem of the identification of art in the public mind with certain socioeconomic levels. The general feeling is that only those with upper-middle and above incomes "belong" at arts events. Whatever the source of this assumption, its presence reinforces the "I don't care" attitude held by most Americans about the arts.

Those who do care about art and arts education are divided primarily because they can't agree on what art is. Some see art as a commodity and project it as such exclusively in order to ensure its funding. Others see art as a management problem based in economics and promote concepts based on pay-as-you-go theories and policy by plebiscite mechanisms. Others see art as a technical profession, the practice of which earns them a living. And a few see art as a means of cultivating individual minds as well as whole civilizations. Too many in each camp suffer from a terminal myopia that prevents holistic and common efforts.

There are also divisions over what the purpose for art should be. To what extent should art be for art's sake or for politics' sake, for religion's sake, for high society's sake, for psychological health's sake, for entertainment's sake?

Then there is the problem of reflected glory—the ability of art to reflect glory on those who sponsor it as well as those who create it. Some argue forcefully that priority-reversing confusions on this point are rampant in contemporary American culture and that these confusions are produced primarily by an advocacy mentality that places arts support before art itself.

Finally, let us note the primary division with respect to values. This involves positions concerning the role of art in the cultural formation of individuals as opposed to the role of art in creating a mass culture.

To summarize, we must ask ourselves whether the general value system in the United States provides a conducive climate for the delivery of rigorous, sequential, curriculum-based arts education at the K–12 level. To the extent that the answer is no, we have a serious problem, because without a commonly held set of values that support our enterprise, it is almost impossible to have the basis for debating arts education as a policy issue at any level.

Delivery Systems

Three distinct nonmedia communities are involved in the delivery system for K–12 arts education. These are the arts community, the general education community, and the arts education community. Of the three, only the arts education community has arts education as its primary business. Unfortunately, maddening dysfunctions in policy formulation arise from the fact that each of these major communities seems to misperceive the role, purpose, and influence of the other two communities on the arts education product. The arts community chronically fails to make a distinction between the education community and the arts education community. In return, the arts education community recognizes a philosophical and content connection with the arts community but is worried about an operational connection lest the roles and responsibilities of artists and teachers become confused. The education community tends to minimize the importance of art as a basic component of the curriculum. In summary, we must face the fact that the arts community and the arts education community are not sufficiently unified to influence the operational values of the education community, much less the values of the public in general.

The delivery systems for art, education, and arts education also differ with respect to funding patterns and protocols. The socioeconomic parameters present in each delivery system are not the same, nor are decision-making processes affecting the flow of funds and the setting of priorities.

In addition, the national, and perhaps international, market for art is centered in New York City. Fortunately, there is no central source of arts education policy equivalent to the power that New York exerts in the world of art or that New York and Los Angeles exert in the world of entertainment. This structural difference, however, has major ramifications for public relations, national debate, and policy development.

Arts and arts education delivery systems are also quite different with respect to mechanisms for policy formulation. Arts policies are most often dictated by those with credentials of wealth and power. Arts education policies are determined for the most part through the negotiations of professional teachers and administrators after funding levels are set by those with wealth and power. An issue that must be faced is the steady effort of arts advocates with wealth and power to achieve strategic control over K–12 arts education, thus confining arts education experts to the tactical realm.

Another issue is the extent to which the structures and operations of our delivery systems for art, education, and arts education influence the values and cultural formation issues discussed previously. I mention this specifically because our current basic delivery systems have elements of success built into them. But whether the composite system achieves or fails to achieve depends on the values and competencies of those entrusted with operating it. Therefore, an issue we must face is our ability to make evaluative distinctions among structural flaws, value flaws, and individual competence lest we find ourselves proposing or supporting baby-and-bathwater solutions every time a problem arises.

Demographics

We are all aware that the continuing decline in the numbers of school- and college-age students has made a serious impact on educational policy development. We are also aware of projections telling us that the ethnic profile of our population is rapidly changing.

The problem with declining numbers goes far beyond the meaning of those numbers for funding. Declining numbers can serve to mask the more serious problems in arts education that reside primarily in the realm of values. If we allow the demographic situation to become the immediate explanation for most of our problems, we are simply deluding ourselves.

The issue of ethnic profile is also serious for arts education. It calls forth highly charged feelings about content that quickly establish battle lines between those who believe that some basic common experience should be shared by all of those who have achieved graduation from high school and those who believe that each ethnic group should focus primarily on retaining its own identity. Since the arts disciplines provide cultural signatures as surely as languages and religions do, arts education will be in the vortex of discussions and debates arising from the changing ethnic profile of our society. The arts education community's positioning on this particular issue must be done with great care to balance the humanistic concerns we all share with the realities of educational decision making. An impossible situation results when the study of particular artistic subject matter becomes viewed primarily as part of the struggle to establish any particular ethnic presence. In these circumstances, the subject has become social policy or politics, not art. To the extent that we can develop public understanding of the arts as disciplines universally applied to various cultural manifestations, to that same extent we can prevent art from being viewed primarily as a means for imposing one culture on another. Early focus on the acquisition of basic skills in one or more of the arts is the best approach for obviating this destructive argument.

Policy Climate

The advent of mass communication has created a climate for policymaking in art, education, and arts education far removed from the New England town meeting concept lauded in our eighth-grade civics courses. While the administrative, legislative, and judicial branches of government remain in legal control of affairs and while business, industry, labor, and the citizenry remain powerful, tremendous influence is now exerted by think tanks and policy study groups, all peopled with individuals having high levels of education and deep commitments to issues. Most Americans are blissfully unaware of this stunningly influential policy development complex and the web of connections between policy intellectuals, the media, and specific traditional mechanisms for making decisions.

Clearly, the field of K–12 arts education shows little activity that can be characterized as having the same types of analytical or operational objectives. In fact, the same can be said for the arts community. The reason for this latter assertion is that arts advocacy carries all of the outward characteristics of policy studies and political action based thereon without a significant foundation in either artistic content or overall cultural analysis.

We have now arrived, through a circuitous route, at one of the thorniest issues confronting the arts and arts education communities. This involves the policy climate that we are generating for ourselves by our approach to the promotion of our cause. My own bias is that the techniques and values arts advocates have used to promote art during the last twenty years have done as much harm as good. Many advocates ubiquitously link art with leisure in order to sell it. The result is confirmation of many people's suspicions that art is a frill. Many advocates have focused on personalities rather than work. The result is that concepts of artistic value become based on social rather than intellectual distinctions. Many advocates have developed criteria for the success of arts enterprises based primarily on quantitative rather than qualitative measures. The result is loss of distinctions between art and entertainment on either an individual or institutional basis.

In summary, many promotional approaches have made the error of embracing techniques that are fundamentally inimical to building individual cultural capabilities and thus to the basic requirements for a thriving cultural life centered on active participation in the arts disciplines. In making the choice between individualist and mass approaches to cultural formation, most advocates are clearly on the mass side.

The result is an enervated policy climate for arts education created by attempts to hold two very different positions within the same enterprise. On the one hand there are philosophies and operations based on an arts and leisure connection. On the other are philosophies and operations based on an arts and intellectual work connection. Only one of these is consistent with renewed public aspirations for serious education that produces demonstrable results.

Finally, the policy climate is affected in an imbalanced way by the fact that some entities are able to command media attention while others doing equal or more important work cannot command such attention. Everyone knows that media attention produces recognition and that recognition produces funding and other kinds of support, including additional recognition. Therefore, the influence and funding game has been handicapped against those heroes of arts education who actually enter the classroom daily and teach students. Decisions about media attention do not seem to be made by use of criteria focused on ideas or even product, but rather on images of wealth, name recognition, and the relationship between the two. For example, would Project Zero receive much attention if it were located at Oklahoma State University rather than Harvard? Would the idea of discipline-based visual art education ever have received much notoriety if it had not been embraced by the Getty Trust, even though the ideas and the issues generated therefrom have been important policy considerations in visual art education for many years?

The arts education community must face the ugly little fact that the policy development climate is made doubly difficult by this image-chasing syndrome which pervades not only what is being done but how it is being reported. In proposals and discussions on arts education emanating from foundations, arts agencies, and arts centers, one rarely sees credit for anything given to specialist teachers of the arts disciplines or to any institution between the coasts.

The arts education community must also face the fact that it is neither in a socioeconomic position nor in a political position to prevail in a policy climate dominated by values promoting image over substance, personality over work, and entertainment over art. Therefore, in order to make improvements for arts education, these values which poison the policy climate against us must be changed.

New Times

There has been a significant change over the last five years in the approach of the American people to issues of education and culture. Whatever our particular views about this situation, it seems clear that the reshuffling of issues and priorities when new times arrive gives us a magnificent opportunity to make advances for our cause.

For example, economic and trade conditions have shown us the fallacy of our laissez-faire approach to education. Our nation seems now determined to find a new philosophical place for work in the education process. Of course, this attempted reversal is not without the evils of oversimplification, media hype, and political opportunism. However, public consensus that more substance is desirable in education could be a powerful plus for the cause of rigorous arts education.

One of the most significant evidences of new times is the change of policy direction on arts education at the National Endowment for the Arts. Most researchers are surely aware that at the May 1986 council meeting, five years of patient effort by Chairman Hodsoll, council member Samuel Lipman, and many other individuals paid off in the ratification of a newly formed arts-in-education program which will include curriculum-based arts education as well as artist residencies. The fact that this more holistic approach to arts education could be achieved in the National Endowment for the Arts is a tribute to outstanding personal leadership; however, it is hard to imagine such a change in the context of the American mood of the sixties and early seventies.

Additional evidence is available in the changed statements of such organizations as the American Council on the Arts, several state arts agencies, and philosophical leaders in the arts presentation sector. The extent to which action will follow words is yet to be determined; however, all this activity indicates that things are moving and changing with respect to the position of curriculum-based arts education on the whole spectrum of arts concerns.

We must face the fact that new times are upon us and that they are likely to be with us for a while to come. Although no time is perfect or without its challenges, there is much that is favorable in the present situation. The mood of seriousness is more in our interest than a mood of frivolity. The focus on rigorous study and individual application is more in our interest than emphasis on mass entertainment. Concern for the historical and cultural values undergirding our civilization is more in our interest than hedonistic wallowing in a never-ending succession of fad periods. A posture sustaining high cultural aspirations is more in our interest than bovine acceptance of mass-cultural products pegged at the lowest common denominator of intellectual achievement and moral behavior.

Issues the Arts Education Profession Must Confront

New Times

Taking advantage of our opportunities in new times requires investments of our own resources. Since the professional arts education community is not rich enough in either funds or personnel to buy its way out of its difficulties, each individual in the field must somehow find extra energy and extra time to grasp these opportunities for making change before new times become old times and conditions become solidified again. We must not allow ourselves to think that we are working with an open-ended time frame and that current opportunities will be around forever.

New times have caused some damage to arts education. Focus on the three R's and more restrictive college preparatory programs have diminished arts curricula in many schools. As real as this is, one cannot deny the fact that the issue is, after all, based in the values placed on art by the American people and, therefore, by the educational system. If we are unable to use these new times to address this root cause of our problems, we will be unable to make any substantial progress in the immediate future. This is why we must continue to articulate a case for, and fight operationally for, the inclusion of art as a basic in the K–12 curriculum and why we must make sure that the types of arts education we deliver are based in rigorous pursuit of the arts disciplines.

Basic Principles

The arts education community must confront the fact that it does not agree sufficiently on basic principles. Part of the reason for this is the variety of value systems supporting current operation of arts education programs throughout the United States. For example, in some communities there would be no school music program at all were it not for the perceived need to have music to raise the school spirit at athletic contests. Other communities have different values based in various mixtures of social, economic, cultural, or political criteria. The point is that arts educators attempting to survive in situations where any of these specific values are prominent come to regard their approaches as the only ones appropriate or possible for arts education as a whole. The result is too little fundamental agreement about the purpose, content, and evaluation mechanisms operationally appropriate for all basic arts education in the country. We do not have sufficient unanimity on what is central.

For example, while there is no question in most people's minds about the value of mathematical study in the development of intellect, the mention of rigorous intellectual skills with regard to art sends many advocates and arts educators into paroxysms of concern that such approaches will remove the creative aspect of art from the classroom.

In addition to such disagreements over content, there is too much emphasis on method over function in K–12 arts education. For example, many teachers and parents seem prouder of student involvement with an Orff, Kodaly, or Suzuki program than of student involvement in the study of music. Although this is not particularly the fault of the Getty Trust, one is already hearing proponents and arts advocates talk about a "Getty program" rather than a visual arts program. And so it goes. All this does is fragment and factionalize the field even more with respect to its basic goal of teaching the arts disciplines and keeping art first in our public relations efforts. These conditions also confuse the public about what the real purpose of arts education is. Such focus on method over function also disadvantages and discourages the capable teacher who is able to create his or her own methods of presenting subject matter to students.

In fact, the rampaging pettiness of methods debates gives strong evidence that the field as a whole has not realized it is in a massive struggle in the cultural formation system, the outcome of which will determine the quality of our cultural future and with it the place and possibility of the existence of sequential arts education in the nation's schools. This is not the time to vitiate our energies. We must find common principles, unify behind them, articulate them in every possible policy forum, and leave matters of methodology to local option.

I hope to be forgiven for departing for a moment from simply listing issues to propose the kind of principles around which we should unify. I would like to quote four presented in the document entitled "K–12 Arts Education in the United States: Present Context, Future Needs," published by eight organizations of professional teachers and institutions in the art disciplines.[1]

> 1. Teaching the various arts disciplines and supporting such teaching is the primary goal of the arts education community. Winning contests; entertaining students, parents, or school board members; providing mechanisms for socialization or markets for new technologies, methods, and equipment must not become the primary reasons for our existence.
>
> 2. Art is a medium with possibilities for the highest intellectual content, not simply entertainment or an ornament for a variety of life-styles.
>
> 3. The arts education community has the responsibility to be a serious contender in the ongoing struggle for influence in cultural

formation: its intellectual and economic competitors must be challenged. A fundamental purpose of arts education is to enlarge the number of active participants in the art forms, not just the number of passive spectators.

4. The content of the education we provide must enable individuals to produce and understand work in as many art forms as possible. However, our first priority in the educational setting must be providing the knowledge and skills necessary to work with and understand the techniques and traditions of art from the highest intellectual heritage of civilization.

In summary, the arts education community must focus on the articulation of basic principles which describe functions to be served rather than methods to be followed. To the extent that we can have unity at this level, to that same extent we have an opportunity to be effective in the new times that are upon us.

Curriculum Content

Surely we would all agree that students need to make art, study art, and experience art. We must then confront the fact that severe problems arise when proponents of any one of these approaches capture the means to emphasize that approach over the others through the media and in various policy development processes. Unfortunately, the economics of art and education seem to leave many individuals and organizations no short-term choice but unilateral promotion of their approach. All too rarely does one find programs integrating curriculum-based instruction and arts experiences. Without such integration, students provided arts experiences alone are left with misimpressions about art, feeling perhaps that it is something that only someone else can do or, more specifically, that art provides an entertaining time away from subjects deserving rigorous study. There are equally serious problems with programs focused on making art that provide no real study of art. Here, making art becomes a technical exercise that is not enriched by the development of artistic modes of thought. Likewise, the study of art isolated from making art usually teaches approaches unrelated to the mental processes inherent in artistic expression. Here, art becomes history, psychology, philosophy, anthropology, sociology, and so forth. Everything but art.

We must all confront the issue that there are sufficient protectionist forces behind each of these concepts to prevent the proponents of any one from gaining the upper hand. Therefore, it is not only philosophically wrong but also tactically imprudent to expect that anything but a program of appropriate integration can unify the field. Such integration will be difficult to achieve. Furthermore, it cannot be imposed from the top down. By that I mean no national curriculum or panacea can solve this problem since arts education practice varies so widely from community to community, and rightly so. The best approach is one that focuses on principles related to functions to be served. We must encourage every community to find its own way to achieve programs implied by those principles. We must also encourage communities to build on the strengths they already have in arts education. We must try to bypass the protectionist impulse so continuously honed in the arts and arts education communities and so ultimately destructive to the development of improved curricular integration. Above all, we must emphasize the early acquisition of basic skills to provide each student with the tools for advanced work. Aesthetic education is a result, not a curriculum.

Teacher Preparation

Unquestionably, an excellent arts teacher must be able to practice his or her discipline at a basic professional level. Teachers also must be able to work effectively with students in an educational setting. Given these basic requirements, what types of individuals with what kinds of backgrounds should teach the arts and in what settings? For example, what are the roles of the arts specialist, the general classroom teacher, and the visiting artist?

Clearly, some powerful individuals and groups seem to be more comfortable with a system that relies on visiting artists supported by general classroom teachers, thus eliminating arts specialists. While such concepts are clearly problematical, perhaps worse is the rhetoric prevalent among arts advocates that denies artistic credentials to specialist arts teachers. This is another manifestation of the arts community's failure to recognize a distinction between the education community as a whole and the arts education community specifically. The constant reference in advocacy literature to artists and educators, with no mention of arts educators, simply reinforces this error in the public mind and provides a convenient rationale for bypassing the arts education community in activities concerned with arts policy development.

At a more academic level, the issue of curricula used for teacher preparation arises. While the literature is replete with studies, reports, and diatribes on the subject, new influences have entered the picture with calls for five-year undergraduate programs in teacher education, career ladders, new programs of examination and certification, and more accountability mechanisms. What do these proposals mean for K–12 arts education?

Of course, all teacher preparation concerns must be looked at in the light of rewards and expectations available to those who enter the teaching profession. We are all familiar with dreary statistics about careers in teaching; however, we must confront the fact that in terms of public understanding and local respect, the arts teacher is at a severe disadvantage in comparison with colleagues in scientific and humanistic disciplines.

Teachers of the performing and visual arts are seen by the public more as creators of entertainment than as purveyors of intellectual content. Without attention to this problem, arts education is likely to feel the operational results of trends evident in current statistics showing that only 10 percent of the college students expecting to teach in secondary schools actually want to be in that career. By contrast, 83 percent of those preparing to be professional musicians actually want to be in that career, the highest of any field cited.[2] Given working conditions and salary levels generally available in both professions, the contrast is particularly vivid.

Promotion/Public Relations

The arts education community must confront the fact that, in modern terms, its public relations position represents a failure of monumental dimensions. For example, our community is unable to achieve major recognition of its concerns or even major recognition of the subject of arts education unless the issue is raised by nationally powerful advocates who have no expertise in the field. In most cases this means that the expertise developed after years of practice is bypassed unless an advocacy organization decides to take notice of it.

Techniques of advocacy normally prevent such notice because the primary purpose of advocacy is to draw attention to the importance of the advocate and not to the work of others. Advocacy technique also focuses on "the arts" rather than the separate arts disciplines; it de-emphasizes reliance on individual thought; it obscures the meanings of terms; it focuses on personalities rather than work; it is inimical to the idea of learned expertise and professional continuity; and it is on the opposite side of the human development spectrum from liberal education. Advocacy is a mind-set as much as it is anything else, a mind-set focused on image over substances. The result of twenty years of advocacy is that those with the power to influence the public by commanding media attention or political influence in the arts are not those with the expertise developed from a lifetime of commitment to teaching art.[3]

As I have already mentioned, there are movements under way that could begin to reverse this dichotomous approach and put our image and substance resources together in new and effective ways. This will be difficult in the best of circumstances. However, we must not allow ourselves to luxuriate in cynicism by saying that it cannot be done at all.

There is not much hope that the professional arts education community can be effective in the policy climate previously discussed unless there is significant change in the way we present ourselves. I say this respectfully as a matter of reality. I do not know where resources will come from; however, I do know that both the content and the style of our presentation too often are insufficient to compete in the circles where we must compete if we are to be regarded as major players in policy development concerned with cultural formation. Astute readers will certainly wish to call me on the point that I am advocating an image-over-substance approach after being somewhat negative about the presence of such preferences in others. My potential critics, however, are only partly right. What is needed in public relations and promotion for arts education is the fusion of image and substance. In too many cases image is in one camp, substance in another. The two must be brought together either by a fusion of the resources between camps or by each gaining the other's capability. Otherwise, the vacuous advocacy message sent with a slick image is the one most likely to get through in a media-oriented society. In other words, the message most damaging to the cause of rigorous arts education has the best chance of being heard. This presents a chilling prospect for all serious policy work on behalf of both the arts and arts education. This is why agreement on and continuous promulgation of basic principles are so important. This is why enhanced self-esteem is so vital. This is why we must seek sophistication in our approach to trendsetters and decision-making institutions if we want to be taken seriously. The penchant for the corny, the cutesy, the silly, and the superficial in promotions for arts education simply has to be squelched. The times demand it; our sense of importance as professionals demands it. And perhaps it is not too much to say that our survival as a professionally practicing entity in cultural formation demands it.

Policy Development

Finally, our own policy development mechanisms are not sufficient to deal with the broad range of concerns we must face in contemporary society. For many years, arts education could act rather autonomously. The field was left to itself. Those who preceded us worked hard to establish a system of arts education throughout the nation. Places were carved out for curricula in elementary and secondary schools. Teacher preparation programs were established in colleges and universities. The system as it was built and as it continues to operate was never tooled to deal with the cultural formation system that confronts us today.

Perhaps the best example is the lack of research being done about how education in the various arts or in arts education in general relates to the context of contemporary American society. Much of arts education research is consumed with inward-looking studies extremely important for developing a body of knowledge about the field for those within the field. However, there seems to be little academic thinking devoted to how the field should relate to the larger society in operational terms. We do not have many programs in arts education at the doctoral level focused on what in other fields are called policy studies.

Unless the arts education community can develop a rapid capability in sophisticated policy analysis, it is quite likely that the arts enterprise will expand its present building tendency to rely on such organizations as the Brookings Institution, the Rand Corporation, various university-assisted institutes of advanced studies that normally deal with domestic and foreign policy issues, and other commercial think tanks. These entities are long on policy analysis technique but short on knowledge about art, especially about arts education. If this happens, the arts community as a whole will simply repeat in the policy analysis arena what has come to be a major problem in the promotion and public relations arena. Somehow, it should be possible to confront this issue head on and do something about it. Otherwise, major proposals for arts education will be developed by those with neither hands-on experience nor expertise. While there is nothing new in this, the public image of expertise developed by these entities in other fields will give tremendous weight to their recommendations, irrespective of their merit, feasibility, relationship to the needs of art, or viability in advancing the sort of rigorous arts instruction needed for continuous cultural advancement.

Our approach to policy must focus on research that delineates policy issues and gathers data that can be extrapolated for use in analytical situations. Our research and policy analysis must then result in carefully considered action plans that carry intellectual weight and that are focused on the needs of art and the development of civilization.

We must be able to analyze such things as postures of force influencing the context of arts education. For example, what plans do we have to maintain an intellectually credible approach to arts education in an age dominated by MTV, stupid soap operas, and the lowest-common-denominator mentality? What are the assets we cannot afford to trade? What can we trade and under what circumstances? What ideas are opposed to our best interests and the best interests of our students? Surely not everything in the cultural formation system deserves our support. Surely not everything being suggested under the flag of art, arts education, or arts support is a good idea. How sophisticated are our individual and collective mechanisms for deciding what is good and what is bad for our cause? Right now these mechanisms seem pitifully small and under tremendous pressure. The interests of students often seem tragically lost in the search for funds or even a pat on the head from the powerful.

Of course, there are many other policy development issues: college admission requirements, the specifics of arts curricula, high school graduation requirements in the arts, and other concepts articulated by the goals of MENC, NAEA, NDA, AATY, and other organizations. All of these have serious policy ramifications. The positive move by governmental arts agencies to deal with arts education more holistically is an important new factor. There are many other specific questions; however, unless we develop a capability for sophisticated policy analysis within those colleges, universities, and independent schools of art that are committed to the cause of arts education, we are going to be increasingly controlled by those who know little about our field.

Unfortunately for us, it is not as though we live in a house with peeling paint and have the option of going about our business, being sure that the house will be left alone. If we do not paint the house the color that we want it to be painted, a group or coalition of groups will come along and paint the house for us, and it probably won't be in the color we like. Not only will they paint the house for us, but they will move inside and knock down walls, redecorate, and finally cast us aside. Instead of deciding what our house will look like, we will wind up with assignments from the new owners about how it is to be maintained. When the new owners have made uninformed structural changes that cause the house to break apart, they will move on to their next cause and leave us with the mess. We will be far worse off than before.

The current policy climate is such that this could be done not because there is some particular disdain for our existence, even though this sometimes seems the case, but because we will be perceived as having no influence in the policy development arenas that count. The fact that we do have something to say and that we are busy about what we ought to be doing will have little effect unless we are involved with current policy development mechanisms. We must find our own policy intellectuals and weigh in with our own sophisticated capabilities. This will require significant reorganization and reorientation to expand our concept of research and scholarship on arts education. Let me re-emphasize that I am not talking about writing curricula, important as that is, but I am talking about working on the conditions determining whether curricula for the arts disciplines in American K–12 education will exist at all.

In light of this concern, the petty fights we often are engaged in pale by comparison. The cultural formation matrix has much that is antagonistic to the achievement of our goals. New times bring us the opportunity to redress this situation. Perhaps the greatest issue before us is whether we will have the will, the courage, and the foresight to face this great need which confronts our profession.

Conclusion

Obviously, many other issues are evident, some strategic, some tactical, some operational. Just as obviously, we arts educators have much to do if we are to succeed in our goal of providing competence in one or more of the arts to individual students. We have little choice but to heighten our aspirations, seek new levels of competence in policy analysis, and develop more influence in cultural formation. In doing all of this, we would do well to heed the old admonition that educators should fight ignorance instead of each other.

Notes

1. "K–12 Arts Education in the United States: Present, Context, Future Needs" (Reston, Va.: MENC, NAEA, NDA, ATA, NASM, NASAD, NAST, NASD, January 1986), pp. 23–24.
2. Carnegie Endowment for the Advancement of Teaching, "The Price of College Shaping Students' Choices," *Change* (May–June 1986): 30.
3. "Advocacy: Substance or Fluff?" *Design for Arts in Education* 87, no. 2 (November–December 1985).

Contributors

Ralph A. Smith is professor of cultural and educational policy at the University of Illinois at Urbana-Champaign where he teaches courses in aesthetics and arts education and edits the *Journal of Aesthetic Education.* The author of *Excellence in Art Education* and *The Sense of Art: A Study in Aesthetic Education,* he has also coauthored *Art Education: A Critical Necessity* and edited or coedited *Cultural Literacy and Arts Education, Aesthetics and Arts Education,* and *The Arts, Education, and Aesthetic Knowing.* His criticism of public policy for arts education has been widely discussed. He is a distinguished fellow of the National Art Education Association and recipient of two of its prestigious awards.

Ronald Berman is professor of literature at the University of California at San Diego. A former chairman of the National Endowment for the Humanities, his interests include literature, intellectual history, and cultural policy. Among his publications are *A Reader's Guide to Shakespeare's Plays, America in the Sixties, Culture and Politics, Advertising and Social Change,* and *How Television Sees Its Audience.* During his tenure with the Humanities Endowment the agency experienced notable growth and contributed significantly to the support of museum exhibitions, educational programs, and basic research in the liberal arts. For his efforts he was awarded the Medal of the City of New York. He is currently completing a book on F. Scott Fitzgerald.

Edward C. Banfield is George D. Markham Professor of Government, emeritus, at Harvard University. Among his numerous works are *Political Influence, City Politics,* with James Q. Wilson, *The Unheavenly City,* and *The Democratic Muse: Visual Arts and the Public Interest,* which raised a number of questions about government support of the arts and arts education.

Jacques Barzun is literary adviser to Charles Scribner's Sons and University Professor Emeritus at Columbia University. Among his major writings are: *Teacher in America, The House of Intellect, The Energies of Art, Science: The*

Glorious Entertainment, The Use and Abuse of Art, Clio and the Doctors, A Stroll with William James, and *Critical Questions.*

Monroe C. Beardsley (1915–85), after teaching at Swarthmore College for many years, was professor of philosophy at Temple University at the time of his death. His major works include *Aesthetics: Problems in the Philosophy of Criticism, The Possibility of Criticism, Aesthetics from Classical Greece to the Present: A Brief History, Philosophical Thinking,* with Elizabeth Beardsley, and *The Aesthetic Point of View,* edited by Michael J. Wreen and Donald M. Callen.

Noel Carroll is a member of the Cornell Sage School of Philosophy and the Center for Performing Arts. He is the author of *Mystifying Movies* and *The Philosophy of Horror* and has published in such journals as *Daedalus,* the *Journal of Aesthetics and Art Criticism,* and the *Journal of Aesthetic Education.*

Laura Chapman is an educational consultant and specialist in the visual arts who has worked with schools, museums, and other cultural organizations. She has taught at the Ohio State University, the University of Illinois, and the University of Cincinnati, and is the author of *Approaches to Art Education, Instant Art, Instant Culture: The Unspoken Policy for American Schools,* and a series of textbooks for the elementary grades entitled *Discover Art.*

Charles Frankel (1917–79) was for many years professor of philosophy at Columbia University. *High on Foggy Bottom: An Outsider's Inside View of the Government* is an account of his tenure as assistant secretary of state for educational and cultural affairs from 1965 to 1967. He also wrote *The Faith of Reason, The Case for Modern Man, The Democratic Prospect,* and *Education and the Barricades.*

Herbert Gans is professor of sociology at Columbia University. His book *Popular Culture and High Culture* has been widely discussed for its analysis of taste cultures. He is also the author of *Deciding What's News* and *The Urban Villagers.* He is currently studying unemployment policies and the impact of the news media on politics.

Ernest van den Haag is a retired psychoanalyst and former John M. Olin Professor of Jurisprudence and Public Policy at Fordham University. Among his publications are *Passion and Social Constraint, Political Violence and Civil Disobedience,* and *Capitalism: Sources of Hostility.*

Samuel H. Hope is a composer and served in a number of performing arts administrative posts before accepting his current position as executive director of the National Office for Arts Accreditation in Higher Education. The author of numerous articles on policy issues, he is also executive editor of the journal *Design for Arts in Education.*

HILTON KRAMER is a former art critic for the *New York Times* and current editor of *The New Criterion.* His two major collections of critical writings are *The Age of the Avant-Garde: An Art Chronicle of 1956–1972* and *The Revenge of the Philistines: Art and Culture, 1972–1984.* His *Abstract Art: A Cultural History* is forthcoming.

E. LOUIS LANKFORD is associate professor of art education at the Ohio State University, where he teaches courses in aesthetics and art education. He has published numerous articles on the arts and education in such journals as *Studies in Art Education, Art Education,* and the *Journal of Aesthetic Education.* He is currently completing a book on aesthetics and art education.

BARBARA LEONDAR, coeditor with A. N. Perkins of *The Arts and Cognition,* taught English and literature at a number of universities and held several administrative posts, including the presidency of the University of Maine from 1986 to 1989 and senior associate of the Presidential Search Consultation Service of the Association of Governing Boards of Universities and Colleges. She is now retired and lives in New Hampshire.

ALBERT WILLIAM LEVI (1911–88) was for many years David May Distinguished University Professor of the Humanities of Washington University. Among his major works are *Philosophy and the Modern World, Literature, Philosophy, and the Imagination, Humanism and Politics,* and *Philosophy and Social Expression.* At the time of his death he was coauthoring, with Ralph A. Smith, a volume titled *Art Education: A Critical Necessity,* which presents a humanities interpretation of visual arts education.

MARK LILLA is a member of the Department of Politics at New York University. A former associate editor of the *Public Interest,* he has contributed articles to such magazines as *Harper's,* the *New Republic, Partisan Review,* and *The New Criterion.*

SAMUEL LIPMAN is music critic for *Commentary* magazine and publisher of *The New Criterion.* He has written widely on cultural and educational topics and has served as a member of the National Council of the Arts. Among his major writings are *Music after Modernism, The House of Music,* and *Arguing for Music, Arguing for Culture.*

KEVIN V. MULCAHY is director of the Institute of Government Research of Louisiana State University in Baton Rouge. The author of numerous publications and member of several advisory groups on the fine arts and policy, he is coeditor of *Public Policy and the Arts* and *The Challenge to Reform Arts Education,* and coauthor of the forthcoming *American Notes* and *White House Government.*

SIR ROY SHAW was influential in the Worker's Educational Association in Great Britain, studied literature and philosophy, and became professor of adult education. Before his retirement he served for eight years as secretary-general of the British Arts Council, a time he recalls in *The Arts and the People.* He continues to write and lecture.

JOHN WILSON is a fellow of Mansfield College, Oxford University and a lecturer and tutor in Oxford's Department of Educational Studies. He is the author of *Dialogue on Moral Education, Preface to the Philosophy of Education, Thinking with Concepts,* and, with Barbara Cowell, *Education: An Introduction.*

Index